ENGLISH ROMANTIC DRAMA

1795–1843

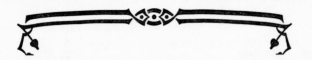

English Romantic Drama

Drama

1795-1843

A Critical History

BY

Richard M. Fletcher

AN EXPOSITION–UNIVERSITY BOOK

EXPOSITION PRESS   *New York*

EXPOSITION   PRESS   INC.

386 Park Avenue South   New York, N.Y. 10016

FIRST EDITION

© 1966 by Richard M. Fletcher. *All rights reserved, including the right of reproduction in whole or in part in any form, except for short quotations in critical essays and reviews.* Manufactured in the United States of America. Library of Congress catalog-card number: 66–28840.

EP 44127

Preface

At first glance it may seem curious that so little attention is paid by present-day scholars and critics to the history and development of Romantic Drama, in view of the uncomplimentary nature of what little has been written about that area of English literature. Possibly the reason is that those who might be interested in the field have been frightened off. The standard work on poetic drama of the early nineteenth century, Allardyce Nicoll's *A History of Early Nineteenth Century English Drama*, published in 1930, regards Romantic drama as an aberration and a mistake. Nicoll, however, merely mirrors attitudes presented some fifteen years earlier by Samuel C. Chew in his study *The Dramas of Lord Byron*. Nor does Bertrand Evans in *Gothic Drama from Walpole to Shelley* (1947) offer views which differ significantly from theirs. Otherwise, work in the field has been restricted to studies of the influence on the playwrights of the period of sentimental, Gothic, and Elizabethan drama—and never has treated Romantic drama itself as an organic whole.

Since Nicoll's *History*, however, a body of fresh material has become available which is extensive enough to warrant a reappraisal of the subject. Of first importance are the four volumes of Coleridge's *Letters* (dating to 1819), edited by Earl L. Griggs. This correspondence, which embraces the period of Coleridge's contribution to the drama, is extremely helpful in piecing together Coleridge's development as a playwright as well as in deriving his probable dramatic theories. The publication of the Preface to *The Borderers* by Ernest de Selincourt, in 1926, provides us with Wordsworth's statements on dramatic theory and on the theatre. *Bulwer and Macready* (1958), edited by Charles H. Shattuck, a compilation of the correspondence between Edward Bulwer and theatre manager William Macready, presents a seamless and coherent account of the motives of one writer who was concerned with the development of Romantic drama, as well as of the conditions that prevailed in the early Victorian period.

But of course other material has become available since 1930 as well, so that at last it has become possible to examine Romantic drama in considerable detail and depth—and with considerable accuracy. With these facts kept in mind, the purposes of this study can be simply stated: they are, not to refute what has been said already, but rather to correct evaluations which have been based on erroneous assumptions and conceptions about Romantic drama; and to bring poetic tragedy as a genre into sharper focus, both as it reflected and as it delineated the spirit of its age. If in the process Romantic drama can be demonstrated to be more vibrant, more vital—and more artistic—than it generally is acknowledged to be, then the cause of English drama as a whole will also have been served.

I wish to acknowledge my indebtedness during the writing of the book to Professors William H. Marshall, Frederick L. Jones, and Matthew W. Black, all of the University of Pennsylvania, for their invaluable assistance in pointing out its more glaring weaknesses. I wish also to express my appreciation to the staffs of the libraries of the University of Pennsylvania and of Haverford and Bryn Mawr colleges for permission to use their facilities.

R. M. F.

Contents

CHAPTER I

Romantic Drama and Its Theatre

TODAY the many blank-verse dramas that were written by the great Romantic poets and by their lesser contemporaries, when they are not totally ignored, are passed over as trivia or as vagaries from the natural concerns of the Romantic mind. Actually they deserve a more consequential fate. Admittedly Romantic drama is in certain respects trite and banal; yet in others it is a more faithful mirror of its age than is commonly supposed. To be sure, we can rationalize our indifference and neglect on the grounds that English Romantic drama is nothing less than colorless and unimaginative; and we can add that its rhetoric is dry and awkward and its plots are both puerile and insipid. To reflect that this stiff, mechanical drama once seemed to many the betokening of a new day dawning in the history of the English theatre is enough, certainly, to give us pause at the fickleness of time, the ways of the world, and the idiosyncracies of the critical mind and the quixotic in human taste. In any case there are examples aplenty for meditation here.

Yet objectivity should entail a dispassionate point of view as we scrutinize the workings of the past. When we see that dramatic works by acknowledged poetic geniuses are not up to their customary standards, what should draw us on in our investigation is fact rather than fancy or conjecture. Otherwise, what we understand by faults or weaknesses can lead us into bias or misinterpretation, particularly if in our study we examine merely works of individuals and not the total product of a given literary period.

Of course, this does not mean that there is anything necessarily wrong in examining the dramas, let us say, of Byron apart from the other poetic dramas of his age. The point is that those few critical investigations which have been undertaken in Romantic drama have applied generalizations from individual works to the medium as a genre, from individual playwrights to the canon as an entity. Granting that the quality of Romantic drama makes the evident lack of interest in it understandable, the truth remains that illuminating and perceptive criticism of it as a whole is virtually unknown.

There is a second point we must recognize. Once we have agreed that most of the blank-verse dramas of early-nineteenth-century England are inferior by almost any standard, we must add that this same observation can be applied to the dramas of many another literary period. Indeed, honesty must constrain us to admit that our present vantage point, whatever else it contributes to critical and evaluative standards, inclines us to judge the drama of the past by criteria which were not necessarily those that either the playwright or his audience believed to be significant. Every age has its standards of taste, its critical fashions. A great deal hinges, too, on captious prejudice or esthetic appeal, factors always difficult to explain rationally or justify objectively. Nevertheless, it must be confessed that although we seem unwilling to be interested in the plays that have come down to us from the period of early-nineteenth-century Romantic poetry, we seem to muster a remarkable tolerance for the drama, let us say, of the Restoration Age, remoter in point of time, or even for the Jacobean Masque, a more esoteric and conventionalized dramatic type than Romantic drama ever was.

All of this may be another way of saying that we have come to regard the early-nineteenth-century Romantic solely as a poet or as an essayist; that is, so far as they concern the Romantic, drama and poetry are opposed to each other as genres. This in turn would seem to imply that the poet and the playwright are going in different directions, the one toward lyricism, the other toward——?

But here we call to mind a judgment that customarily is leveled against the Romantics: what might be termed their inability to "dramaticize." The preponderance of shorter works in the Romantic canon can be cited as proof of the essentially "undramatic" quality of the Romantic mind, as an instance. What to do, then, about *Don Juan, Christabel, The Eve of St. Agnes, The Rime of the Ancient Mariner,* and so on, remains something of a problem, although admittedly advocates of this undramatic school of thought have a point. As a matter of fact, criticism of and complaints about Romantic drama depend in general on some kind of variant remark about its lack of dramatic action, the absence in it of realism, and the like. Not that dramatic action and realism are necessarily synonymous, although lurking in the mind of the anti-Romantic there appears to be established some sort of link between the two, which by itself presents a problem of terminology we must deal with in due course. But as for their objections to the lack of drama, of movement, of "flair," in Romantic poetry, which, in turn, concerns us in our interest here more specifically with the quality of the blank verse in Romantic plays, we must grant that the Romantic poet was no different in his attitude toward dramaturgy than he was in his attitude toward prosody. The meditative, reflective, dreamy quality of his sonnets was something he carried over to the stage. But here, as elsewhere, what obtains in one medium is not expected to obtain in another. The Romantic is permitted by the modern critic to write Romantic poetry if it is in the form of a sonnet, a ballad, or the like; but when he continues to write Romantic poetry for the stage, his efforts are called unrealistic, undramatic, and inept.

Damned, therefore, if he does and damned if he doesn't, the Romantic playwright was fortunate to precede the modern critic. In his own day the blank-verse dramatist was regarded as something akin to an advance wave of future promise. And for a time many presumably sober, respectable Englishmen were convinced that Romantic drama would help restore the theatre to its former—Elizabethan—splendor. After all, it has been better than a century and a half since Coleridge witnessed the premiere of his blank-verse play, *Remorse,* the first of the Romantic plays to cross the boards of a London theatre. And one might mention the numerous other attempts that have been made from that time on to the very present to revive blank-verse drama on the English as well as on the American stage. It may be facetious or impertinent to remark on Maxwell Anderson's efforts to revive "the language of common men" in terms meaningfully relevant to contemporary requirements; or the ofttimes electrifying experiments with stage poetry of Christopher Frye; or even T. S. Eliot's efforts to awaken the poetic impulse for the theatre (not to neglect those many other playwrights who from time to time have believed that somehow the theatre of prose is not vibrant, dynamic, vital enough, that drama by its nature demands a medium of expression more stylized than pedestrian non-poetic dialogue). The point is that in one way or another, we find ourselves boats against the current, borne ceaselessly back into the past, each in our own way influenced by Elizabethan, and especially Shakespearean, precedent. In many ways we are not so different from the Romantic in our attitudes as we might believe. He in any case looked unabashedly to Elizabethan models for his guide and inspiration; and if in our own day we do not consciously look to the Romantic to justify our infrequent nagging suspicion that prose is not quite so appropriate a medium for dramatic expression as poetry, possibly we cannot bring ourselves to it because he, the Romantic playwright, with the Elizabethans as his gods, somehow failed.

And so let us turn to what is available to us of "modern" criticism that deals with Romantic drama. The term is quoted because aside from Allardyce Nicoll's *A History of Early Nineteenth Century English Drama*, old-fashioned and opinionated though it may sound today, there is really little else. Without quoting him at too great length, certain of his remarks are worthy of attention, among them, for example, his objections to the Romantic poet as dramatist:

> Not one of them . . . really gripped the imagination of the age . . . ; not one produced a dramatic masterpiece which can be looked upon as the starting-point for further art development . . . each in his own way had something of a talent for the theatre, each produced works which may, even in this

century, be read with pleasure . . . All this we may confess; but the fact remains that they did not provide that for which the age was seeking and which it found dimly suggested by Robertson and robustly by Ibsen.[1]

In sum, Nicoll's objection is not so much to the inferior quality of Romantic drama as to its seeming inability to express dramatically what he believes the audience of the Romantic Period was looking for. Yet who is to say what Romantic audiences were looking for? We cannot say that they were yearning for realism in drama any more than we can demonstrate that if they had nothing else to choose from, modern audiences would not flock to see poetic tragedies. In our age we seem to be witnessing the heyday of the musical. But this does not mean that legitimate plays cannot command audiences, too; or that the same audience cannot enjoy both straight plays and musical comedies. Nevertheless, the continuing popularity of melodrama during the Romantic Period indicates to some critics that audiences viewed the melodrama form as an escape from having to view poetic tragedy. And latter-day critics have been only too willing to regard melodrama as a kind of sublimation for nineteenth-century craving for "realism" in its dramatic bill of fare. Nicoll, for example, refers to melodrama as being "realistic in tendency," whatever that may mean; and adds that melodrama contained "all that was vital and popular in the theatrical world of the time,"[2] the period, that is to say, roughly from the beginning to the middle of the nineteenth century.

Unfortunately, attitudes, once they become clichés, prove difficult to discard. Possibly Nicoll borrowed his convictions about melodrama from Ernest Watson, who, in his study of the nineteenth-century English theatre, declares: "Even in the melodrama there was a new spirit which made a fresh and unmistakable appeal, and that spirit, strange as it may seem now, was the first suggestion of what we to-day call realism."[3]

---

[1] (2 vols., London, 1930), I, 63–64.

[2] *Ibid.*, pp. 75, 119.

[3] *Sheridan to Robertson: A Study of the Nineteenth-Century London Stage* (Cambridge, Mass., 1926), p. 127.

To this can only be added—strange indeed! What, then, about the realism, if it may be so termed, of Shakespeare and the other Elizabethans, with whom audiences of the Romantic Period were also familiar? For even more remarkable than Nicoll's believing melodrama to be "realistic in tendency," Watson declares that the later Victorian audience found Shakespeare's realism—by which, I suppose, he may mean Shakespeare's truth to life—to be "remote and poetical."[4] Why this should have been so is difficult to fathom—remote, possibly—but why should Victorian audiences have objected to Shakespeare's being poetical? They, like the Romantic audience, grew up knowing him by heart, after all.

No, the difficulty seems to rest with the acting styles of the Romantic Period rather than with latter-day critics' objections to there being no realism in the early-nineteenth-century English theatre. We may agree, as Watson suggests, that audiences were fascinated by melodrama because of its freshness and its novelty, having grown "frankly tired of the ineffectual imitations of the Elizabethan stage."[5] Once more, however, the evaluation is a subjective one, which may well be based on wish fulfillment as much as on fact. The truth is that if melodrama enjoyed an immense vogue, so did burlettas, burlesques, comedies—forms of what we might call vaudeville—and other kinds of admission entertainment. Indeed, the English theatre of the early nineteenth century was but continuing in the widening tradition of its eighteenth-century predecessor; it was also reverting to customs in entertainment which went far back into English cultural history. For the demands of theatrical audiences for diversity were seemingly unlimited; and no single medium would have been able in any case to satisfy every taste. In this light it is evident that melodrama and poetic drama could exist side by side, realism to the contrary, and both be enjoyed by a wide, if possibly not by the same, audience.

Still, evidence enough has come down to us that early-nineteenth-century writers were becoming increasingly impatient

---

[4] *Ibid.*

[5] *Ibid.*, p. 126.

with contemporary legitimate drama. By legitimate drama we mean, to be sure, the fare offered in the two patent houses, Covent Garden and Drury Lane. But for the present let us remind ourselves that we are still faced by the objection that its atmosphere of romantic unreality is the inherent weakness in Romantic drama; and let us first attempt to lay this objection to rest before we proceed to a discussion of the theatre and the audience of the Romantic Period. Even more cogently than by Nicoll, the attitude of the detractors of Romantic drama has been stated by Samuel Chew in his study of Byron's dramas:

> The domestic themes that had been employed in a number of plays during the preceding century were quite ignored. None of the poets turned to ordinary, daily modern life for the subjects of their plays. Thus it happens that the poetic drama, though more serious than the stage-plays, was almost equally removed from life; it reflected, inadequately but not distortedly, the thought and aspirations of the age, but it did not afford a criticism of the life of the people. It was as far removed as possible from realism.[6]

All of this, we must admit, sounds like so much gibberish, which unhappily it is. Yet before we attempt to refute Chew, let us note the distinction that he draws between "stage-plays" and "poetic drama," as if the latter were simply printed plays which would never be, nor ever had been, acted. Such, we must note, is not altogether the case; we shall see that a considerable body of poetic dramas has been presented on the stage. Granted, the poetic dramas of Wordsworth and Keats have never been acted in the theatre—but theirs were by no means the only ones that were written during the Romantic Period. Next let us observe Chew's circular logic: although he declares that the dramas of the Romantic poets "reflected, inadequately but not distortedly, the thought and aspirations of the age," he declares that their authors did not offer "a criticism of the life of the people." And they did not offer it, he maintains, because their plays were "as far removed as possible from realism." Yet since he ac-

---

[6] *The Dramas of Lord Byron* (Göttingen, 1915), p. 28.

knowledges in the previous breath that these Romantic poets nevertheless somehow managed to reflect "the thought and aspirations of the age," we begin to wonder, what, then, is he objecting to? If the Romantic poets were able, by the means most suited to their temperaments, to reflect in their writings "the thought and aspirations of the age" in which they lived, then at least in terms of their contemporary milieu they must have created valid and pertinent forms of art. To condemn them for not having written in a manner more suited to theatrical conventions of a later day is both absurd and illogical. Nonetheless, the fact remains that aside from a single defense by U. C. Nag of the style and content of the plays of the Romantic poets, based on problems that have to do with staging in the period,[7] critics of Romantic drama are agreed that since it is not "realistic," for that reason, if for no other, it cannot be very good.

There are other points on which latter-day critics rest their case: that the Romantic dramatists were pampered children; they refused to accept adverse criticism; disdained lowering themselves by mingling in the arena of the stage; were unconversant with staging and stage techniques; and by temperament were egocentrics whose dramas should be regarded as little more than dramatic monologues about themselves. As Nicoll remarks:

> We must look at these Romantic poets honestly, and, if we do we must realize that, in spite of their high-sounding Pantisocracies and their revolutionary views, they were too aristocratic and affected—thin-skinned, too, preferring to write their lyrics which might be ridiculed or loved in private rather than attempt dramas the open condemnation of which might ruffle their dignity. Perhaps criticism has been overkind in the past to these Romantic poets. They have long been the spoilt children of our literature; we have been too readily inclined to bow to their pettish wills, to find excuses for their failures, instead of treating them honestly, and perhaps a little severely, as spoilt children ought to be treated.[8]

---

[7] "The English Theatre of the Romantic Revival," *Nineteenth Century and After,* CIV (1928), 384–398.

[8] *A History of Early Nineteenth Century English Drama,* I, 63.

Although such criticism undeniably brings little light to bear on the value of Romantic drama per se, what has been cited up to this point indicates that critical prejudice is commonly so strong that critics leave themselves little time to weigh intrinsic merits and deficiencies. Instead, their thesis is that the Romantic dramatists

> never grasped the basic principle that "those who live to please must please to live." They did not cater to the public taste. Their subjects were mostly remote from contemporary interests and their style was derivative. Mistakenly, they laid their stress upon poetry at the expense of action. Naturally exuberant (not to say long-winded), they made no attempt to master the condensation and restraint required for effective drama. The self-centeredness of most of them was ill-suited to the playwright's art. It may also be that they shrank from the rude ordeal of facing the approval of ill-mannered audiences.[9]

If we look more closely at these remarks, we note that they are applicable to playwrights of any age. Playwrights must naturally be exuberant, how else can they communicate in a dramatic vein? Artists customarily are self-centered (although in this respect not unique). Remote subjects need not be displeasing ones. A great deal of all great drama is verbose and unconstrained. Once style and tone become common property, any succeeding efforts can be termed derivative. The ordeal of facing critics in our own day has no doubt replaced the ordeal of facing ill-mannered audiences, but the principle is the same. Stress upon poetry at the expense of action has been demonstrated to be no mistake in the case of writers other than the Romantic dramatists. And, what is more, to judge from contemporary comment, the Romantic playwright did indeed cater to public taste.

Let us, then, turn from the critics to Romantic drama itself, to ask what it is and who wrote it. To answer the first question: Romantic drama is drama in blank verse. We need not think of

---

[9] Samuel C. Chew, "The Drama in Decline," in *A Literary History of England,* ed. Albert C. Baugh (New York, 1948), p. 1266.

it as drama written in blank verse exclusively, for Edward Bulwer, a writer who for a variety of reasons must be considered a Romantic playwright, wrote Romantic dramas in which he included elements of prose as well; but aside from Bulwer the rule applies that the serious drama of the English Romantic Period was drama in poetry.

Since many writers of the early nineteenth century tried their hand at poetic tragedy, the list of performed and unperformed plays of this type is very large, though this fact is not necessarily astonishing, since blank-verse dramas which can be considered Romantic were being written well into the fourth decade of the century. And a remarkable fact must be noted about the Romantic impulse which governed the writing and production of the plays: if the movement can be said to have started with Wordsworth and his play *The Borderers*, which he began to write in 1796, the end of the period during which Romantic drama flourished can be established as the year 1842, when this same play was finally published. If our ends are truly in our beginnings, then this observation surely applies to Wordsworth and the influence which he exerted on the course of Romantic tragedy.

But to say that the first poetic tragedy of any importance was by Wordsworth is not to imply that it is he who reintroduced poetic drama into English literature. The true father of Romantic drama is not Wordsworth, but Coleridge. Although the idea embodied in poetic drama is of primary importance—and in more than merely a cursory sense this idea incorporated principles which can justifiably be called Wordsworthian—Wordsworth's *The Borderers* was destined never to reach the stage. The first contemporary drama to be performed on a nineteenth-century London stage composed wholly in blank verse was Coleridge's tragedy *Remorse*. As with any other artistic form, poetic drama could draw for inspiration only on plays that were being published or were being presented concurrently on the stage—and by the time *The Borderers* was published Romantic dramas had virtually vanished from the London theatre. Yet Wordsworth's play is of crucial importance to our study, for its concern both with philosophical problems and with problems of diction. If Coleridge's play was the first to be offered for public viewing, in addition to its providing a convenient landmark to indicate the beginning and the ending of the development of Romantic tragedy in point of time, it was Wordsworth's that first dealt with poetic drama as a concept and as an idea.

There are questions that have to do with the theatre and with theatrical conditions from 1796 to 1843 which must be dealt with in our study of the dramas of the Romantic Period, too. It is in the state of the theatre as much as in the plays themselves that the rebuttals to many of the detractions of Romantic drama can best be found; so before we examine the interrelationships which unite the plays into a relatively seamless whole, let us first turn to the theatre and to the problems that faced the writer for the early-nineteenth-century English stage. Once we do, we must face the truth: in eighteenth-century and early-nineteenth-century England drama had come to such a pass as to be aptly called a "literary by-product"[10] of the cultural scene. There were interesting exceptions to this rule—and for interesting reasons: if in the late eighteenth century plays by Richard Brinsley Sheridan and Oliver Goldsmith captured the fancy of London theatregoers, in the decade of the 1820's plays by Sheridan Knowles became equally popular, as did plays by T. N. Talfourd and Edward Bulwer in the decade of the 1830's. Even though the theatre was thus not totally devoid of interest, mediocrity was not the exception but the rule—despite native artists who turned out plays in almost stupefying quantities; and despite foreign plays, particularly from the French, in translation.

If to modern tastes the years from 1780 to 1830 or so seem a wasteland of turgid, dull drama, we nonetheless should not be surprised to discover that what was performed was not only attended, it seems to have pleased its audience. Emerson's words, "the experience of each new age requires a new confession, and the world seems always to be waiting for its poet," should remind us that the Romantic Period was apparently as able as any other to produce in the theatre what the public wanted to see

---

[10] A. H. Thorndike, *Tragedy* (Boston, 1908), p. 321.

and hear. To be sure, this public was not of the same composition as the one Sheridan and Goldsmith had written for, since
eighteenth-century audiences, like those during the Restoration,
were prepared to see themselves satirized; but the successors to
the domestic comedy of Lillo had maintained general favor by
conforming to current sentimental tastes; and there were numerous "Gothic" dramas, which for a time so grew in vogue
and popularity that they threatened to drive everything else
off the stage altogether. So the conjunction of these various elements lent a certain vitality and diversity to the London theatre.

But by the turn of the eighteenth century it becomes increasingly apparent in retrospect that the theatre was suffering from
a dearth of ideas. For one thing, the popularity of Gothic drama
led rapidly to its becoming fixed and stereotyped. And, bound up
partly with the increasing population of London, a change occurred in the composition of the theatrical audience which conspired to maintain a fixed, stereotyped status quo in the kinds
of stage productions that were being offered long after that situation might logically have ended: during this same period the
fashionable audience began to desert the theatre in favor of
opera, performed at the King's Theatre, where, until its destruction in 1867, Italian opera enjoyed an unrivaled popularity.

H. B. Baker, in his *History of the London Stage*, calls the
period from 1824 to 1846 the "golden age of opera" in England,[11] and, judging by the reputations of the singers who performed at the King's Theatre during those years, there is hardly
reason to question his word. More than that, until the time of
Queen Victoria the ruling house took no more than a casual
interest in the destiny of the drama, nor, except for the tradi-

---

[11]*History of the London Stage and Its Famous Players (1576–1903)*
(London and New York, 1904), p. 184: "From 1824 to 1846 was the
golden age of opera in this country [England], if not for the *impresarii*,
at least for the public, as between those two dates the lyric drama was
interpreted by artists such as, perhaps, those of no other period in its
history can compare." The decade of the 1810's saw the first productions
in England of Mozart's *Le Nozze di Figaro, Cosi fan tutte, Il Flauto
Magico (Die Zauberflöte), Don Giovanni,* and Rossini's *Il Barbiere di
Siviglia.*

tional annual command performance, did any of the first three
rulers of the century see fit to encourage the theatre to any ap-
preciable degree on other nights. It was not until 1849, when a
series of theatricals was established at Windsor Castle, that
Queen Victoria began to give any real encouragement to actors,
either, notably to Charles Kean.

Another deterrent to the expansion or diversity of theatrical
performances was the Licensing Act, which permitted only the
two patent houses, Covent Garden and Drury Lane, to perform
"legitimate" plays. The other houses, of which seven were operating in the winter of 1800, for the most part had to content
themselves with burlettas, Gothic mysteries, comedies, farces,
equestrian acts, and other forms of "popular" entertainment.
Although by 1832 many non-patent theatres were offering plays
as a matter of course which earlier had been reserved solely for
the legitimate theatres, the fact remains that during the French
Revolution and for many years thereafter, when the best dramatic
talents of the times might have been at work examining current
political and economic problems in the form of stage works, the
audience to which such efforts could best have been directed
was looking elsewhere for edification and entertainment, the
theatre by default becoming the province of the mob.

The elite of London did not desert the theatre altogether.
Despite the vexation of being among rowdy, undisciplined audiences; of sitting on uncomfortable wooden benches sold on a
first-come, first-served basis; of being stupefied by the heat, the
noise, and the glare of uncertain gas-light lamps that were kept
constantly aglow in the auditorium; of being forced to mingle
with cabmen, fishmongers, and prostitutes, and all of the other
low life for whom the theatre was a place both of business and
of pleasure,[12] the theatre continued to maintain its share of
ardent devotees among the literati. It is merely that the theatre
was no longer the plaything of the aristocracy. This might have
been all to the good had not the middle class followed the ex-

---

[12] E. B. Watson in *Sheridan to Robertson,* pp. 80–86, presents an
interesting fictional account of a visit to an early nineteenth-century
London theatre.

ample of the English aristocracy by discovering opera, too, which left the legitimate theatre to the uncertain mercies of the plebs. Understandably the hapless theatre manager, plagued by cut-throat competition and by the ever-present fear that raising prices might precipitate a riot, sought with commendable zeal to sell out his house by giving the public what it wanted, even though in the process what might be characterized today as art was as often as not ignored. Lessons once learned die hard: even the mighty Kemble, subjected to seventy consecutive nights of rioting by irate theatregoers under the banner of "Old Prices" after he attempted to raise prices to mark the reopening of Covent Garden in 1809—even Kemble knuckled under and (save for the boxes) grudgingly restored admissions to their former levels; and this lesson, undeniably, other managers soberly took to heart.

We have been speaking of the "plebs," the "mob." If it was a lower-class public which for the most part now filled the theatres from the pit to the galleries, it was a public, whatever its deficiencies in conduct and morals, that showed itself vociferous in appreciating what it liked. And what it liked was, above all, Shakespeare. This "Shakespeare Idolatry"[13] the early-nineteenth-century audience had inherited from its eighteenth-century forebears—from, among others, Garrick during his long tenure at Drury Lane. But during the early nineteenth century, too, a succession of young new actors began making their debuts in the patent theatres for whom Shakespearean interpretations were singularly congenial, actors who, having grown up with Shakespeare, felt him in their bones. Nor was the public indifferent to their efforts: no matter how low their tastes in other respects, they seemed never to grow weary of Kean as Hamlet or Macready as Macbeth.

Those of either literary ability or literary pretension were as stirred by Shakespeare's genius as was the general public. Although many of them professed to prefer their Shakespeare read rather than acted, they, too, flocked to the patent houses to witness performances of Shakespeare's plays. Unfortunately, their

[13] See Robert W. Babcock, *The Genesis of Shakespeare Idolatry, 1766–1799* (Chapel Hill, N. C., 1931).

attitudes toward Shakespearean drama did not reflect the fact
that manifold changes had occurred in stagecraft since Shakespeare's day. Indeed, ironically enough, the condition of the
theatre actually contributed to the paucity of outstanding dramas.
Before him in his mind's eye the aspiring playwright of the Romantic Period visualized Shakespeare revitalized upon the stage;
the while, he would only discover to his chagrin that his own
efforts would have to be written under radically different conditions from those that were the norm in Shakespeare's day. This
dichotomy between the ideal and the real impelled more than
one hopeful neo-Elizabethan to turn his back on the legitimate
theatre altogether in favor of closet drama; and those who remained found the problem of grappling with the intricacies of a
constantly shifting *mise en scène* almost insurmountable. A dur-
able kind of stability in the internal arrangement of the theatrical stage would not be achieved until the century had nearly
ended, until the later era of Pinero and Bernard Shaw.

The many dramatists who remained struggled ardently and
steadfastly to adapt themselves to the fluid theatrical conditions
of the period. Seeing the immortal bard's plays in production
but fired them the more with the desire to re-establish a vital
new Elizabethanism. But, however commendable their ambitions, and to whatever reaches his genius extended in other respects, problems in staging that had confronted Shakespeare
were far less complex from those that faced Coleridge and his
successors in Romantic drama. These exponents of what they
so sanguinely believed would be a renaissance in English drama
found that their best efforts were continually in conflict with
certain inescapable realities in the theatrical conditions of their
day. And if no better plays were written during the period than
those that saw production, the wonder is not so much that they
were poor but that the drama that was being written could ever
be produced. Problems of the stage and staging grew more
formidable with each passing year.

During the eighteenth century few specific changes had occurred in the theatrical structure with which the Restoration
dramatist had been familiar. As to internal alterations in the

structure of theatre auditoriums themselves, innovations were equally limited, and those few that were suggested, notably efforts to eliminate the doors to the wings at either side of the stage, the public bitterly resisted. (It was not until 1822, during a renovation, that the doors to the wings were finally eliminated at Drury Lane.)

In that they wrote for an open theatre, Shakespeare and his contemporaries had not had to be concerned with artificial illumination or lighting effects: they could write, as the Romantic dramatist ruefully sought to do, for the imagination rather than the eye. And when the enclosed Restoration theatre brought with it candlelight, the dramatist adjusted himself to the new conditions by substituting static action, wit, and formal poetry for spectacle and pageantry. Garrick introduced one noteworthy innovation in lighting by replacing "the six chandeliers of twelve candles each, that had previously hung over the stage, by concealed lamps and footlights,"[14] but continued innovation in this line was scarcely feasible—until, that is, new lighting methods should become available.

Suddenly, with gas lighting, there they were. If this new means of creating lighting effects served as a curse as well as a boon—the gas diffusing noxious odors throughout the auditorium—it was soon discovered, too, that totally original effects could be created by means of it. Why the uses to which it could best be put were not instantly seized on is a question which really need not concern us long; almost inevitably a time lag occurs in most fields after some new medium has been introduced into it—and in this respect early-nineteenth-century theatre was scarcely unique. No more than the theatre manager, the dramatist could no longer keep up with the changing theatrical conditions of his times; the theatre itself was evolving too rapidly. The dramatist soon became little more than a supernumerary in a world in which only the manager could expect to be familiar with the theatre under his direction and with the exigencies of its idiosyncrasies.

The adaptability of gas for new and striking techniques was

---

14 E. B. Watson, p. 92.

not something that went unrecognized for long. Yet it was as late as 1826 before a commentator, in the *Theatrical Observer*, was moved to remark on it in print (a "gas light and coke company" having been incorporated in London as early as 1812):

It would be ridiculous to deny that in the present state of the stage pictorial effects are of the first importance; indeed, when called to the aid of poetical imagination, there is no reason why they should not rank high and be essential to the drama. . . . A very little ingenuity would enable the light to be cast principally or even solely on any single object, the beauty of which would soon be found in all spectral attempts, which, as they are now managed, are generally the most abortive of the dramatic art. The nymphs in *The Tempest* might swim in indistinct moonlight, the witches in *Macbeth* might glower over the murky flame of the caldron, and the ghost in *Hamlet* walk surrounded by a halo of dim light.[15]

It was not until the 1860's that gas lighting would be employed in private houses, and the changes that took place in general theatrical conditions during the nineteenth century were scarcely numerous. E. B. Watson has observed, "In general, then, we may say that the first seventy years of the nineteenth century contributed little to the improvement of the playhouse histrionically. Changes which affected acting were: a gradual disuse of the stage 'Apron'; an improvement in the audience as a result of introducing orchestra stalls; and a slight betterment of lighting effects through the use of a great chandelier in the audience part of the house."[16] Yet any contention that gas illumination was not employed for stage purposes can hardly be substantiated. One spectator records a performance at Covent Garden in 1826 whose lighting effects could only have been achieved with gas; and we note here as well this passage on

---

[15] No. 1491 (September 15, 1826); quoted by Watson, p. 93.

[16] E. B. Watson, pp. 95–96. It will be observed that Watson does not consider stage lighting by gas important enough to merit attention. By "an improvement in the audience" he means the gradual return to the theatre of the middle and upper classes beginning around the middle of the nineteenth century.

gauze—or, as we would call it, a scrim: "At the rising of the curtain a thick mist covers the stage and gradually rolls off. This is
remarkably well managed by means of fine gauze. In the dim
light we distinguish a little cottage, the dwelling of a sorceress;
in the background a lake surrounded by mountains, some of
whose peaks are clothed with snow. All is misty and indistinct;
the sun then rises triumphantly, chases the morning dews, and
the hut with the village in the distance now appears in perfect
outline."[17]

Gauze to create scenic effects, heightened by directed illumination, was employed by James Robinson Planché, too, in several of his theatrical productions. In addition, panoramic devices
were utilized by managers during the period, notably panoramas
invented by Daguerre and Bouton, and a device from the
eighteenth century called the eidophusikon. No wonder, with
such scenic and optical competition available, that Nicoll was
moved to remark that in the early nineteenth century "the playwright became of less importance than the machinist."[18]

But only half the story would be told if we limited our investigation of the condition of the London theatres to the first
seven decades of the nineteenth century; or to lighting and
other scenic effects. Other specific changes with which dramatists
of the first two decades had to be concerned were almost without
exception occurring as Romantic drama began to make its first
hesitant appearance in the London theatres; and the decade
of the 1830's, when the problems raised by these recent innovations began to be resolved, was the decade that witnessed the
high-water mark in the number and the importance of staged
poetic plays. So far as they concern the drama of the early part
of the century, these problems of stagecraft and stage production
are more than cursorily related to each other; much of the tenta-
tive and experimental quality of the drama of the entire period

---

[17] Prince Hermann Ludwig Heinrich Pückler-Muskau, *A Tour in
England of a German Prince* (3 vols., London, 1832), III, Letter
10; quoted in George Rowell, *The Victorian Theatre: A Survey* (Oxford, 1956), p. 21.

[18] Nicoll, I, 35—36, 26.

can be explained by the time that was required to bring them into balance. Especially is this so as regards the burgeoning size of the theatres, for it is largely in terms of the changes in size of the patent theatres that concurrent transformations in staging and lighting first begin to assume their proper perspective. Technical innovation arrived at nearly the same time as theatrical renovation and expansion—and technical competence in handling the new media underwent perpetual re-examination as, under the pressures of patrons, directors, and prestige alike, the dimensions of theatres began to be renovated as well as their capacities.

The first of the houses to be completely rebuilt was Drury Lane. Designed by Christopher Wren in 1674, throughout the eighteenth century this theatre had been held substantially to its original design, in a period that included the tenures of both Garrick and Sheridan. The new Drury Lane that opened in 1794 was a far more elaborate structure. Equipped with "five tiers instead of the former three, the seating capacity has been estimated at over 3,500 and the depth of the stage, 92 feet, was only 20 feet short of the overall length of Wren's Drury Lane,"[19] surely an impressive transformation indeed! A bit earlier, in 1792, Covent Garden had been substantially renovated and enlarged, too. Yet change did not stop at that point. Fire gutted Covent Garden in September, 1808; the following February a similar calamity befell Drury Lane. The two theatres, after they were rebuilt, Covent Garden in 1810 and Drury Lane in 1812, again maintained their late-eighteenth-century seating capacities of slightly over 3,000, feats achieved as much "by internal arrangements as by overall dimensions."[20] For legitimate theatres, both houses remained uncommonly large.

There also began to be developed new techniques in staging and stage management. During the eighteenth century the

---

[19] Rowell, p. 6. *The Annual Register,* April 30, 1794, lists Drury Lane as accommodating 3,611 spectators.

[20] *Ibid.* The alterations and probable capacities of Drury Lane and Covent Garden are discussed by Harry W. Pedicord, *The Theatrical Public in the Time of Garrick* (New York, 1954), pp. 3–8.

construction of elaborate sets and wings was already becoming a highly sophisticated art. De Loutherbourg, an Alsatian hired by Garrick for the old Drury Lane, perfected a system of cutouts and backdrops and intricate backpieces which could be dismantled rapidly, permitting intricate changes in scenery; the ballet and opera, too, during this same period acquired their fair share of more than merely standard scenic effects. But the more varied the development of different types of scenery and sets, the more rapacious became the demands of audiences for refinements that should be even subtler and more "realistic," until even the basic theatre machinery became so inordinately complicated and cumbersome that to understand its ramifications and to make it function smoothly required a high degree of technical competence. Eventually the "stage-traps of the Elizabethan and Georgian eras were greatly elaborated in the nineteenth century to include 'Vampire' traps, 'Corsican' traps, and 'star' traps, all of which contributed not only to the effect of spectacular drama but also to the pantomime and musical stage."[21] A stage manager recalls of the Olympia Theatre around 1836, a house which specialized in burlettas and other extravaganzas, that its stage floor was divided into no fewer than six such traps.[22] Related to this efflorescence of stage machinery, additional features were present in theatres which could be employed for various subsidiary purposes, such as the notorious proscenium doors, through which a favored actor might make a grand entrance, or a spectator a noisy exit, entirely according to predilection or momentary whim.

And so as we return once again to the hero of the piece, the author, if now we better understand the magnitude of the problems he was confronted with, we may well repeat: the wonder is that any worthwhile drama was written at all in the Romantic Period. Certainly, if a basic requirement for any art, and for drama in particular, is that the artist must be assured that the medium of his labors offers some easily conjecturable stability,

---

[21] Rowell, p. 20.

[22] Mathew Mackintosh, *Stage Reminiscences by an Old Stager* (London, 1866), p. 70; quoted by Rowell, p. 19.

this is a requirement which the early-nineteenth-century English theatre was woefully unable to satisfy.

Moreover, because most dramatists for almost the first half of the century were dazzled by Shakespeare's genius, they obdurately insisted on composing poetic masterpieces which, though possibly stageworthy in the Globe Theatre, only displayed a naive lack of understanding for the restrictions that an enclosed theatre places upon flights of fancy. The playwrights who succeeded best in this age were Coleman the Elder, who wrote comedies for his own two theatres, Covent Garden and the Haymarket, and Sheridan Knowles, who over a period of years managed to develop considerable conversance with staging and stage techniques. The rest, those who at most wrote one or two stageworthy dramas, succeeded either by accident or because a knowledgeable stage manager, like Macready, was willing to adapt their efforts for the theatre. Not until the latter half of the century, through the pioneering efforts of Robertson and Boucicault, was the stage prepared once again to embrace the playwright—and vice versa; and of course we then had the easily staged productions of Wilde, Pinero, and Bernard Shaw, and under managers who knew all there was to know about the stage. Writers of the order of Wordsworth, Coleridge, or Browning, however well endowed they might have been with poetic ability, when it came to transforming a poetic ideal into theatrical reality, made their ignorance evident at every turn. Blinded by the brilliance of Shakespearean precedent, they erroneously assumed that imagination and technique do not necessarily go hand in hand, and this without having more than the haziest notion how to manipulate their characters on and off stage.

And so, as we judge Romantic drama, this common-sense recognition must play an important part in our evaluation: we must weigh our judgment, certainly, on the basis of merit, yet we must not forget that lurking pervasively in the background is the physical structure of the nineteenth-century theatre, ever changing, ever shifting.

There remains a final factor, the notorious Licensing Act. Since the Licensing Act and its bearing upon the direction pursued by the drama will become crucially important only at a later point in our discussion of poetic tragedy, we will wait until then to discuss it in detail. By the time the Act was ultimately repealed, in 1843, it was discovered, much to the astonishment of everyone concerned, that it had never been a reality so much as a long-perpetuated fantasy, whose provisions had been observed simply because the legality of the Act had never been thoroughly investigated. But until at least 1832 the Licensing Act was soberingly real to both theatre manager and playwright; and it did much to stifle any original or daring idea that management might harbor about presenting contemporary life or contemporary problems to the English audience. There would have been little point for the playwright to devote himself to burning issues, knowing well that the Lord Chamberlain would only forbid their being staged. Thus a lengthy hiatus in topical drama could be the only logical consequence of such restrictive censorship—that and the fact that since only the two patent houses were authorized to present legitimate plays, censorship was easy to impose.

Although wily theatre managers resorted to stratagems to circumvent the worst restrictions, what remains is drama which is frankly Romantic in its inclinations—not necessarily Romantic, that is to say, because the Romantic dramatist was blind to the world of reality around him, but because if he wished to see his play in production, he had to feign a kind of blindness which all too easily can be mistaken for moral indifference or lack of concern. We shall soon discover that however romantic the product of the period may be characterized as to mood and emotional appeal, this does not mean that it was escapist in tone or in its commitment to the problems of the age. On the contrary, the Romantic playwright often seems remarkably modern in his involvement with the problems of his period—it is merely that his manner of presenting his material tends at times to conceal what actually is a purpose of considerable depth and intensity.

We have now set the stage, and it is time to open the curtain. Much will be explained in due course; and much that now may seem illogical will gradually fit into its proper place. Even though Romantic drama may be no better at the end than at the beginning, at least it may appear less murkily veiled in the reaches of time, as well as more purposefully projected by its creators. To begin at the beginning we must turn back the calendar from the year 1813 and the first performance at Drury Lane of Coleridge's *Remorse;* for our story can properly be said to have opened in the much earlier year of 1796, when Wordsworth was working on *The Borderers.*

CHAPTER II

Wordsworth and Coleridge

The Borderers is first mentioned in a letter of Dorothy Words-worth's dated October 24, 1796: "W. is ardent in the composi-tion of a tragedy."[1] By then she and her brother had been settled at Racedown somewhat more than a year. The background for the play, as Wordsworth's nephew suggests,[2] had occurred to the poet either when he lived at Penrith or when he visited Kes-wick, a town steeped in the atmosphere of the period of Henry III, in whose reign the drama was laid. Passing reference to *The Borderers* is again made somewhat later that same year in a letter by Wordsworth himself: "I have lately been employed in writing a tragedy, the first draught of which is nearly finished."[3]

In June of the following year the manuscript was read to Coleridge. The acquaintance of the two poets dated from 1795, when they met in Bristol; but they first became fast friends after Coleridge moved to Stowey in December, 1796. Shortly there-after Coleridge also began work on a play. In a letter to Richard Brinsley Sheridan, dated February 6, 1797, he remarks: "I re-ceived a letter last Saturday . . . importing that *You* wished me 'to write a tragedy on some popular subject.' "[4] The expression

---

[1] *Memoirs of William Wordsworth,* ed. Christopher Wordsworth (2 vols., London, 1851), I, 96.

[2] *Ibid.*

[3] *Early Letters of William and Dorothy Wordsworth (1787–1805),* ed. Ernest de Selincourt (Oxford, 1935), p. 161. Hereafter referred to as S. I, followed by the page number.

[4] *Collected Letters of Samuel Taylor Coleridge,* ed. Earl Leslie Griggs (4 vols., Oxford [1956, I and II; 1959, III and IV]), I, 304. Hereafter referred to as G. I, etc., followed by the page number.

'popular subject,' he admits in the same letter, "has a little puzzled me. Mr. Bowles perhaps will be able to inform me, whether you meant by it to recommend a fictitious and domestic subject, or one founded on well-known History." But by March 16 the plan apparently had become clearer in both Coleridge's and Sheridan's minds. To Josiah Wade, Coleridge confides: "Sheridan has sent to me to write a Tragedy, which he promises me to introduce on Drury Lane Theatre with every possible advantage, and wishes me to sketch one out immediately and send him the sketch, when he will give me his opinion on it" (G. I,316). The same day, in a letter to another correspondent, Coleridge is somewhat more explicit concerning his general intentions for this drama: "The plan I had sketched is too chaotic to be transmitted at present—but immediately I understand it myself, I will submit it to you: and feel greatly obliged to you for your permission to do it.—It is 'romantic and wild and somewhat terrible'—and I shall have Siddons and Kemble in my hand" (G. I,316).[5]

On June 6, 1797, Coleridge visited the Wordsworths at Racedown. "The first thing that was read after he came was William's new poem *The Ruined Cottage* with which he was much delighted; and after tea he repeated to us two and a half acts of his tragedy *Osorio*. The next morning William read his tragedy *The Borderers*," writes Dorothy Wordsworth of this meeting (S. I,169). Coleridge's enthusiastic response is recorded in his famous letter to Joseph Cottle, June 8, 1797: "Wordsworth admires my Tragedy—which gives me great hopes. Wordsworth has written a Tragedy himself. I speak with heart-felt sincerity and (I think) unblinded judgement, when I tell you, that I feel myself a *little man by his* side; and yet do not think myself the less wonderful. You know, I do not commonly speak in such abrupt and unmingled phrases—and therefore will the more readily believe me.—There are in the piece those *profound* touches of the human heart, which I find three or four times in

---

[5] The date given is on Griggs's authority, based upon his comments in a footnote appearing on the same page.

'The Robbers' of Schiller, and often in Shakespere—but in Wordsworth there are no *inequalities*" (G. I,325).

It is possible that the two poets had become familiar with each other's plays during a visit paid by Wordsworth to Coleridge at Nether Stowey in early April, when Wordsworth was on his way back to Racedown from Bristol.[6] Coleridge mentions this visit by a cryptic reference to "Wordsworth's conversation, &c roused me somewhat" from a state of depression (G. I,319); and he refers to *Osorio* in this same letter by saying: "I employ myself now on a book of Morals in answer to Godwin, and on my Tragedy" (G. I,320). Since *The Borderers* is so directly concerned with refuting Godwinian doctrine, the supposition is not implausible that the plays with which the two writers were concerned were among the topics discussed during this April meeting. Coleridge by this time had dissociated himself from his previous admiration for Godwin's *Political Justice,* a point of view that coincided with Wordsworth's own disenchantment; Coleridge, who had attacked Godwin's philosophy in the *Watchman,* reiterated his position somewhat later in answer to a letter signed "Caius Gracchus" in a subsequent issue of April 2, 1796: "I do consider Mr. Godwin's Principles as vicious; and his book as a Pander to Sensuality. Once I thought otherwise— nay, even addressed a complimentary sonnet to the author, in the *Morning Chronicle,* of which I confess with much moral and poetical contrition, that the lines and the subject were equally bad" (G. I,199–200).

The supposition that the two playwrights were already familiar with each other's dramas by the time of the readings of June 6 is strengthened by a statement made by Dorothy Wordsworth on May 28: "W. has nearly finished a tragedy which he has good hopes of getting shown to Sheridan" (S. I,166). As Miss Moorman points out in her biography, Wordsworth "had certainly had no thought of writing it for the stage when he began it in the previous autumn."[7] Of his visit to the Wordsworths the

---

[6] See comments made in G. I, 316, *n.* 5.

[7] Mary Moorman, *William Wordsworth: The Early Years, 1770–1803* (Oxford, 1957), p. 311.

following month, Coleridge writes on June 9: "I am at present sojourning for a few days with Wordsworth, at Racedown Lodge, near Crewkherne: and finishing my Tragedy. Wordsworth, who is a strict and almost severe critic, thinks *very* highly of it—which gives me great hopes" (G. I,326).

Thus, concurrently, the two poets were working on their tragedies in the same milieu, Wordsworth's almost completed and Coleridge's more than half so. How near Coleridge had come to bringing *Osorio* to a close is indicated by a letter written the next day: "I shall have quite finished my Tragedy in a day or two: and then I mean to walk to Bowles, the poet, to read it to him, and have his criticisms—and then, accordingly as he advises, I shall either transmit the play to Sheridan, or go to London and have a personal interview with him" (G. I,327). But personal contact with the Wordsworths seems to have taken up time Coleridge might otherwise have been devoting to this other work, for the next reference in his correspondence is to Wordsworth's play rather than to his own, in a letter to Thomas Poole: "I pray you, come over if possible by eleven o'clock that we may have Wordsworth's Tragedy read under the trees" (G. I,332). It is not until August that he again mentions *Osorio,* in a letter to Joseph Cottle: "I shall now stick close to my Tragedy (called *Osorio,*) and when I have finished it, shall walk to Shaftesbury to spend a few days with Bowles" (G. I,344). But the tragedy was not completed until early October. In a letter to John Thelwall, written about October 14, Coleridge reports: "Oh! my Tragedy —it is finished, transcribed, and to be sent off to day—but I have no hopes of it's success or even of it's being acted" (G. I,352). Two copies were dispatched, one to Bowles, to whom Coleridge writes on October 16: "At last I send you the Tragedy complete and neatly transcribed—I have sent another to Mr. Linley" (G. I,355). By early December, Linley, Sheridan's brother-in-law, had replied. Coleridge presents a report of the results to Thomas Poole in a letter of December 2: "I received a letter from Linley, the long and the short of which is that Sheridan rejects the Tragedy—his sole objection is—the obscurity of the last three acts" (G. I,358).

Although Coleridge entertained few hopes for the ultimate production of his play, its style pleased him somewhat more. In the letter to Bowles of October 16 he declares: "In truth, I have fagged so long at the work and see so many imperfections in the original and main plot, that I feel an indescribable disgust, a sickness of the very heart, at the mention of the Tragedy. If there be any thing with which I am at all satisfied, it is—the style. I have endeavoured to have few sentences which *might not* be spoken in conversation, avoiding those that are *commonly* used in conversation" (G. I,356). At the same time Coleridge remained active on behalf of *The Borderers*. On November 20 he writes to Joseph Cottle: "I have procured for Wordsworth's Tragedy an Introduction to Harris, the Manager of Covent Garden—who has promised to read it attentively, and give his answer immediately— and if he accept it, to put it in preparation without an hour's delay" (G. I,358).

That same day, November 20, we learn from Dorothy Wordsworth: "William's play is finished, and sent to the managers of the Covent Garden Theatre. We have not the faintest expectation that it will be accepted" (S. I,174). Nonetheless the cause seemed so favorable that the Wordsworths journeyed to London. On December 21, Dorothy Wordsworth writes from Bristol: "We have been to London; our business was the play, and the play is rejected. It was sent to one of the principal actors at Covent Garden, who expressed great approbation and advised William strongly to go to London to make certain alterations. Coleridge's play is also rejected" (S. I,175). Coleridge's next reference to *Osorio*, on February 8, 1798, is expressed somewhat more feelingly:

As to my Tragedy, the story is briefly this—last year in the spring Sheridan wrote to me thro' Bowles (the poet) requesting me in very pressing and complimentary language to write a Tragedy—he promised me his assistance in adapting it for the stage, and that he would bring it on with every possible advantage.—I knew the man's character too well, to suffer myself to be inflated by hope—however I set myself in good earnest about it, finished the piece in a much better style than I had supposed myself capable of doing, and transmitted it to Sheridan, in October—From that time to this I have received no answer from him, altho' I have written to him—and the only intelligence, I have received, was from Linley, Sheridan's brother in law, who told me that Sheridan spoke to him in extravagant terms of it's merits.—In all probability, Mrs. Sheridan has made thread-paper with it. (G. I, 384-385)

Thereafter Coleridge considered having his play brought out in a collected edition of his works. But once again Sheridan renewed his offer, some time early in May. Coleridge writes on the fourteenth: "Sheridan has again promised to fit it for the stage and bring it on, which promise he will . . . certainly break" (G. I,400). Coleridge's surmise apparently proved to be correct, for he does not refer to *Osorio* again until 1800, and then to his intention to "re-write my Tragedy" (G. I,585). The desire to have either his own or Wordsworth's play produced nevertheless had not ceased to occupy his attention. On July 15, 1800, he expresses himself to Daniel Stuart:

With regard to the play business, Wordsworth has a Tragedy by him, in my opinion, a most masterly one this he would transmit by you to Mr Sheridan, for Mr Sheridan's opinion, provided *you* would engage that the *Copy* shall be returned to him—as he has but this one perfect Copy. Mr Sheridan will see by this of what kind Mr Wordsworth's dramatic Talents are; and if he should find the Tragedy unfit for representation, he might put Mr W. in the way of writing a play that *should* be fit for representation, by pointing out to him the defects that render the present one untheatrical. Mr Sheridan's conception of my obstinacy is a mistake—. When I sent my play to him, I gave at the same time expressly to him the whole and absolute power of alteration, addition, and omission—. I did indeed defend some parts of my play against Young Linley, but only as a *metaphysician;* never supposing myself to have any voice or suffrage, or even *opinion,* as to what was or was not suited for representation. After all, I never blamed Mr Sheridan for not bringing my play on the stage. God knows my inmost heart, and knows that I never for an hour together thought it likely to succeed—I blamed Mr Sheridan solely for taking no kind of notice whatsoever, and for withholding from me the copy of my play after repeated applications; and these applications too made at a time when I had no copy in my possession, and wished to have disposed of it to the Book-sellers. . . . But this is all gone by!—I am convinced, I have no Talents for so arduous a species of composition as the Drama. (G. I,603-604)

From these remarks we may assume that Sheridan never actually saw *Osorio* when it was first presented to the Covent Garden committee. Presumably the play was rejected solely on Linley's authority, and the same was probably true for Wordsworth's play. That Coleridge was uncertain concerning the disposition of the matter by the Covent Garden committee is evident from a letter addressed the same day to Humphry Davy, in which he repeats: "Sheridan has sent to me again about my Tragedy—I do not know what will come of it—he is an unprincipled Rogue" (G. I,606). On July 24, in expressing his continued indignation at Sheridan's most recent renewal of the offer that originally had been made three years earlier, Coleridge reports: "Sheridan has sent me a strange sort of message about my Tragedy—wishing me to write for the stage, making all his old offers over again, and charging the non-representation of my play on my extreme obstinacy in refusing to have it at all altered!—Did you ever hear of such a damned impudent Dog?" (G. I,608). By September 22, 1800, to judge from a letter to William Godwin, it is evident that the episode with Sheridan has drawn to its unfortunate close.

That which Lamb informed you, is founded in truth. Mr. Sheridan sent thro' the medium of Stewart a request to Wordsworth to present a Tragedy to his stage, and to me a declaration that the failure of my piece was owing to my obstinacy in refusing any alteration. I laughed and Wordsworth smiled; but my Tragedy will remain at Keswick, and Wordsworth's is not likely to emigrate from Grasmere. Wordsworth's Drama is in it's present state not fit for the stage, and he is not well enough to submit to the drudgery of making it so. Mine is fit for nothing except to excite in the minds of good men the hope, that "the young man is likely to do better." In the first moments I thought of re-writing it, and sent to Lamb for the copy with this intent—I read an act, and altered my opinion and with it my wish. (G. I,624)

Yet in a letter to Southey, on July 22, 1801, Coleridge again is considering altering *Osorio* and having it published: "If I am well enough, I mean to alter, with a devilish sweep of revolution, my Tragedy, and publish it in a little volume by itself with a new name, as a Poem" (G. II,745).

During this time, however, Coleridge remained convinced that his play was superior to other dramas of his day. As early as the end of May, 1798, we find him expressing this sentiment in a letter to Joseph Cottle: "As to the Tragedy, when I consider it [in] reference to Shakespear's and to *one* other Tragedy, it seems a poor thing; and I care little what becomes of it—when I consider [it] in comparison with modern Dramatists, it *rises:* and I think it too bad to be published, too good to be *squandered.* —I think of breaking it up; the planks are sound, and I will build a new ship of old materials" (G. I,412). But many years were to elapse before Coleridge would achieve this goal. Meanwhile, his interest in the theatre continued unabated. In the September 22, 1800, letter to William Godwin, he begins with effusive congratulations on the imminent production of Godwin's tragedy, *Antonio; or, The Soldier's Return,* acted but once (on December 13) in the 1800–1801 season at Drury Lane:

Your Tragedy is to be exhibited at Christmas!—I have indeed merely read thro' your letter; so it is not strange, that my heart still continues beating out of time. Indeed, indeed, Godwin! such a stream of hope and fear rushed in on me, when I read the sentence, as you would not permit yourself to feel. If there be any thing yet undreamt of in our philosophy; if it be, or if it be possible, that thought can impel thought out of the visual limits of a man's own scull and heart; if the clusters of ideas, which constitute our identity, do ever connect and unite into a greater Whole; if feelings could ever propagate themselves without the servile ministrations of undulating air or reflected light; I seem to feel within myself a strength and a power of desire, that might dart a modifying, commanding impulse on a whole Theatre. What does all this mean? Alas! that sober sense should know no other way to construe all this except by the tame phrase— I wish you success. (G. I,624)

Certainly there is no evidence of indifference to theatrical fame here!

Although Godwin's play was harshly reviewed, Coleridge advises his friend not to despair: "If your interest in the Theatre is not ruined by the fate of this, your first piece, take heart, set instantly about a new one . . ." (G. I,657). And in a somewhat earlier letter to Godwin, besides indicating once again his own theatrical ambitions, Coleridge offers an interesting picture of the current plight of the theatre:

The success of a Tragedy in the present size of the Theatres . . . is in my humble opinion rather improbable than probable—. What *Tragedy* has succeeded for the last 15 years? You will probably answer the Question by another—What Tragedy has *deserved* to succeed? and to that I can give no answer.—Be my Thoughts therefore sacred to Hope—! If EVERY *Wish* of mine had but a pair of Hands, your Play should be *clapped* thro' 160 successive nights—and I would reconcile it to my conscience (in part) by two thoughts, first that *you* are a good man; and secondly that the divinity of Shakespere would remain all that while unblasphemed by the applause of a Rabble, who if he were now for the first time to present his pieces would hiss them into infamy. (G. I,653)

Elsewhere, to Godwin, Coleridge remarks on other plays being presented in London concurrently.

Have you seen Sheridan since your return? How is it with your Tragedy? Were you in town, when Miss Bayley's [sic] Tragedy was represented? How was it, that it proved so uninteresting? Was the fault in the Theatre, the Audience, or the Play?—It must have excited a deeper feeling in you than that of mere curiosity: for doubtless, the Tragedy had great merit. I know not indeed, how far Kemble might have

watered and thinned it's consistence—I speak of the printed
Play.—Have you read the Wallenstein?—Prolix and crowded
and dragging as it is, yet it is quite a model for it's judicious
management of the *Sequence* of Scenes—and such it is held
on the German Theatres. Our English Acting Plays are many
of them woefully deficient in this part of the dramatic Trade
and Mystery. (G. I,621)

The one thing not surprising about this letter to Godwin is
that Coleridge should here be mentioning Schiller's *Wallenstein*,
for by this time he himself had translated two parts of this trilogy
into English. Indeed, by this period Coleridge had already served
a lengthy apprenticeship in his efforts to write for the stage; and
despite the protestations to the contrary indicated by his correspondence, he had succeeded in mastering more than the bare
rudiments of stage technique. His admiration of the "judicious
management of the *Sequence* of Scenes" in Schiller's *Wallenstein*
stands in juxtaposition to what, as he himself recognized, was a
besetting weakness in his own plays. His first attempt at play-
writing had been "An Historic Drama," *The Fall of Robespierre,* written in collaboration with Robert Southey in 1794.
Coleridge wrote only the first act of this play, but it was agreed
that since his name was then the better known, *The Fall of Robespierre* might sell more readily if attributed solely to him. In the
Dedication to this drama, Coleridge states his intentions as being "to imitate the empassioned and highly figurative language
of the French orators, and to develope the characters of the chief
actors on a vast stage of horrors." And indeed, both young poets
were so deeply disturbed by the aftereffects of the French Revolution that it was their object in this piece of juvenilia to express
their own political positions by depicting the inhumanity of the
Registry in all of its actual horror. In his contribution of some
275 lines, however, Coleridge does little more than indicate for
the first time those weaknesses in composition that were to plague
him in his other dramatic works: skill in moving his characters
in an explicable fashion on and off stage would ever elude him.
He does show an ability to handle dialogue capably, even though
the dialogue in *The Fall* is chiefly rhetorical. The speeches (all

of the set type) abound in rhetorical flights of fancy that are elevated, if not especially elevating—and, it might be added, as figurative as the intentions indicated in the Preface of developing "the characters of the chief actors on a vast stage of horrors" would serve to indicate. In this act by Coleridge is a "Song" subsequently reprinted among his collected poetical works as "To Domestic Peace." Otherwise, Coleridge's contribution to this play gives little hint of future dramatic promise.

If nothing else, *The Fall of Robespierre* proved to be the first step in his dramatic career. By 1796 Coleridge had begun his study of German. That same year he began entertaining "some thoughts of making a proposal to [George] Robinson, the great London Bookseller, of translating all the works [of] Schiller, which would make a portly Quarto, on the conditions that he should pay my Journey and wife's to and from Jena, a cheap German University where Schiller resides" (G. I,209). With the extinction of his hopes for the production of *Osorio* within a reasonable period of time, Coleridge evidently felt impelled to return to this earlier project. If he could not see his own plays staged, he would be able to have a hand in the production of someone else's for which he could claim partial credit. The choice of Schiller to translate is understandable when we remember how great was Coleridge's admiration of Schiller at this time; four years and two translations later saw his views somewhat modified, as can be gathered from a letter to Daniel Stuart of October 7, 1800: "To be known to Schiller was a thought, that passed across my brain and vanished—I would not stir 20 yards out of my way to *know* him" (G. I,628). But in 1796, when he had addressed an extravagant apostrophe to Schiller entitled "To the Author of 'The Robbers,'" Coleridge's admiration was still fresh.[8] In ad-

---

[8] The poem is worth quoting, if for nothing else, to show the intensity of Coleridge's feelings at the time.

> Ah! Bard tremendous in sublimity!
> Could I behold thee in thy loftier mood
> Wandering at eve with finely-frenzied eye
> Beneath some vast old tempest-swinging wood!
> Awhile with mute awe gazing I would brood:
> Then weep aloud in a wild ecstasy!

dition to his remarks about the merits of *Wallenstein* that he imparted to Godwin, in a letter to Robert Southey he finds it to be a "dull heavy play; but I entertain hopes, that you will think the language for the greater part, natural and good common-sense English—to which excellence if I can lay fair claim in any book of poetry or prose, I shall be a very *singular* writer at least" (G. I,610).

As for the actual task of translation, in a letter to Thomas Poole dated February 25, 1800, Coleridge speaks of "translating three manuscript plays of Schiller—and positively for the last week have worked with my pen in my hand 14 hours every day" (G. I,574). It required but six weeks for him to complete this task he had set himself, in itself a remarkable achievement. The resulting product has been criticized for this hastiness in its composition;[9] yet, taken together, *The Piccolomini* and *The Death of Wallenstein* constitute one of the finest dramatic translations into English from a foreign language.[10] Besides their literary excellence as translations, they are of interest because of the skill with which Coleridge was able to render into poetic English even

---

[9] P. Machule, "Coleridge's Wallensteinübersetzung," *Englische Studien,* XXXI (1902), 182-239, presents derogatory comments that stand in opposition to most English criticism. Among other things, the author says: "Die Wallenstein-übersetzung Coleridge's gehört zu den büchern, die bei einer oberflächlichen lektüre durch gefällige züge bestechen, bei einer eingehenden prüfung günstige urteil in das gegenteil umzuschlagen droht. Die übersetzung beweist, dass ihr verfasser in seltener weise für ein so schwieriges werk befähigt war, aber er hat sich augenscheinlich nicht die zeit genommen oder nehmen können, jede einzelne stelle ruhig und sorgfältig zu erwägen und immer wieder die feilende und bessernde hand an den ersten entwurf zu legen." (P. 236.)

[10] For comments on the initially unfavorable reception of Coleridge's translation by the English press, notably in the *Athenaeum* and the *Monthly Review,* and specific comments by later critics on its literary excellence, see J. L. Haney, *The German Influence on S. T. Coleridge* (Philadelphia, 1902), pp. 21-23. For more recent criticism in the vein of the Machule article noted above, including an evaluation of the inaccuracies in the various editions of Coleridge's *Wallenstein,* see Bayard Q. Morgan, "What Happened to Coleridge's *Wallenstein,*" *MLJ,* XLIII (1959), 195-201.

Schiller's most difficult idiomatic passages. At these points he gives reasons for his emendations and includes the original text for purposes of comparison.[11] At other times, again with reasons given for his deletions, Coleridge omits passages that he feels are superfluous.[12] While admitting the growing number of liberties he has been taking with the original, Coleridge justifies himself on one occasion by declaring: "I fear that I should not have done amiss, had I taken this liberty more frequently."[13] In general, however, he does succeed in fulfilling his express intention of remaining "bound by the sense of my original, with as few exceptions as the nature of the language rendered possible,"[14] a problem rendered all the more difficult, and surmounted all the more brilliantly, by his having to duplicate the blank-verse meter of the original.[15]

In other respects Coleridge shows himself to be somewhat less successful. His shortcomings are most apparent where we might logically expect them to be least intrusive. In the dramatic passages he is at his best; invariably he translates the set speeches with consummate skill. It is in narration and especially in rendering antecedent action intelligible that Coleridge seems least at ease. Whenever possible, he severely compresses linking passages, effecting an ambiguity that is detrimental to the sense of what comes after;[16] but since these points, for purposes of the trans-

---

[11] See, for example, footnote, p. 632, in *Poetical Works,* ed. E. H. Coleridge (London, 1912).

[12] Viz., "The Piccolomini," II, iv, *Poetical Works,* pp. 646-647, where Coleridge confesses having "taken more liberty than in any other part of the play."

[13] "The Death of Wallenstein," *Poetical Works,* p. 753n.

[14] Preface of the Translator to the First Edition, *Poetical Works,* p. 725.

[15] For a more complete discussion of the technical aspects of Coleridge's translation, see H. F. G. Roscher, *Die Wallenstein-übersetzung von S. T. Coleridge* (Leipzig, 1905), especially the summary, pp. 169-170.

[16] This is especially evident in the extensive prose passage, *Poetical Works,* pp. 662-672, which is in blank verse in the original; possibly Coleridge felt it improper to put poetry into the mouths of servants and boon drinking companions, yet as a consequence there are instances here of certain declarations that are left unexplained.

lation, are minor enough, they do not seriously impede the reader's comprehension of the action as a whole. Rather more incomprehensible is Coleridge's having chosen to add the first two
acts of *Wallensteins Tod* to his translation of *The Piccolomini*,
whereby the latter play is brought to a close upon a note of mysti-
fication.[17] Hence, when the Coleridgean *Death of Wallenstein*
commences, no indication can be given of what has come previously, since the antecedent action from Schiller's *Wallensteins
Tod* is now an integral part of *The Piccolomini*. The only reasonable explanation is that Coleridge did not wish to begin his
Death of Wallenstein with the scene that shows Wallenstein con-
sulting with his astrologer; in a flyleaf notation Coleridge takes
Schiller very much to task on this point.[18] Whatever the reason,
here in particular Coleridge demonstrates a singular ineptitude
when it comes to fitting scenes together logically, whatever facility
of imagination he possesses for stage dialogue and whatever gift
of language for mastering linguistic problems of stage poetry.

When we turn from these *Wallenstein* translations to the
earlier *Osorio,* immediately we conjecture what might have resulted had Coleridge written this play after he gained experience
from studying Schiller's dramas, rather than before. Superficially,
the errors in composition and stage direction in *Osorio* are of
insurmountable proportions. Since the play is often poorly
constructed and impossibly ambiguous, it is little wonder that
Coleridge should once have remarked that he experienced
"an indescribable disgust . . . at the mention of the tragedy"
(G. I,356). One of *Osorio's* principal drawbacks is the fact that

---

[17] *Die Piccolomini* ends with the question of Wallenstein's duplicity
unresolved in the younger Piccolomini's mind; Schiller drew the cli-
mactic scene in this fashion to intensify the trilogy's main theme of
the conflict of love vs. obedience to royal prerogative. Coleridge ends
The Piccolomini with the more dramatic scene of the rupture between
father and son, leaving the opening of the second play to weak, secondary action.

[18] The quotation reads: "Astrology is made prophetic, and yet
treated ludicrously; the author as philosopher is in compleat discord
with himself as Historian. This is a most grievous fault." (Preface,
Poetical Works, p. 955.)

the scene takes place in a nebulous Moorish hinderland pur-
porting to pass for Castilian soil, a place presumably where anything can occur without its straining an audience's credulity.
Fortunately, by the time of the production of its readaptation
bearing the title *Remorse*, Coleridge had corrected a number of
the weaknesses occasioned by his choice of locale. But the plots of
the two plays unluckily remain unchanged. His sincere admiration for *The Borderers* and the almost mystical admiration the
play aroused within the Wordsworths' circle[19] reflect, however,
more upon Wordsworth's solidly grounded sense of continuity of
construction than upon any inability of Coleridge's to create
logically developed action. Dramatically speaking, there lies the
difference between the two plays; and certainly it is the reason
why Coleridge did not slavishly choose to imitate the example
established by Wordsworth in *The Borderers:* for his own play,
despite its incongruities, is dramatic, whereas Wordsworth's is
too static for theatrical production. Coleridge's drama would
stage better than it reads, Wordsworth's the opposite.

It is a pity we do not know the exact extent to which either
was influenced by the work of the other in the writing of these
plays. But a number of conjectures can be made that in themselves are pertinent to the dramas of the later poetic playwrights
and to the course the theatre was to adopt in the period of Romantic drama as it developed in the early nineteenth century.

---

[19] Charles Lamb once remarks in writing to Coleridge: "By-the-by,
I have a sort of recollection that somebody, I think *you*, promised me
a sight of Wordsworth's Tragedy. I should be very glad of it just now;
for I have got Manning with me, and should like to read it *with him*.
But this, I confess, is a refinement." Lamb also confides to Coleridge,
on another occasion: "The names of Tom Poole, of Wordsworth, and
his good sister, with thine and Sara's, are become 'familiar in my mouth
as household words.'" (*Works,* ed. E. V. Lucas [7 vols., London, 1903–
1912], VI, 184, 108.) For William Macready's familiarity with *The
Borderers,* see p. 164. Swinburne is less complimentary. *The Borderers*
he calls "unparalleled by any serious production of the human intellect
for morbid and monstrous extravagance of horrible impossibility"
("Wordsworth and Byron," Miscellanies in *Bonchurch Edition,* ed.
Edmund Gosse and Thomas J. Wise [20 vols., London, 1925–1927],
XIV, 207).

Both plays contain elements of the Gothic and sentimental drama,[20] elements that by the decade of the 1790's had become inextricably intertwined. By this time stage plays had grown into an amalgamation of tear-drenched horror, making it possible for the audience to enjoy the privilege of shrieking and weeping in almost the same breath. Although Horace Walpole's *The Mysterious Mother* (1768) introduced this new genre of Gothic drama to English audiences, if we consider the tastes of the immediately subsequent period, it is logical to suppose that if not from Walpole, Gothic drama would probably have come onto the stage from some outside—German—source. Given the concurrent decline in native English drama of other types, the Gothic play gradually assumed an increasingly influential position throughout the latter half of the eighteenth century. Soon these Gothic dramas and French importations began to flood the English stage.[21] The motive of terror, or sheer horror, was combined in these German imports of the 1790's with an overlay of sentimentality that, by itself, grew so extreme that there resulted in reaction to it a widespread form of burlesque.[22] This excess of "feeling" contributed in turn to a revulsion against Gothic drama in favor of psychological analysis of character, combined with investigation of a single, or multiform, passion. In their totality this attitude is best represented by *The Plays of the Passions*, a series of dramas by Joanna Baillie; the same tendency is noticeable in Wordsworth's *The Borderers* and Coleridge's *Osorio* (*Remorse*).

It is not that Baillie, Wordsworth, and Coleridge were attempting to reject the traditions, the heritage, that had come

---

[20] See pp. 73–74.

[21] Bertrand Evans, in *Gothic Drama from Walpole to Shelley* (Berkeley and Los Angeles, 1947), p. 13, comments: "In relation to the total number of plays of all kinds, the number of Gothic plays between 1768 and 1823 is fractional. Yet it is certain that the period saw as many Gothic plays as any other single kind."

[22] Somewhat later mention will be made of *The Rovers* by Canning, Ellis, and Frere. Samuel C. Chew, in *The Dramas of Lord Byron* (pp. 4–5), has discovered another burlesque entitled *On the Prevalence of the German Drama on the British Stage*.

down to them. They and subsequent writers were not necessarily interested in theatrical reform. There were, to be sure, others, from Gifford in his *Maeviad* (1794) to Lord Byron in the Prefaces to his plays, who urged a fundamental reform in theatrical presentation; but those most actively concerned with writing for the theatre were more interested, in the words of Coleridge, in making "something that would do for the Theatre in its present state" (G. IV,971).[23] In short, intellectually the Romantic playwrights did not regard themselves as being at odds with the age in which they lived; nor did they find it incongruous, when setting pen to paper, that their techniques and locales in large measure should be indebted to Elizabethan, and especially Shakespearean, precedent. An instance of the fealty of Romantic dramatists to Gothic and Elizabethan models can be cited from a letter written by Thomas Lovell Beddoes in 1825: "With the greatest reverence for all the antiquities of the drama, I still think that we had better beget than revive—attempt to give the literature of this age an idiosyncrasy and spirit of its own and only raise a ghost to gaze on, not to live with—just now the drama is a haunted ruin."[24] Yet in that very same year, 1825, as if he had never written these sentiments, Beddoes commenced *Death's Jest-Book*, the most famous and most Gothically antique of all his works. Or we might turn to Joanna Baillie, who passed judgment in much the same vein as early as 1802 in the Preface to her *Plays*: "[The] spirit of imitation and attention to effect, has . . . confined [contemporary playwrights] very much in their choice of situations and events to bring their great characters into action: rebellions, conspiracies, contentions for empires, and rival ships in love have alone been thought worthy of trying those heroes; and palaces and dungeons the only places magnificent or solemn enough for them to appear in."[25] Miss

---

[23] Written on the flyleaf of a copy of *Zapolya* and headed: "To the author of Peter's Letters to his Kinfolk."

[24] *Works of Thomas Lovell Beddoes,* ed. H. W. Donner (Oxford and London, 1935), p. 595.

[25] *A Series of Plays* (2 vols., London, 1802), I,35.

Baillie continued writing plays in an equally Gothic and Shakespearean vein for another twenty years.

Either the Romantic dramatists could perceive faults, not in their own works but only in the works of others; or possibly the paradox can be explained on the grounds of their being incorrigibly obtuse. But given these evidences of self-criticism and the fact that they persisted in writing in a vein with which they themselves were the first to find fault, we can only conclude that the manner itself must not have been what displeased them; rather it must have been the weaknesses in the method of presentation that aroused their wrath. And if we recognize their conviction that they should write within the framework of a literary tradition, then, instead of regarding them as mere imitators, we should begin to perceive tangible reasons why they persisted in writing in this particular dramatically poetic vein.

For corroboration let us turn to Coleridge's "Critique on Bertram" in the *Biographia Literaria. Bertram,* a play by Charles R. Maturin, was accepted by the Drury Lane Theatre committee in place of Coleridge's own play, *Zapolya,* in 1816. This fact may partly explain the vituperativeness of Coleridge's attack against Maturin's play (although *Bertram* had been submitted to the committee before *Zapolya,* and that quite possibly may have weighed in its final decision). From his analysis and the reasons for his critique, however, Coleridge does not seem to have allowed his criticism to be prejudiced by personal bias. He condemns *Bertram* for catering to the sensationalism of popular taste; he affirms that the so-called German school, far from being of Teutonic origin, is nothing other than a corruption of Shakespearean influence that once more has been transported by importation to its true source, English soil. Rather than expecting from this a plea for the renovation or reform of the English stage, we can understand Coleridge's argument only when we realize that both he and many of his contemporaries believed they were writing in the mainstream of an English tradition when they regarded reverently and observed sedulously the manners of Shakespeare and the Elizabethan stage. Coleridge says:

Eighteen years ago I observed, that the whole secret of the modern jacobinical drama (which, and not the German, is its appropriate designation) and of all its popularity, consists in the confusion and subversion of the natural order of things in their causes and effects: namely in the excitement of surprise by representing the qualities of liberality, refined feeling, and a nice sense of honor (those things rather which pass among us for such) in persons and in classes where experience teaches us least to expect them; and by rewarding with all the sympathies which are the due of virtue, those criminals whom law, reason and religion have excommunicated from our esteem.[26]

It is these weaknesses, and not what latter-day scholars have termed "Shakespeare Idolatry,"[27] that, from Coleridge's point of view, stood in need of reform in the English theatre. Coleridge himself would have been astounded were he to know that his own play, *Zapolya*, shows "how heavy the dead hand of Elizabethanism lay upon the talent of the time,"[28] for in conjunction with this drama after its rejection in favor of *Bertram*, he mentions "the insolence and unfeeling caprice with which I was treated by the classical committee [of the Drury Lane Theatre], one of which coolly informed me that after *Bertram* [the public] would not be contented but with something truly Shakespearian, if not equal to yet *like* the BERTRAM!!" (G. IV,971).[29] No, the dramatists of Coleridge's age, no matter what their reservations in other respects, felt that when they wrote "romantic drama" they were neither being derivative nor writing pseudo-Shakespearean plays. What they were endeavoring to do was to demonstrate, through an examination of the characteristics of particular "passions" of the soul, the stresses experienced by

[26] *The Complete Works of S. T. Coleridge,* ed. W. G. T. Shedd (7 vols., New York, 1853) , III,567.

[27] Reference has been made to Babcock's book in Chapter I and, specifically, to Nicoll in his *Early Nineteenth Century English Drama.*

[28] Samuel C. Chew, "The Drama in Decline," in *A Literary History of England,* p. 1268.

[29] Written on the flyleaf of a copy of *Zapolya.*

the individual mind. Baillie, for one, believed that the chief object of a playwright is

> to delineate passion in its progress, to trace it from its early beginning, and to show the fearful gulf toward which it hastens, if not checked in the earlier portions of its career. . . . [Miss Baillie] has thus a high moral purpose in her design; which, if the drama can warn and save, will not altogether have been defeated. . . . The sole difference between her design and the usual practice of dramatic composers is, that while they have in most instances selected a story for the striking nature of its details, which rendered the prominence of one master passion necessary, she proposed to render her plots subservient to her main end, the development of one predominant and overruling passion.[30]

Coleridge finds, in turn, that "of all intellectual power, that of superiority to the fear of the invisible world is the most dazzling. Its influence is abundantly proved by the one circumstance, that it can bribe us into a voluntary submission of our better knowledge, into suspension of all our judgment derived from constant experience, and enable us to peruse with the liveliest interest the wildest tales of ghosts, wizards, genii, and secret talismans."[31]

When we turn to the way in which passions were utilized for the stage, the reasons why Coleridge adopted the theme of remorse for *Osorio* become immediately understandable. Coleridge believed that "power is necessarily an object of our desire and of our admiration. But of all power, that of the mind is, on every account, the grand *desideratum* of human ambition. . . . And the co-existence of great intellectual lordship with guilt has never been adequately represented without exciting the strongest interest, and for this reason, that in this bad and heterogeneous co-ordination we can contemplate the intellect of man more exclusively as a separate self-subsistence, than in its

---

[30] "Introduction," *Dramatic Works of Joanna Baillie* (London, 1851), p. x.

[31] *Complete Works of Coleridge*, III,564.

proper state of subordination to his own conscience, or to the will of an infinitely superior being."[32] And these remarks should be compared with that of Wordsworth about his play, *The Borderers*.

> My care was almost exclusively given to the passions and the characters, and the position in which the persons in the Drama stood relatively to each other, that the reader (for I had then no thought of the Stage) might be moved, and to a degree instructed, by lights penetrating somewhat into the depths of our nature. In this endeavour, I cannot think, upon a very late review, that I have failed. As to the scene and period of action, little more was required for my purposes than the absence of established Law and Government; so that the agents might be at liberty to act on their own impulses . . .[33]

How far such a unified concept could be carried out within a poetic framework for stage representation can also be illustrated through the works of other poetic dramatists who were equally insistent on upholding much this same point of view. In their dramas there is to be found

> a substitution of spiritual for external action, an increasing interest in the psychology of situation, a growing inattention to mere plot, a new and (judging by old standards) disproportionate insistence upon motive. This is illustrated by Miss Baillie, Coleridge, and others; and especially by Byron. It reaches its climax in Browning's dramas. In *Luria*, for example, there is a minute examination and revelation of every thought and impulse from the moment of its birth, and this in the character, not only of the protagonist but of each lesser person, as his or her deeds affect the significance of the spiritual motive which is behind the mere act.[34]

That this is old-fashioned and derivative it would be difficult to

---

[32] *Ibid.*

[33] *The Poetical Works of William Wordsworth*, ed. Ernest de Selincourt and Helen Darbishire (5 vols., Oxford, 1940, repr. 1952), I,324.

[34] Chew, *The Dramas of Lord Byron*, pp. 28-29. As will be pointed out in the next chapter, however, a "disproportionate insistence upon motive" by Byron does not necessarily correspond with what Chew would seem to imply.

maintain. Strindberg, O'Neill, and even Tennessee Williams have made experiments in much the same line.

But since these works of the other poetic dramatists are yet to come, for the time being let us return to the plays of Wordsworth and Coleridge. Coleridge's remarks on the state of the contemporary literary scene already have been quoted; Wordsworth, in the Preface to the second edition of *Lyrical Ballads*, expresses himself with almost equal forcefulness: "The invaluable works of our elder writers, I had almost said the works of Shakespeare and Milton, are driven into neglect by frantic novels, sickly and stupid German Tragedies, and deluges of idle and extravagant stories in verse. When I think upon this degrading thirst after outrageous stimulation, I am almost ashamed to have spoken of the feeble endeavour made in these volumes to counteract it."[35] These sentiments give Wordsworth's probable reasons for having written *The Borderers*. Although in his written works he is never explicit concerning these reasons— and certainly not so direct as Coleridge—the remarks he makes to his daughter upon the publication of *The Borderers* in 1842 are revealing.

> I am glad you like the tragedy. I was myself surprised to find the interest so kept up in the fourth and fifth acts. Of the third I never doubted, and quite agree with you that Herbert's speech is much the finest thing in the drama; I mean the most moving, or rather, the most in that style of the pathetic which one loves to dwell upon, though I acknowledge it is not so intensively dramatic as some parts of the fifth act especially.
>
> As to the first, my only fear was that the *action* was too far advanced in it. I think the scene where the vagrant tells her false story has great merit; it is thoroughly natural and yet not commonplace nature. Some of the sentiments which the development of Oswald's character required will, I fear, be complained of as too depraved for anything but biographical writing.[36]

---

[35] *The Poetical Works of William Wordsworth,* ed. Thomas Hutchinson (Oxford, 1933), pp. 935–936.

[36] *The Letters of William and Dorothy Wordsworth: The Later Years,* ed. Ernest de Selincourt (3 vols., Oxford, 1939), III,1122.

There are two considerations here. First is the evident attention that Wordsworth paid to language when he composed *The
Borderers*. It will be recalled that Coleridge was equally concerned with language that should be "natural" without being
"commonplace." Hence we may surmise that the precepts of the
Preface to *Lyrical Ballads* were being worked out by the two
poets as early as this period of the writing of their two plays.
This theme of naturalness of diction, certainly, runs as a leit-
motif through the few remarks each chose to make about their
still-fumbling attempts at satisfactorily rendering in verse the
"language of real life." A conscious effort to accomplish this task
was surely a characteristic each saw in the work of the other, and
by itself this must have been an important factor in Coleridge's
unstinting admiration for Wordsworth's play.

A second consideration is the peculiar problem of "autobiography" that has grown up around *The Borderers* by those
who regard this drama as some sort of atonement for Wordsworth's desertion of his French mistress, Annette Vallon. The
ingenious theory advanced by Campbell and Mueschke is no
longer widely credited.[37] De Selincourt has pointed out that
undoubtedly they are correct in their contention that "*The Borderers* is 'the result of a clash between Godwin's philosophy and
his [Wordsworth's] own bitter and searching experience' ";
yet "in their limitation of that experience to one element in it
they throw over all the evidence in favour of pure hypothesis."[38]
F. O. Matthiessen has shown the pitfalls awaiting any analysis
when the attempt is made to recast fiction into autobiography,
by remarking how impossible it is "for the literary critic to produce more than long-shot hunches in trying to get at an author's
particular conflicts through his novels or plays."[39] And although

[37] O. J. Campbell and Paul Mueschke, "*The Borderers* as a Document in the History of Wordsworth's Aesthetic Development," *MP*,
XXIII (1925–26), 465–482. "This drama offers clear evidence that its
initial aesthetic impulse was the remorse that his abandonment of
Annette had aroused in him" (p. 466).

[38] Ernest de Selincourt, "Wordsworth's Preface to 'The Borderers,' "
Oxford Lectures on Poetry (Oxford, 1934), p. 176.

[39] *American Renaissance* (New York, 1941), p. 479.

superficially relevant in the light of Wordsworth's life history previous to his having written *The Borderers,* such a long-shot hunch is based solely on the formulation that "all of Wordsworth's poetry is rightly to be regarded as thinly disguised expression of his personal experience. Even his most loyal admirers have remarked his lack of dramatic power—what Coleridge called his 'dramatic ventriloquism.' "[40] The second premise here, however, does not logically follow from the first; nor does this hypothesis prove that Wordsworth's *Borderers* for the given reason is thinly disguised autobiography. Rather, Wordsworth's remark that "the sentiments which the development of Oswald's character required will, I fear, be complained of as too depraved for anything but biographical writing" should offer a better clue to the poet's actual intentions, intentions best substantiated by similar statements that appear in the play's Introduction.

> I may observe that while I was composing this Play I wrote a short essay illustrative of that constitution and those tendencies of human nature which make the apparently motiveless actions of bad men intelligible to careful observers. This was partly done with reference to the character of Oswald, and his persevering endeavour to lead the man he disliked into so heinous a crime; but still more to preserve in my distinct remembrance what I had observed of transition in character, and the reflections I had been led to make during the time I was a witness of the changes through which the French Revolution passed.[41]

If this sounds reminiscent of Shakespeare, de Selincourt has pointed out that *"The Borderers* owed far more to *Othello* than to any other influence outside the poet's own experience."[42] It cannot be denied that both Wordsworth and Coleridge, aside from their studies of character, brought no new material as such into their dramas. Gothic and sentimental elements are present in both; nor does either *The Borderers or Osorio (Remorse),* structurally speaking, deviate markedly from the direction being

40 Campbell and Mueschke, pp. 470–471.

41 *Poetical Works,* ed. de Selincourt and Darbishire, I,343.

42 De Selincourt, *Oxford Lectures on Poetry,* p. 174.

pursued in other plays of the period.[43] But it was not the intention of either poet to introduce new directions that the theatre
might follow: both merely wished to write something that would
"do for the Theatre in its present state." Certainly, in company
with their contemporaries, their plays "are directly out of the
sentimental tradition of long-suffering, virtuous heroes and
heroines whom we are asked to pity. Through the offices of that
pity and the terror evoked by Cenci, Auchindrane, Oswald or
Ordonio, we are asked to strengthen our sensitivity. To understand the plays fully, we must realize that they are written out of
the materials, the motives and the whole framework of their
time."[44] And in their plays Gothic elements are equally in evidence. This fact is not surprising, considering that when Wordsworth was writing *The Borderers*, Gothic drama was at the very
height of its popularity.[45] The important thing to remember is
that "Wordsworth was the first to use the Gothic mode for a
purpose other than the mere exploitation of the elements which
composed it."[46] And this purpose is most succinctly expressed
in the statement that in *The Borderers* "the villain tries to de-
stroy the hero's remorse, and fails; in Coleridge's play, the hero
tries to arouse the villain's remorse, and succeeds. Thus, pro-
ceeding from opposite directions, both poets reached the same
conclusion. Philosophical analysis by two great minds approved
the trait that had been for a generation a principal subject of
dramatic spectacle."[47]

Both poets are explicit on this point concerning their philosophical intentions, and these intentions are emphasized in
specific statements in the plays themselves. After the premiere

---

[43] The structure of plays contemporary with Wordsworth's and
Coleridge's will be discussed more fully in Chapter III.

[44] George Bair, "The Plays of the Romantic Poets: Their Place in
Dramatic History" (unpublished dissertation, University of Pennsylvania, 1951), p. 188.

[45] Evans, *Gothic Drama from Walpole to Shelley*, p. 217. Evans also
points out that between 1795 and 1797 twelve Gothic dramas were produced, including some of the outstanding specimens (p. 256n.).

[46] *Ibid.*, p. 218.

[47] *Ibid.*, p. 220.

of *Remorse*, for example, in a letter to Robert Southey, Coleridge explains: "By *remorse* I mean the Anguish and Disquie-
tude arising from the self-contradiction introduced into the Soul
by Guilt—a feeling, which is good or bad according as the Will
makes use of it. This is exprest in the lines chosen as the Motto—
and Remorse is everywhere distinguished from virtuousness"
(G. III,433-434). And this "Motto" to which he refers is to be
found in lines that come near the beginning of the play:

> Remorse is as the heart in which it grows:
> If that be gentle, it drops balmy dews
> Of true repentance; but if proud and gloomy,
> It is a poison-tree, that pierced to the inmost
> Weeps only tears of poison! (I,i,20-24)

Interestingly, these lines do not appear in the play's earlier version, the one entitled *Osorio*. In both versions there is one other
speech in which the word "remorse" is apostrophized, but it
does not appear until Act III.

There is an even earlier point in this drama at which Wordsworth's influence comes clearly to the fore. It will be recalled that
when the poets read their plays to each other at Racedown,
Coleridge recited the "first two and a half acts" of his *Osorio*.
It cannot be proved that he had progressed no further in its
composition by the time of that meeting; still, so striking is the
similarity between two speeches on "remorse" in *The Borderers*
and *Osorio* that it seems hardly coincidental. The one in *The
Borderers* is spoken by the villain, Oswald:

> . . . Remorse—
> It cannot live with thought; think on, think on,
> And it will die. What! in this universe
> Where the least things control the greatest, where
> The faintest breath that breathes can move a world;
> What! feel remorse, where, if a cat had sneezed,
> A leaf had fallen, the thing had never been
> Whose very shadow gnaws us to the vitals. (III,1560-67)

And, appropriately, it is the villain, Osorio, who utters sentiments in a similar vein in Coleridge's play:

> . . . Remorse! remorse!
> Where gott'st thou that fool's word? Curse on remorse!
> Can it give up the dead, or recompact
> A mangled body—mangled, dash'd to atoms!
> Not all the blessings of a host of angels
> Can blow away a desolate widow's curse;
> And tho' thou spill thy heart's blood for atonement,
> It will not weigh against an orphan's tear. (III,ii,198-205)

So we are able to find a fairly close connection in content between the two plays, a connection intensified by one or two other rather remarkable resemblances. Again, in *Osorio* these occur after the beginning of the third act.[48] Mention has been made of Coleridge's "Motto" in *Remorse*; a similar expression appears in Act III of *The Borderers*:

> . . . Pain is of the heart,
> And what are a few throes of bodily suffering
> If they can waken one pang of remorse? (III,1399-1401)

And there are parallel references to serpents that seem somewhat more than accidental:

> . . . If a snake
> Crawl from beneath our feet we do not ask
> A license to destroy him: our good governors
> Hedge in the life of every pest and plague
> That bears the shape of man; and for what purpose,
> But to protect themselves from extirpation?
> (*Borderers*, III,1578-83)

> What if one reptile sting another reptile,
> Where is the crime? The goodly face of Nature
> Hath one trail less of slimy filth upon it.
> Are we not all predestined rottenness
> And cold dishonor? (*Osorio*, III,212-216)

---

[48] Coleridge acknowledges having unconsciously borrowed a line from Wordsworth for *Remorse;* see footnote to *Poetical Works,* ed. E. H. Coleridge, p. 823. Elsewhere he says: "As to my thefts from the Wallenstein, they were on compulsion from the necessity of Haste—and do not lie heavy on my conscience, being partly thefts from myself, and because I gave Schiller 20 for one I had taken" (G. III,435).

It can be argued that with Coleridge's "cormorant reading" and phenomenal memory such similarities can scarcely be called plagiarism, particularly if they happened to impress him upon hearing *The Borderers* read for the first time. J. L. Lowes demonstrates how strongly the figure of the Wandering Jew affected both poets, Marmaduke becoming essentially the representation of the Wanderer himself in the last ten lines of *The Borderers*,[49] whereas "the unfathomable Stranger of *Der Geisterseher* and *The Monk* was hovering in the background of *Osorio*."[50] As Lowes points out, *Osorio* was freely drawn from Schiller's *Der Geisterseher*.[51]

On yet another count the resemblance between *The Borderers* and *Osorio* seems more than accidental. In the fourth act of *Osorio* appears what was later to be included as one of Coleridge's contributions to the *Lyrical Ballads* of 1798, "The Foster-Mother's Tale: A Dramatic Fragment," a short scene that contributes nothing to the action of the drama, and for which Coleridge possibly received inspiration from part of a scene in *The Borderers*, Act I, the account given by a beggar woman of a dream. In the version by Coleridge are the lines

> And all alone set sail by silent moonlight,
> Up a great river, great as any sea,

and we see how closely in point of time *Osorio* is related to both *The Ancient Mariner* and *Kubla Khan*.

Philosophically Wordsworth had the greater, the more sublime, idea; Coleridge, even though he possessed the better dramatic talent, did not have the weight of philosophy upon which to peg his play. Possibly this is because Coleridge was not so obsessed with the problems presented by Godwinian doctrine as was Wordsworth. The essay written by Wordsworth on the speculative background with which his play is concerned, from its opening sentence in any case presents the problem he

---

[49] *The Road to Xanadu* (New York, 1927; rev. ed., 1936), p. 224 and *n*.

[50] *Ibid.*, p. 235.

[51] *Ibid.*, p. 221 and *n*.

had set himself to resolve by dramatic action: "Let us suppose a young man of great intellectual powers, yet without any solid principles of genuine benevolence. His master passions are pride and the love of distinction. He has deeply imbibed a spirit of enterprise in a tumultuous age. He goes into the world and is betrayed into a great crime.—That influence on which all his happiness is built immediately deserts him."[52] Iago comes to mind, and as de Selincourt says, if "Iago is one of Shakespeare's most notable triumphs we can hardly be surprised that Wordsworth failed in his harder task. It was always his fate, in his more ambitious writings, to attempt something more difficult than his great models, and thereby to court artistic failure."[53]

Coleridge, by the same token, if less ambitious than Wordsworth, ultimately was more successful, at least so far as stage representation is concerned. But the effort cost him considerable toil. Infrequent references to revisions to *Osorio* appear in his correspondence for more than a decade after he had completed his translation of *Wallenstein*; briefly, too, before apparently losing interest altogether, he visited the theatre almost nightly.[54] Then, unexpectedly, in 1807 a singular incident revived it again: in a conversation with Godwin, Coleridge reports: "I was speaking with some asperity of Sheridan's late conduct in parliament; and Godwin with a half-sneer implied that my *resentment* was the cause of my *dislike* and that I confounded the *patriot* with the *Manager*" (G. III,14). Concurrently, a copy of *Osorio* was found among Godwin's papers, and in typical fashion Coleridge once again begins making forecasts of his future plans: "I certainly will correct it; and changing both the title, and the names of the Dramatis Personae, procure it to be presented to Covent Garden" (G. III,14).

---

[52] *Poetical Works,* ed. de Selincourt and Darbishire, I,345.

[53] *Oxford Lectures on Poetry,* p. 175.

[54] "[George] Greenough [a friend of Coleridge] was told that he [Coleridge] went to Drury Lane pit four times a week, in order to make himself known, and was introduced to Sheridan 'whom he detests,' " during Coleridge's residence in London while writing for the *Morning Post,* 1799–1800. (E. K. Chambers, *Samuel Taylor Coleridge* [Oxford, 1938], p. 122.)

The wonder is that despite a subsequent anguished recapitulation of his former woes incurred with Sheridan, and despite other grievances that had arisen in the interim,[55] this time Coleridge managed to fulfill his intentions—and in that same year. "I have re-written my play—and about doubled the length of *Christabel*—2 thirds are finished" (G. III,39), he writes to Dorothy Wordsworth, who ecstatically transmits this information as: "The best news contained in his letter was that he had been going on with the *Christabel*, and had written almost as much as we have already seen and *re*written his tragedy."[56] The emphasis by author and correspondent here is exactly reversed, an indication of the relative importance each attached to these two separate works. Although again Coleridge had "reasons for belief, that a Tragedy of mine will be brought on the stage this season" (G. III,34), we learn nothing more until 1812, when once more he is consumed with the "anxiety to finish 1. the re-writing of my Play . . ." (G. III,415). This time his long struggle finally was to be crowned with success, for on December 1, 1812, he proudly remarks to Josiah Wedgwood: "I am sure, that I shall have your good wishes on my behalf, when I tell you that I have had a Play accepted at Drury Lane, which is to come out at Christmas, and of the success of which both Manager, Comm-Men, and actors speak sanguinely" (G. III,421).

From a structural point of view, *Remorse* is a great improvement over its predecessor. The antecedent action, which in the original version is never completely clear, here is better integrated by the addition of a new first scene. In the revised version the original opening that now follows it is both strengthened and compressed: the utterances of the principal characters are on occasion modified to make their statements less abrupt; and their frequent outbursts of rhetoric are refined and made more

---

[55] See G. III,17–18. It may be noted that some fifteen years earlier Lamb had written Coleridge: "Lloyd tells me that Sheridan put you upon writing your tragedy. I hope you are only Coleridgeizing when you talk of finishing it in a few days." (*Works,* ed. E. V. Lucas, VI,104.)

[56] *Letters of William and Dorothy Wordsworth: The Middle Years,* ed. Ernest de Selincourt (2 vols., Oxford, 1937), I,458.

meaningful. The plot itself is not especially dynamic, but an air of definite tension is established and the characters speak both dramatically and well. Don Alvar, believed lost at sea, in this new first scene is discovered in conversation with Zulimez, his servant. Following a lengthy exile they have reached home safely. Alvar erroneously believes that his beloved, Doña Teresa, had been involved in a plot instigated by his younger brother, Don Ordonio (Osorio in the original play), to murder him; in his certainty that she and his brother have been married subsequent to his presumed death, he has adopted the disguise of a Mohammedan, not with the intention of wreaking revenge, but in the hope of bringing his brother to repentance for his misdeeds by arousing within him a feeling of remorse. Ordonio's deep-dyed villainy, however, thwarts his brother's purposes: not only does he remain unrepentant, he murders an accomplice he had hired years earlier to assassinate his brother; and in turn is then murdered by this same assassin's wife. Doña Teresa, meanwhile, who has remained true to her lost lover, is unaware of Ordonio's perfidy. Indeed, only when he is in his death agonies does Ordonio truly repent, the play then ending upon this note of moral admonition:

> That Conscience rules us e'en against our choice.
> Our inward Monitress to guide or warn,
> If listened to; but if repelled with scorn,
> At length as dire Remorse, she reappears,
> Works in our guilty hopes, and selfish fears! (V,i,288-292)

Any sketch of the plot of *Remorse*, however, merely lends confirmation to the inference that the action is patently absurd. This "tragedy" does not direct itself toward the intellect, but allows free play to the sensibilities, not so much by the story as by the aura of the romantic evoked by the situation in which the scene takes place. It is evident that Coleridge was faced with the task of wringing from his audience a "willing suspension of disbelief" for credibility of the events depicted; to deny him success in this venture would be the same as to say that his contemporary audience must have been incredibly naive. Since within the confines of the never-never land in which they figure the predicaments of his characters are credibly rendered and since the author has managed to make the action intelligible within the self-imposed framework to which he has chosen to limit himself, there is little point in challenging the fact that this work will win a positive response from its audience. The theatre public of Coleridge's day, accustomed to a rhetorical acting style, to oratory, and to a renaissance in stage poetry, in all probability did not miss the absence of "realism" in *Remorse*. And when Coleridge compliments himself on "the variety of metres, according as the Speeches are merely transitive; or narrative; or passionate; or (as in the Incantation) deliberate and formal Poetry" in the play (G. III,434), he is complimenting himself for writing in a manner that his contemporaries were attempting, too.

The difference between their efforts and his, lies, of course in the fact that Joanna Baillie, William Godwin, and Charles Maturin, to mention only three, were less successful than Coleridge was at writing blank verse. By the same token, *Remorse* contains more merits in its favor than merely the one of being written in a superior brand of poetry. There are three scenes that are of more than passing interest. One follows the other in rapid succession; each is Gothic in its atmosphere of mystery and gloom; and one of the principal characters in the play undertakes a step in each of these scenes that for the action as a whole turns out to be decisive. In the first, guided by motives of hatred and revenge, Ordonio slays Isidore, the assassin he once had hired to murder his brother; in the second the heroine, Teresa, resolves out of pity to free the imprisoned Don Alvar, not realizing that he is her beloved in disguise; and in the third Isidore's wife determines to revenge herself upon Ordonio. The three scenes act as contrasts to the divergent motives of pity and revenge; each ends abruptly, the first and third upon a note of horror, the second upon a note of resolution. Each in its own way is effective; and as an entity these three scenes demonstrate the care and skill with which Coleridge synthesized and juxtaposed the previously chaotic elements of *Osorio* to form a dramatic unity.

By contrast Wordsworth's *Borderers* is static and philosophical. To convince Wordsworth against his better judgment that the play would be effective upon the stage, Coleridge must indeed have employed his best powers of persuasion, for as it stands too little happens in *The Borderers* and it contains too frequent monologues and shifts in scene. The reign of Henry III was a period analogous for Wordsworth's purposes to the French Revolution, in which the absence of established law and government permits the individual to give free license to his best or worst impulses. A band of former Crusaders, led by the idealistic Marmaduke, through its leader has fallen under the influence of the wily Oswald, an outcast by his own conscience for the perpetration of past misdeeds. Although initially overcome by remorse, Oswald with time has gained a stoic indifference to crime by adopting the (Godwinian) philosophy that all human emotions are merest weakness, whereas all of his own desires are manifestly the expression of his own reason and intellect. Finding himself in the presence of the idealistic Marmaduke and seeing through him his own past history recreated, Oswald conceives the plan of reproducing in this man of feeling his own downfall. By abandoning a virtuous woman, Marmaduke, too, will be freed from the fetters of conscience and from a sense of common humanity. Oswald convinces Marmaduke that Lord Herbert, recently returned from the Holy Land, is a depraved scoundrel who for insidious purposes bought his purported daughter, Idonea, from a beggar woman. The two outlaws abandon the innocent and blind Herbert upon a desolate moor, Marmaduke, repenting, returning too late to save the dying man. Idonea is informed of Marmaduke's part in the crime, the beggar woman repents of her part in the conspiracy, while Oswald, who remains unrepentant, is killed by the other outlaws, and for his part in the catastrophe Marmaduke is left to seek a life of solitary expiation.

If this summary sounds un-Wordsworthian, it is because we

are accustomed to think of the speculative, philosophical Wordsworth, dissociated from the world of action and limited to a
self-restricted view of the world and of life in which violence and
action play only the most tangential roles. That Wordsworth
himself felt ill at ease in the world of intrigue and rapacity of
his creation is more than probable, for almost a relieved note
of satisfaction is evident in the comments made to his daughter
on *The Borderers'* merits and drawbacks that have been remarked on earlier; and to judge from his former reticence on
the subject, the confident tone of his Introduction of 1842 had
been absent when he first offered the play for staging in 1797:

> This Dramatic Piece, as noted in its title-page, was composed
> in 1795–6. It lay nearly from that time till within the last
> two or three months unregarded among my papers, without
> being mentioned even to my most intimate friends. Having,
> however, impressions upon my mind which made me un-
> willing to destroy the MS., I determined to undertake the
> responsibility of publishing it during my own life, rather
> than impose upon my successors the task of deciding its fate.
> Accordingly it has been revised with some care; but, as it
> was at first written, and is now published, without any view
> to its exhibition upon the stage, not the slightest alteration
> has been made in the conduct of the story, or the composition
> of the characters.[57]

This is a far cry from the days when Mrs. Wordsworth felt compelled to inform Crabb Robinson concerning the play's where-
abouts: "The tragedy is in existence, but say nothing about it,
lest its destruction should follow."[58]

Possibly, in his re-examination of the work that had pro-
ceeded from his pen some forty-six years before, Wordsworth
discovered other reasons, too, for approving this piece of late
juvenilia. First is the extent of the dramatic evolution that had
occurred in the intervening period. In 1842 *The Borderers* was
not quite so old-fashioned as Wordsworth might easily have

---

[57] *Poetical Works,* ed. de Selincourt and Darbishire, I,341–342.

[58] *Correspondence of Crabb Robinson with the Wordsworth Circle,*
ed. Edith J. Morley (2 vols., Oxford, 1927) , I,323.

suspected beforehand; on the contrary, drama had caught up with *The Borderers* instead of leaving it behind: the ideas, the interest in philosophical speculation, the concern with psychological analysis and investigation—these elements that with a certain degree of satisfaction Wordsworth found to be present in his play in 1842, by then in fact had become the common property of poetic dramatists. The idea of an historical framework upon which to construct the action had also become a unifying factor in poetic drama, even though this factor did not depend upon tendencies which the first of the poetic dramatists had developed in their own dramatic works. In a letter to T. N. Talfourd, written in 1836, Wordsworth says: "You have most ably fulfilled your own purpose [in the play *Ion*], and your poem is a distinguished contribution to English literature. . . . I cannot help catching at the hope that, in the evening of life, you may realize those anticipations which you throw out."[59] So it is possible that although he long since had lost interest in writing drama himself, in Talfourd Wordsworth perceived a successor in the kind of drama that he had envisaged philosophically in his *Borderers*.

Another consideration that makes *The Borderers* of particular interest is the way it illustrates the difference between Coleridge's and Wordsworth's attitudes toward superstition. Coleridge, relates Hazlitt, "lamented that Wordsworth was not prone enough to believe in the traditional superstitions of the place, and that there was something corporeal, a *matter-of-fact-ness*, a clinging to the palpable, or often to the petty, in his poetry, in consequence."[60] And this "clinging to the palpable" is nowhere better evidenced than in the Preface to *The Borderers*:

> There is a kind of superstition which makes us shudder, when we find moral sentiments to which we attach a sacred importance applied to vicious purposes. In real life this is done every day, and we do not feel the disgust. The difference

---

[59] *The Later Years*, III,817.

[60] "My First Acquaintance with Poets," *Complete Works of William Hazlitt*, ed. P. P. Howe (21 vols., London and Toronto, 1933), XVII, 117.

is here. In works of imagination we see the motive and the
end. In real life we rarely see either the one or the other;
and when the distress comes it prevents us from attending
to the cause. This superstition of which I have spoken is not
without its use; yet it appears to be one great source of our
vices; it is our constant engine in seducing each other. We
are lulled asleep by its agency, and betrayed before we know
that an attempt is made to betray us.[61]

Coleridge would never be so disturbed by the potential dangers
inherent in such "works of imagination." Instead of being "lulled
asleep," the reader in his presence, as though in some transient
vision, is rather awakened into a sense of the inexplicable and
the wondrous, unreal, yet nonetheless perceived. Although the
same, quite naturally, can be said of Wordsworth's *The Borderers*—and of Romantic drama in general—this is particularly true
of Coleridge's plays. At the very least he and his peers wrote
drama that was definitely of, and for, their time. It is possible
that their plays could no more be produced today than, let us
say, the heroic tragedies of Dryden or the bulk of Restoration
drama; but it would be incorrect to say that Romantic drama
lacks power and poetic art.

Whether the plays of the Romantic dramatists deserve to live
and whether they are worth reading—on this question we must
turn from the more pedantic, unsuperstitious Wordsworth to
the visionary Coleridge. And our answer must depend upon the
Coleridgean plea, and our acceptance of it, for an individual
willing "suspension of all our judgment derived from constant
experience . . . to peruse with the liveliest interest the wildest
tales of ghosts, wizards, genii, and secret talismans."

---

[61] *Poetical Works,* I,348.

CHAPTER III

A Hero Complex and the Urge to Elizabethanize

AND SO, with Coleridge's *Remorse,* poetic drama in blank verse returned to the English stage. The anxious Wordsworth, writing to Daniel Stuart several months before its premiere, earnestly inquires: "Do you hear or see anything of Coleridge? Lamb writes to Lloyd that C's. play is accepted. Heaven grant it success."[1] Soon after the play's debut, Dorothy Wordsworth remarks to a correspondent: "Coleridge's play has been completely successful—Mrs. Coleridge is much excited as you may guess."[2] Genest, in his *History of the London Stage,* is dubious of the complete success of the drama;[3] but the press was cordial in its reception, the *Morning Post* noting those same qualities of language and morality that Coleridge, too, admired in this play: "The language is equally poetic and impassioned, the incidents are sufficient to keep the attention alive during the whole of the representation, and some of the situations are strikingly calculated for dramatic effect. . . . The moral is perfect . . . The style is throughout poetical and classical, and far above the common level."[4]

The jubilant Coleridge, two days after the play's first performance on January 23, had no need of critical encomiums. To a correspondent he declares: "I have not yet read what the *remorseless* Critics of the 'ano-abstersurae Chartae' (more often

---

[1] *Letters:The Middle Years,* II,523.

[2] *Ibid.,* 552.

[3] Genest writes: "this is a tolerable T. by Coleridge—some parts of it are beautifully written." (*Some Account of the English Stage* [10 vols., Bath, 1832], VIII,355.)

[4] January 25, 1813, p. 2.

defiled than f[iled]) say of the Play; but I hear that Hazlitt i[n the] M.C. [*Morning Chronicle*] has sneered at my presumption in [entering] the Lists with Shakespear's Hamlet in Teresa's Description of the two Brothers: when (so help me the Muses) that Passage never once occurred to my conscious recollection, however it may, unknown to myself, have been the working idea within me. But mercy on us! is there no such thing as two men's having similar Thoughts on similar Occasions—?" (G. III,429). To his wife he proudly reports: "*Hitherto* the Remorse has met with *unexampled* APPLAUSE—but whether it will *continue* to fill the *House*, that is quite another Question—and of this my Friends are, in my opinion, far, far too sanguine" (G. III,429-430). The play ran for twenty performances, an eminently respectable number. *Percy*, by Hannah More, was the single new tragedy (tragedy in the sense that leading characters are killed in the course of the action) that played in London for more than ten performances between 1777 and 1802. It ran for nineteen performances, followed by "about ten," according to Genest, for "Monk" Lewis's *Alphonso, King of Castile* in 1802. No other tragedy achieved even that number of performances until Coleridge's *Remorse*, but thereafter a significant increase took place in the frequency with which those surpassing the magic number ten were offered upon the stage. Of "poetic" tragedies,[5] the plays and the number of performances are: Charles Maturin, *Bertram*, 1816 (22); Richard Sheil, *The Apostate*, 1817 (12); Henry Hart Milman, *Fazio*, 1818 (15); Richard Sheil, *Evadne*, 1819 (30); Sheridan Knowles, *Virginius*, 1820 (14).

Although such a total can scarcely be said to constitute a renaissance in poetic tragedy, at least the drama itself was on the way toward making more of a comeback than when *Osorio* was written in 1797. "You will have heard," writes Coleridge to his wife,

---

[5] Other tragedies given during the same period include: Joseph Addison, *Cato*, 1811 (16); William Dimond, *The Bride of Abydos,* 1818 (14); John Payne, *Brutus,* 1818 (52); Horace Twiss, *Carib Chief,* 1819 (10).

that on my entering the Box on Saturday Night I was discovered by the Pit—and that they all turned their faces
towards our Box, and gave a treble chear of Claps. I mention
these things, because it will please Southey to hear that there
is a large number of Persons in London, who hail with enthusiasm any prospect of the Stage's being purified and
rendered classical. My success, *if* I succeed (of which, I
assure you, I entertain doubts in my opinion well-founded,
both from the want of a prominent Actor for Ordonio, and
from the want of vulgar Pathos in the Play itself—nay, there
is not enough even of *true* dramatic Pathos) but if I succeed,
I succeed for others as well as for myself. (G. III,430-431)

Of course, such sentiments were shared by others besides
Coleridge. We have seen that Wordsworth, too, had once hoped
to at least purify, if not reform, the state of intellectual stagnation into which the English theatre had steadily been sinking
throughout the latter half of the eighteenth century.[6] Robert
Southey, writing in 1799, expresses himself in much the same
terms:

Dramatic writing is very difficult. To make common tragedies
or comedies is easy child's play. I should find it easier to
satisfy an audience than to satisfy myself. Our stage seems
to have reached the very depth of degradation. It is impossible to sink below "Pizarro." Kotzebue's play might have
passed as the worst possible, if Sheridan had not proved the
possibility of making it worse. The London audience is a
very good-natured one; they will be pleased with anything
whatever the manager chooses to provide—the dullness of
sentimental comedy, the vulgarity of broad farce, and the
Lincolnshire-fen flatness of Mr. Whaley's tragedy, or the
puppet-show of "Pizarro," all in their turn![7]

But at last the day seemed ripe for something new, something more in keeping with the legendary "spirit of the times."
This idea obsessed nineteenth-century critics and writers; the

---

[6] See the remarks by Wordsworth from the *Lyrical Ballads,* p. 55.
[7] *Letters of Robert Southey,* ed. J. W. Warter (4 vols., London,
1856), I,87.

term *Zeitgeist*, in fact, captured the imagination of an entire era
in English cultural history. We find this urge to codify the experience of the times reflected even in the title of Hazlitt's critical work, *The Spirit of the Age*. Yet, taken by itself, this fact
is of minor importance; Hazlitt was only one spokesman for the
early nineteenth century, one of the many for whom the French
Revolution and the ultimate fall of Napoleon seemed to foreshadow the beginning of some better, as yet but dimly perceived,
age of peace and plenitude. Why later critics believe that "realism" is the key to what these early-nineteenth-century members
of the *avant garde* were seeking is, in light of the influences to
which the literary and cultural scene of the times was subject,
thereby made doubly difficult, if not impossible, to fathom. If
we take the drama alone, we find that the soil had not been
prepared for the attitudes and points of view required for such
a view of human existence; the soil was of a much different composition. The plays produced in London about the time Wordsworth and Coleridge were writing *The Borderers* and *Osorio*
were Schiller's *Die Räuber, Der Geisterseher*; Kotzebue's *Spanier von Peru (Pizarro)*; Lewis's *Castle Spectre, Monk*; Radcliffe's
Mysteries of Udolpho. There is scarcely a trace of realism to
be found here! As for the audience, their attitude was that

> it was natural to be sensitive. They could learn about nature
> by attuning their sympathy to the pitiable situation of the
> characters being presented on the stage. Or they showed that
> they knew nature by weeping when the strings of their hearts
> were played upon. In giving their audiences plays which
> aroused the emotions of pity and fear, . . . authors achieved
> success. In becoming natural, however, the characters also
> became abstractions of virtue or villainy, of motherhood,
> sisterhood, widowhood. . . . All lose their identities as human
> beings when the dramas of which they are a part are sub-
> verted to the teaching of a moral code.[8]

We have spoken earlier of this interest in the "passions."
Let us turn to other influences that were at work in early-nine-

---

[8] Bair, *The Plays of the Romantic Poets*, p. 114.

teenth-century drama. The two of primary importance were medievalism and the English Renaissance. Today we tend to regard these as if they were mutually exclusive entities—yet the facts scarcely warrant the assumption. As we have seen, several divergent influences were in operation concurrently in the plays of Wordsworth and Coleridge. There were the sentimentality of Kotzebue's *Spanier von Peru,* the historical Gothicism of Schiller's *Geisterseher,* and strong Shakespearean overtones from *Othello* in *The Borderers*; and Coleridge's later fantasy play, *Zapolya,* was devised by its author as a "humble imitation of the *Winter's Tale.*"[9] In this, Coleridge's last drama, it is interesting to observe the diverse sources borrowed from in its construction: Coleridge drew the main plot, the usurpation of an infant's right to the throne, from *A Winter's Tale* and *Cymbeline,* as well as from Douglas's *Merope,* while for the story of the usurper's treachery he utilized elements from *The Rape of Lucrece,* in addition to other minor sources.[10] There is no reason, however, to call either *Remorse* or *Zapolya* pseudo-Shakespearean in point of style. Coleridge himself recognized his indebtedness to the works of others, some instances of which have been mentioned earlier.[11] The main point to remember is that the Romantic dramatists were fully aware of the influences and the background material that went to make up their plays. To separate the two principal streams of medievalism and Elizabethanism in their works is scarcely possible. For they, writing in an age of turbulent reaction and later liberalism—and this is equally applicable to Romantic drama from Wordsworth to Robert Browning—were seeking to express the changes as well as they knew how while using the materials seemingly best suited dramatically for this task.

Perhaps the varied goals they set themselves in their poetic tragedies are best described by Coleridge in a letter concerning *Zapolya* addressed to Byron in 1815. "Before the third week in

---

[9] "Advertisement to *Zapolya,*" *Poetical Works,* ed. E. H. Coleridge, p. 883.

[10] See the remarks by E. L. Griggs in *Letters,* III,627*n.*

[11] See especially Chapter II, *n.* 48.

December," he writes, "I shall, I trust, be able to transmit to
your Lordship a Tragedy, in which I have endeavored to avoid
the faults and deficiencies of the *Remorse* by a better subordination of the characters, by avoiding the duplicity of Interest, by a
greater clearness of the Plot, and by a deeper Pathos. Above all,
I have labored to render the Poem at once tragic and dramatic"
(G. IV,598). Little wonder that here as elsewhere Coleridge
should have failed so signally in his intentions; little reason to
suppose that any writer would have done better in attempting—
consciously—to write a play that in the same breath should be
pathetic, tragic, dramatic, poetic, psychological, and motivated by
"natural" emotions. Of principal importance to these writers
was the mind, the intellect; the creative function of telling a
story, a tale of dramatic interest and vitality for its own sake,
something not tied in with a thesis or moral precept, to them was
too trivial and irrelevant for stage presentation. It was too "low."
Yet to produce through poetic means a dramatic commentary
on human existence that at once will be contemporary and time-
less has in the words of Felix Schelling, always been "the ideal of
most dramatists in most ages."[12] That from our point of view
these poetic dramatists failed offers more of an indication of their
vision and integrity than it does of our present-day greater insights of the difficulties with which they were faced. Possibly
whereas they aspired to do too much, we have set ourselves goals
that, if more dramatic, are also more trivial and less meaningful.

The fact that the plays of Coleridge, and of those other dramatists to whom we must presently turn, were written with the
thought of production in mind—and were seriously considered
for production in their time—ought to serve us as testimony to
the valiant efforts being made by literary artists of the early
nineteenth century to fuse a contemporaneous Gothic and supernatural atmosphere with poetic traditions inherited from the
Elizabethan stage. Slowly these attempts were beginning to take
shape. Not until the Liberal Age of the 1830's were the most
serious critics ready to believe that a renaissance in the drama

---

[12] *English Drama* (London and New York, 1914), p. 394.

was actually taking place; yet with Coleridge the day has faintly begun to dawn.

It is a moot point, however, whether any such poetic revival would have been possible had it not been for two further developments in English dramaturgy during this same period. These two phenomena in themselves helped prepare audiences for poetic drama, for which the public was scarcely ready when Wordsworth wrote his *Borderers*. Even by 1813 one of these, the so-called Elizabethan revival, was still quite new, although if we should wish to mark its commencement by any exact year, the publication of Charles Lamb's *Specimens of the Dramatic Poets* in 1808 offers the most suitable date.[13] Subsequently, there are the lectures on Shakespeare given by Coleridge, starting in 1810, as well as the editions of Massinger, Jonson, and Ford published by William Gifford; and later still, the lectures on Shakespearean and Elizabethan drama offered by Hazlitt from 1817 to 1821.

This first phenomenon was matched by another of equal significance. Suddenly there appeared a new group of outstanding actors to perform this Shakespearean drama. The actors were not all of the caliber of a Roscius;[14] yet of the actors and actresses who emerged at this time, many in some special way contributed to the glories of English dramatic art.[15] Between 1809 and 1821, among those acting in tragedy at Covent Garden were Kemble, Cooke, Macready, Young, Charles Kemble, Conway, Terry, Abbot, Mrs. Siddons, Miss O'Neill, and Mrs. Bunn; comic actors included Munden, Johnstone, Liston, Jones, Charles Kemble, Farren, Fawcett, Blanchard, Mathews, Emery,

---

[13] Used as a *terminus a quo* by Chew, *The Dramas of Lord Byron,* p. 16.

[14] See, for example, Coleridge's comments on the acting in *Remorse, supra,* pp. 71–72, and comments by Nicoll, *History of Early Nineteenth Century English Drama,* I,47.

[15] Accounts of the major actors and their skills have been amply given in numerous reminiscences and histories of the London stage. Among them: C. H. Herford, *Sketch of the History of the English Drama (to 1843)* (Cambridge, 1881) ; J. Knight, *History of the English Stage During the Reign of Victoria* (London, 1901) .

Farley, and Yates.[16] Thus the stage did not lack outstanding talent and unusual ability. Writing about Mrs. Siddons in the *Examiner* on June 16, 1816, Hazlitt eulogizes her acting ability: "The enthusiasm she excited had something idolatrous about it; she was regarded less with admiration than with wonder, as if a being of a superior order had dropped from another sphere to awe the world with the majesty of her appearance. She raised Tragedy to the skies, or brought it down from thence. . . . We can conceive nothing grander. She embodied to our imagination the fables of mythology, of the heroic and deified mortals of older time. . . . She was Tragedy personified."[17] Or, of a leading comic actor, there is Lamb's account from "On the acting of Munden": "There is one face of Farley, one face of Knight, one (but what a one it is!) of Liston; but Munden has none that you can properly pin down, and call *his*. When you think he has exhausted his battery of looks, in unaccountable warfare with your gravity, suddenly he sprouts out an entirely new set of features, like Hydra. He is not one, but legion; not so much a comedian, as a company. If his name could be multiplied like his countenance, it might fill a play-bill."[18]

To continue for a moment with Charles Lamb as our guide, let us observe the effect such actors had on the audiences. After recounting his early rapture with the theatre at the age of six or seven, Lamb describes his growing realization that drama somehow had become inextricably a part and parcel of his very existence:

> The green curtain was no longer a veil, drawn between two worlds, the unfolding of which was to bring back past ages to present a "royal ghost,"—but a certain quantity of green baize, which was to separate the audience for a given time from certain of their fellowmen who were to come forward and pretend these parts. The lights—the orchestra lights— came up a clumsy machinery. The first ring, and the second

---

[16] Mentioned in Baker's *The London Stage,* p. 129.

[17] "A View of the English Stage," *Complete Works of William Hazlitt,* ed. P. P. Howe, V,312.

[18] *Works,* ed. E. V. Lucas, II,169.

ring, was now but a trick of the prompter's bell—which had been, like the note of the cuckoo, a phantom of a voice, no hand seen or guessed at which ministered to its warning. The actors were men and women painted. I thought the fault was in them; but it was in myself, and the alteration which those many centuries—of six short twelvemonths—had wrought in me. . . . Comparison and retrospection soon yielded to the present attraction of the scene; and the theatre became to me, upon a new stock, the most delightful of recreations.[19]

We can scarcely accuse Lamb of surrendering here to fantasies of the typical (or what we might think of as typical) romantic temperament; the quality of his awakening to the theatre as being "the most delightful of recreations" reveals an attitude at once aware and alive to the deficiencies and drawbacks of the theatre with its "clumsy machinery." More characteristic than Lamb's remarks are recurrent complaints during the Romantic Period of "the degradation of our vaunted" stage from writers like Byron, Hazlitt, and Gifford. Byron, always a trenchant commentator, as early as *English Bards and Scotch Reviewers* casts a disdainful glance toward the drama with the introductory comment:

Now to the Drama turn—Oh! motley sight!
What precious scenes the wondering eyes invite:
Puns, and a Prince within a barrel pent,
And Dibdin's nonsense[20] yield complete content. (560–563)

Byron, if acid, was merely expressing in milder terms the sentiments William Gifford gives utterance to in his *Maeviad* of almost a decade earlier: "I know not if the stage has been so low, since the days of Gammar Gurton, as at this hour. It seems as if all the blockheads in the kingdom had started up, and exclaimed with one voice, Come! let us write for the theatres. In this there is nothing, perhaps, altogether new; the striking and peculiar novelty of the times seems to be, that *all* they write is received."[21]

---

[19] *Ibid.*, 114.

[20] Charles Dibdin (1745–1814), a minor playwright noted for his farces.

[21] *The Baviad and Maeviad* (8th ed., London, 1811), pp. 59–60n.

For this state of affairs Gifford, like Southey, finds not so much
the managers or writers to be responsible as the audiences, who
will accept any fare that is offered them. For "if they now and
then experience a slight fit of disgust," Gifford declares, theatrical audiences "have not resolution enough to express it, but sit
yawning and gaping in each other's faces for a little encouragement in their culpable forbearance."[22] In his account of the "woe-
ful stuff" that with monotonous regularity crossed the boards,
Gifford offers a grim picture of an indifference on the part of
audiences to even the most innocuous of theatrical refinements.
As in the *Baviad*, to be sure, the other villains of the piece were
the members of the Della Cruscan school of the "true sublime"—
Cobbe, Andrews, Reynolds, and the chief poetaster of the group,
Robert Merry.[23] Yet in his plea for new directions in theatrical
tastes and theatrical writing, Gifford merely foreshadows a theme
to be repeated and re-emphasized by successive critics of the
drama in these early years of the nineteenth century.

> Then let your style be brief, your meaning clear,
> Nor like Lorenzo,[24] tire the labouring ear
> With a wild waste of words; sound without sense,
> And all the florid glare of impotence.
> Still with your characters your language change,
> From grave to gay, as nature dictates, range;
> Now droop in all the plaintiveness of woe,
> Now in glad numbers light and airy flow;
> Now shake the stage with guilt's alarming tone,
> And make the aching bosom all your own;
> Now—But I sing in vain; from first to last,
> Your joy is fustian, and your grief bombast:
> Rhetoric has banish'd reason; kings and queens,
> Vent in hyperboles their royal spleens;
> Guardsmen in metaphors express their hopes,
> And "maidens, in white linen," howl in tropes. (73–88)

---

[22] *Ibid.*, p. 60n.

[23] See John M. Longaker, *The Della Cruscans and William Gifford*
(Philadelphia, 1924).

[24] "A lamentable tragedy by Della Crusca, mixed full of pleasant
mirth" (*Maeviad*, p. 74n.).

If it be imagined that contemporary commentators were prepared for Wordsworth's "language of real life" to give expression to the depiction of ordinary existence, it becomes evident very quickly that not even Byron was prepared to go that far. On the question of the diction of poetry, in *English Bards* Byron derides Wordsworth as a "mild apostate from poetic rule" (236):

> Who, both by precept and example, shows
> That prose is verse, and verse is merely prose. (241–242)

So we cannot expect from Byron much sympathy in any attempt to render poetically language that will be both "natural" and "real." Byron's credo, best expounded in *Hints from Horace*, calls rather for stage action that does not exceed credulity or reality; nor, according to his argument, should the subject matter of drama necessarily be historical, particularly if its action is violent.

> Many deeds preserved in History's page
> Are better told than acted on the stage;
> The ear sustains what shocks the timid eye,
> And Horror thus subsides to sympathy. (267–270)

Drama must subscribe to a higher moral purpose than merely to shock the audience's susceptibilities. For Byron, "sense of shame" and "talent" are patently dead. The time for reform has come.

> Heavens! is all sense of shame and talent gone?
> Have we no living Bard of merit?—none?
> Awake, GEORGE COLMAN! CUMBERLAND, awake!
> Ring the alarum bell! let folly quake!
> Oh! SHERIDAN! if aught can move thy pen,
> Let Comedy assume her throne again;
> Abjure the mummery of German schools;
> Leave new Pizarros to translating fools;
> Give, as thy last memorial to the age,
> One classic drama, and reform the stage.
>
> (*English Bards*, 576–585)

Obviously the youthful Byron believed British dramatic ability was best exemplified by the comic rather than by the tragic spirit. Although his tastes would begin to undergo a change somewhat later, as late as September, 1811, he writes of sending to Dallas as a contribution to the drama—subsequently lost—"a comedy of Goldoni's translated, one scene."[25] There was good reason for Byron's early interest in comedy. Of all the plays written in the early nineteenth century, none surpassed in influence the successful unstaged closet play of the Anti-Jacobins, *The Rovers* (1798), by Canning, Ellis, and Frere. This famous parody of Gothic drama, in its own way somewhat of a dramatic complement to Jane Austen's *Northanger Abbey,* helped spoof the Gothic vogue out of its greatest, if not its most infamous, popularity. The comic spirit inherent in English drama, the kind of satirical humor so dear to the techniques of the best Restoration and eighteenth-century dramatists, here is to be found employed with deadly effect against, in Coleridge's words, heavyhanded "jacobinical" drama "of German import." Through two issues of the *Anti-Jacobin*, with the sprightly wit of a Goldsmith, and the deft deadpan irony of a Swift, this burlesque holds the tendency in the English theatre to Germanize up to searching ridicule. The plots of *Die Räuber* and *Kabale und Liebe* of Schiller, in addition to those of lesser current German drama, are derided in lines on the dramatist of the German school:

> . . . where no dull maxims bind
> The bold expansion of the electric mind.
> Fixed to no period, circled by no space,
> He leaps the flaming bounds of time and place:
> Round the dark confines of the forest raves,
> With gentle robbers stocks his gloomy caves;
> Tells how prime ministers are shocking things,
> And reigning dukes as bad as tyrant kings.
>
> ("Prologue," 9–16)

When it then comes to dialogue, the parody becomes a minor

---

[25] *Letters and Journals of Lord Byron,* ed. R. E. Prothero (6 vols., London, 1898–1904), II,43. Hereafter cited as L & J I, etc.

masterpiece. A snatch of conversation between Matilda Pottingen, "in love with Rogero, and Mother to Casimere's Children," and Cecilia Mückenfeld, Casimere's wife, will serve as illustration.

> MAT. (*aside*). Thank heaven! I have at last found a heart which is in unison with my own. (*To Cecilia*) Yes, I understand you; the first pulsation of sentiment—the silver tones upon the yet unsounded harp. . . .
>
> CEC. The dawn of life, when this blossom (*putting her hand upon her heart*) first expanded its petals to the penetrating dart of love!
>
> MAT. Yes—the time—the golden time, when the first beams of the morning meet and embrace one another! The blooming blue upon the yet unplucked plum! . . .
>
> CEC. Your countenance grows animated, my dear madam.
>
> MAT. And yours, too, is glowing with illumination.
>
> CEC. I had long been looking out for a congenial spirit. My heart was withered; but the beams of yours have rekindled it.
>
> MAT. A sudden thought strikes me. Let us swear an eternal friendship!
>
> CEC. Let us agree to live together!
>
> MAT. Willingly.[26]

A little of this sort of thing can go a long way, although when written, in 1798, it must have been a tonic to its readers after dramas like *Pizarro*. Considering Byron's tastes and inclinations, there is little reason to doubt the sincerity of his own clarion call:

> Let Comedy assume her throne again;
> Abjure the mummery of German schools;
> Leave new Pizarros to translating fools . . .

Actually Byron's appeal, in *Hints from Horace*, had been heeded by Wordsworth, Coleridge, and Joanna Baillie, attempting to develop a new drama, for some time past. This drama probably was not the comedy that Byron envisioned, but rather a mode of investigating psychologically some "passion of the

---

[26] *Parodies and Other Burlesques of the Anti-Jacobin,* ed. Henry Morley (London, 1890), p. 290.

soul." Gothic drama did not die out altogether; and in the new guise of melodrama it would be carried to self-perpetuated esteem during most of the nineteenth century. Still, as Alois Brandl remarks, to whatever extent horror and terror continued to be popular, they began to be developed "less in the way of robbers, ghosts, and tyrants, external miseries, crass romances, and empty tirades, than in inward commotions of the soul."[27] Even Byron, in his Preface to *Marino Faliero*, makes mention of Miss Baillie's abilities, even though in somewhat remarkable company: "But surely there is dramatic power somewhere,— where Joanna Baillie, and Milman, and John Wilson exist." And we have already seen that both Wordsworth and Coleridge were alive to the genius of Miss Baillie's drama, *De Montfort.* "I tried what I could," reports Byron in this same Preface, "to get 'De Montfort' revived, but in vain, . . . and I endeavoured also to wake Mr. Coleridge to write a tragedy." "Wake" is surely unfair, for somewhat earlier, tried with the ignominy of having his *Zapolya* returned to him and seeing *Bertram* played instead, Coleridge plaintively declares to a correspondent: "I have had a regular Tragedy on the stocks for some years—which it was my purpose to write in the first instance wholly in reference to its representability on a Metropolitan Theatre—and to re-write it altogether as a dramatic Poem for publication. But neither my finances nor my feelings can *afford* it" (G. IV,722). But Byron himself was very much alive to the problems of the theatre and to the direction it was pursuing in psychological drama in the 1810's. Soon he, too, began in his plays to veer in that same direction.

We have his disclaimer, again from the Preface to *Marino Faliero*: "Were I capable of writing a play which could be deemed stage-worthy, success would give me no pleasure, and failure great pain. It is for this reason that, even during the time of being one of the committee of one of the theatres, I never made the attempt, and never will." But this is so much window-dressing, one of those irksome features of Byron's tem-

---

[27] *Coleridge and the English Romantic School* (London, 1887), p. 166.

perament that have earned him the title of "haughty M'Lord";
the facts turn out to be quite otherwise. Dating from the period
of his sojourn at Southwell, we have the charming, if somewhat
unbelievable, picture of a completely ingratiating Byron interested in amateur theatricals. "The chief mover of the project," he
developed, we are told, into "the star of the company" and "re-
peatedly brought down the house with his acting."[28] And he always kept a warm spot in his heart for actors. "The long complaints of the actual state of the drama," he maintains (in the
Preface to *Marino Faliero*), "arise, however, from no fault of
the performers. I can conceive nothing better than Kemble,
Cooke, and Kean, . . . or than Elliston in *gentleman's* comedy
. . ." —recollections dating from the days of his having been a
constant visitor to the theatre.[29] It is perhaps fitting that his
"Address" should have been the one spoken at the opening of the
new Drury Lane Theatre on October 12, 1812, although the
manner in which it happened to be chosen is more open to question.[30] The occasion at the time seemed so auspicious, if not
prophetic, of better theatrical days to come that Byron's fustian
may be excused when he admonishes the audience:

> If e'er Frivolity had led to fame,
> And made us blush that you forbore to blame—
> If e'er the sinking stage could condescend
> To soothe the sickly taste it dare not mend—
> All past reproach may present scenes refute,
> And censure, wisely loud, be justly mute. (56–61)

But Horace and James Smith, sacred to memory for their
Rejected Addresses on this dedication (a total of twenty-one, all
written in brilliant parody of each particular author's style and
temperament), in the poem "*Cui Bono?* by Lord B" were quick

---

[28] See L & J I,117*n.*

[29] Chew, *Byron*, p. 32*n.*, mentions a number of plays Byron witnessed in London theatres before the end of 1813.

[30] Finding none among those submitted by the public that suited
him, Byron adopted the simple expedient of writing, and accepting,
an "Address" of his own.

to put their finger on the weaknesses in the Byronic attitudes toward theatrical reform:

> Hence, pedant Nature! with my Grecian rules,
> Centaurs (not fabulous) those rules efface;
> Back, sister muses, to your native schools;
> Here booted grooms usurp Apollo's place,
> Hoofs shame the boards that Garrick used to grace;
> The play of limbs succeeds the play of wit;
> Man yields the drama to the Houynim race,
> His prompter spurs, his licenser the bit,
> The stage a stable-yard, a jockey club the pit. (91–99)

And indeed, in the drama written in this period, including Byron's, anything like the tone of wit and levity of the Smiths' *Rejected Addresses* is so altogether absent that we ask ourselves why. Why is Romantic drama so deficient in any sort of humor? The "humour of *Beppo* and *Don Juan* and Byron's matchless letters is entirely lacking in his plays; there is not a trace of it in the dramas of Coleridge and Shelley; even Lamb left it behind him, save in feeble imitation of Shakespeare, when he wrote his dramas."[31] We might even go further by saying that Romantic drama is more notable for humorous anecdotes that can be told about it than it is for any sort of humorous content.

An instance that might be mentioned concerns a few lines from *Osorio*. Having come upon the play again by accident, in 1807, through the good offices of William Godwin, and having decided to go to work on it once more, Coleridge remarks to a correspondent that recently Sheridan has been making fun of certain lines from *Osorio*. "I should be less than a man, if I had not been indignant that within the last 12 months," he declares, Sheridan "has made me an object of ridicule among persons disposed to think well of me by misquoting a line, ridiculous enough in itself, and then asserting that it was a fair specimen of the whole Tragedy. But I should have felt much more indignation, if any friend had been so treated; because I should then have encouraged a feeling, which, it being my own case, I

---

[31] Chew, *Byron,* p. 29.

checked and repressed" (G. III,14-15). The wound still rankled when *Remorse* was published in 1813; in the Preface to the first edition Coleridge asserts that a "Person" (Sheridan) has cited a line as "Drip! drip! drip! there's nothing here but dripping," whereas the line originally read "Drip! drip! a ceaseless sound of water-drops."

Unfortunately Coleridge's memory played him false; the lines from *Osorio* (omitted in *Remorse*), are:

> Drip! drip! drip! drip! such a place as this
> It has nothing else to do but drip! drip! drip!
> I wish it had not dripp'd upon my torch.

So we have an example of offended artistic sensibility that refuses to perceive humor in the incongruous—particularly when the work being derided is one's own. How Sheridan came upon *Osorio* in the first place remains unfathomable; possibly Godwin, in whose possession the only extant copy of the tragedy apparently rested, had shown it to Sheridan. It is doubtful whether Sheridan would have remembered the lines after so many years, having, after all, been sent a copy back in 1797—that is, if he had even bothered reading it at that time.[32] Possibly Sir George Beaumont had let Sheridan read it some years before—it is impossible to say. In Coleridge's words, "I have been so lucky as to discover among Mr Godwin's Books the Copy of my Tragedy, which I had lent to poor dear Mrs Robinson—the only copy in existence, that I know of. I was very much pleased with it, still more pleased that I could see at once what it's faults were, and that a week's labor would compleatly remove them. Sir George Beaumont read it about 4 years ago; and he expressed his full persuasion, that with a few alterations which any person acquainted with the mechanics of the stage might easily suggest, it would *act* as well as it reads." (G. III,14.)

In semi-justification of Coleridge's attitude is a revealing comment from the Smiths' "Rejected Addresses" that touches on the humorlessness of Romantic drama. It comes from the selection entitled "*The Theatre* by the Rev. G. C[rabbe]," in whose

---

[32] See remarks on this, *supra,* pp. 40–41.

name it is written that "in the satirical view of life and manners, which I occasionally present, my clerical profession has taught me, how extremely improper it would be by any allusion, however slight, to give any uneasiness, however trivial, to any individual, however foolish or wicked."[33] In short, we are no longer confronted with the satirical free-for-all of an Augustan Age; personalities ought not to be touched—on the stage. In the newspapers and in the journals, yes; a Jeffrey can with impunity write (as he did about Wordsworth's *Excursion*): "This will never do!" In some way having to do with a shift in sensibility in this period, public statement is becoming differentiated from private utterance. The influence of the clergy on sensibility and taste is becoming stronger, and somewhat later for a time members of the clergy were themselves the principal writers of staged and would-be-staged Romantic plays, especially before the dawn of the Liberal Age, when biblical dramas briefly threatened to flood the theatres. The restraints of sobriety and decorum imposed by both the censorship of the Licensing Act and the omnipresent code of proper conduct were elements, too, that no playwright could afford to ignore, nor, from their attitudes, did the Romantic playwrights intend to ignore them, had they been the less in evidence. Francis Jeffrey, a principal watch-dog of correctness and good form, discloses why the type of comedy that Byron advocated in his youth was out of the question in the Romantic Period; and why, by the same token, Romantic drama itself is so humorless—aside from any clerical restraints. The Romantics' lack of humor is tied in with changing attitudes which the weight of this clerical, and Methodist, ascendancy helped bring about.

The issue concerns taste. "All tastes, then," says Jeffrey,

> are equally just and true, in so far as concerns the individual whose taste is in question; and what a man feels distinctly to be beautiful, *is beautiful* to him, whatever other people think of it . . . but it does not follow, from it, that all tastes are equally good or desirable, or that there is any difficulty

[33] Horace and James Smith, *Rejected Addresses* (22nd ed., Boston, 1860), p. 162.

in describing that which is really the best, and the most
to be envied. . . . But, if beauty consist in the reflection of
our affections and sympathies, it is plain that *he* will always
see the most beauty whose affections are the warmest and
most exercised—whose imagination is the most powerful, and
who has most accustomed himself to attend to the objects
by which he is surrounded. . . . It will follow pretty exactly,
too, that all men's perceptions of beauty will be nearly in
proportion to the degree of their sensibility and social sympathies; and that those who have no affections towards
sentient beings, will be as certainly insensible to beauty in
external objects, as he who cannot hear the sound of his
friend's voice, must be deaf to its echo.[34]

Jeffrey argues here for a correspondence between a sense of the
beautiful and the intensity of an individual's "sensibility and
social sympathies." He goes on to aver that "the wisest course,
perhaps, if it were only practicable, would be to have *two* tastes
—one to enjoy and one to work by—one founded upon universal
associations, . . . and another guided by all casual and individual
associations," through which the individual "might still look
fondly upon nature" and upon objects of "secret admiration."[35]
Thus the public or literary man would need two distinct personalities, one in the presence of some important issue, and the
other of private whim or caprice, not interfering with or intrud-
ing upon this other, public, image. Goethe expresses much the
same thing in "zwei Seelen wohnen in meiner Brust," the one
representing the iconoclastic nonconformist, the other the pub-
lic-spirited personality guided by what is "right." The only difference between their attitudes is that Jeffrey feels that only he
who is a sensible, social being can at the same time experience the
"beautiful" and the "true." We might also cite Coleridge's intentions for *The Ancient Mariner*: "my endeavors should be directed to persons and characters supernatural, or at least romantic; yet so as to transfer a human interest and a semblance

---

[34]*Contributions to the Edinburgh Review* (2nd ed., 3 vols., London,
1846) , I,75–76.
[35] *Ibid.,* p. 78.

of truth . . ."[36] A "moral" purpose, combined with "sensibility and social sympathy" for mankind and for all life, is paramount; and in such a scheme of things humor can scarcely play a practical or even a relevant role.

And so let us return to the *Rejected Addresses* of Horace and James Smith, and particularly to their shrewd commentary on Byron's "dramatic philosophy." In speaking of Byron's "Grecian rules," they have hit upon the fundamental weakness in the Byronic conception of the theatre. As Byron conceived it, drama "was not to be romantic. Romantic drama, preeminently that of his own day, had failed. It had not been able to combine both literary and dramatic qualities in enduring products, and it was therefore to be abandoned. Exceptional genius here and there might be its own excuse to follow its own self-appointed course. But the many who would turn to playmaking could not be trusted to manage romantic license in as technical a form as drama. . . . For the sake of the anticipated reform, the first example of the new practice should of course be severer in adherence to regularity than would be expected to prevail once the norm was attained."[37] In order to achieve this severe "adherence to regularity," Byron writes at one point: "It has been my object to be as simple and severe as Alfieri" (L & J, V,323). At another, he remarks: "My dramatic simplicity is *studiously* Greek, and must continue so; *no* reform ever succeeded at first. I admire the old English dramatists; but this is quite another field, and has nothing to do with theirs" (L & J, V,347).

To say that Byron's views represent unity in diversity would be to beg the question, since obviously the disagreements among the Romantic playwrights regarding the specific direction the drama should pursue would in the natural course of events be as numerous as the agreements. Yet Byron, the great *Ewige-Nein-Sager* of the Romantic dramatists, looked, in his dramas as in his poems, to Augustan, neo-classical precedent. In view of his admiration for Pope and Dryden, it should not surprise

---

[36] *Biographia Literaria,* ed. George Watson (London and New York, 1956), pp. 168–169.

[37] Clement Tyson Goode, *Byron as Critic* (Weimar, 1923), p. 109.

us to discover that he was concerned with sedulously observing whatever is *"studiously* Greek" (his "Grecian rules"). Nor should it surprise us that whereas Wordsworth and Coleridge believed they were no more than reverting to tradition when they followed Elizabethan playwriting customs, to Byron his "severity" belonged to "quite another field . . . [which had] nothing to do with theirs" (the Elizabethans' dramatic conventions). Thus at the very time Wordsworth and Coleridge were endeavoring to restore English drama to what they were convinced was its proper classical, pre-jacobinical path, Byron was arguing for something entirely different, something classical in that it should be modeled upon the rules.

It may seem strange that so long after they had been expounded upon by Dr. Johnson in his "Preface to Shakespeare," Byron should be returning to the neo-classical concept of the unities. That he "studied the arguments for and against the unities in the *Essay of Dramatic Poesy* of Dryden is proved by a close verbal reminiscence"[38] in what the author of *Manfred* and *Werner* has uttered in their behalf. In a conversation with Medwin, Byron emphatically recommends their employment, if for nothing else, "as a disciplinary measure."[39] "I was always a friend to the unities, and believe that the subjects are not wanting which may be treated in strict conformity to their rules. No one can be absurd enough to contend, that the preservation of the unities is a defect,—at least a fault. Look at Alfieri's plays, and tell me what is wanting in them. Does he ever deviate from the rules prescribed by the ancients, from the classical simplicity of the old models?"[40] Even more pointed is a statement from the Preface to Byron's most "classical" play, *Sardanapalus*: "The Author has in one instance attempted to preserve, and in the other to approach, the 'unities'; conceiving that with any very distant departure from them, there may be poetry, but can be no drama."

---

[38] Chew, *Byron,* p. 165.

[39] Goode, *Byron as Critic,* p. 111.

[40] Thomas Medwin, *Conversations of Lord Byron* (London, 1824), pp. 108–109.

As for the hero of tragedy, it becomes immediately apparent that Byron's ideas here were based on those of his predecessors, who themselves had thought along strictly classical lines:

> I must remark from *Aristotle* and *Rymer,* that the hero of tragedy and (I add *meo periculo*) a tragic poem must *be guilty,* to excite *"terror and pity,"* the end of tragic poetry. . . . "The pity which the poet is to labor for is *for* the criminal. The terror is likewise in the punishment of the said criminal, who, if he be represented too great an offender, will *not be pitied*; if altogether *innocent* his punishment will be unjust." In the Greek Tragedy innocence is unhappy often, and the offender escapes. I must also ask you is *Achilles* a *good* character, or is even Aeneas anything but a successful run-away? It is for Turnus men feel and not for the Trojan. Who is the hero of *Paradise Lost?* Why Satan,—and Macbeth, and Richard, and Othello, Pierre, and Lothario, and Zanga? (L & J, V,284)

Assuredly Byron was not, in a modern sense, a literary critic; but he was, for the most part, so adept and shrewd a critic of the drama of his day that we might well take his critical dicta seriously. About *Remorse,* he remarks in writing to Coleridge, for example: "We have had nothing to be mentioned in the same breath with *Remorse* for very many years" (L & J, III,191). Even more astutely, Maturin's unsuccessful play *Manuel* he calls "the absurd work of a clever man" (L & J, IV,137) and "as heavy a nightmare as was ever bestrode by Indigestion" (L & J, IV,151).[41] In the remarks quoted above there is in any case a subtle twist.

The fact is, Byron is not echoing Aristotelian principle. On the contrary, by implying that the villain rather than the tragic hero should be the protagonist in the dramatic action, he is insinuating exactly the opposite. Aristotle states: "The poet in like manner, in portraying men quick or slow to anger, or with similar infirmities of character, must know how to represent them as such, *and at the same time as good men,* as Agathon and

---

[41] For other critical comments by Byron, see p. 113.

Homer have represented Achilles."[42] Granted, except possibly
for Othello, that Byron has selected in each play the figure who
is the Lucifer of the piece; but his emphasis is askew. According
to Aristotle's conception, Achilles *is* a "good man"; according to Byron's re-interpretation of Aristotle, Achilles is not.
Where Byron goes astray is in his misinterpretation of the advice
that the "pity which the poet is to labor for is *for* the criminal"
—which is not to mean that the criminal can be purely villainous:
rather, he must exhibit "good" qualities in sufficient measure
for the audience's pity to achieve its cathartic effect, the excita-
tion (from the Byron quotation above) of *"terror and pity"*
over this great (if only partly good) man's fall.

What results from Byron's misapplication of Aristotle's
"Poetics" is not so much a hero in the conventional sense as a
villain who has altogether replaced the conventional hero of
the drama, his sheer wickedness being the sole means by which
the audience's sympathies and interest are to be aroused in his
behalf. The "passion" and the awakening to "remorse" in a villainous nature by Wordsworth or Coleridge, have in the hands
of Byron been corrupted to villainy for the sake of villainy. The
use of a foil-hero as a sop to customary attitudes regarding morality in "giving the villain his just deserts" is also for the most
part ignored. In the Byronic concept classical severity leads to
artistic license that transgresses even the most sacrosanct canons
of biblical retribution. As a critic expresses the case, it is Byron's
Manfred who "best represents the high romantic expression, in
dramatic form, of the Gothic spirit." Elsewhere the same critic
declares that the "crimes of villains in other Gothic plays were
ultimately divulged, after long speculation, in naked words.
Manfred's deed, we are led to suppose, was as appalling as any of
theirs, who were villains; yet Manfred remains a hero, whose
heroic reputation was preserved by extending the traditional
Gothic ambiguity. Byron never lifted the dark veil which en-
velopes him and the past event where the truth lies, and thus
what might have been irreparably ugly, when boldly displayed,

---

[42] *Works of Aristotle,* ed. W. D. Ross (12 vols., Oxford, 1908–1952),
XI,1454[b]. The italics are mine.

retained the fascination of profound mystery. Fleeting glimpses by half-light revealed a hero where full illumination would have disclosed a villain."[43] As a consequence of this reversal of human values, the Byronic hero becomes nothing more than the typical villain of Gothic drama, unabashedly recast into heroic guise.

How Byron managed to reach this singular formulation of classical doctrine is both an interesting and a perplexing problem. Partly it is bound up with the complex psychology of Byron as a person. But it would be fruitless here to go into the tangled issue of Byron's career, although his connection with the theatre of his day is too important for its own sake to be fully ignored, not to mention the flickering light that it may cast upon questions entailed by the "Byronic hero" in Byron's plays. That he was deeply concerned with the parlous state of the contemporary theatre is indisputable. And he was appalled by the licentiousness and vulgarity of contemporary plays:

> True Briton all beside, I here am French—
> Bloodshed 'tis surely better to retrench:
> The gladiatorial gore we teach to flow
> In tragic scenes disgusts, though but in show;
> We hate the carnage while we see the trick,
> And find small sympathy in being sick.
> Not on the stage the regicide Macbeth
> Appals an audience with a Monarch's death;
> To gaze when sable Hubert threats to sear
> Young Arthur's eyes, can *ours* or *Nature* bear?
> A haltered heroine Johnson sought to slay—
> We save Irene, but half damned the play.
>
> (*Hints from Horace,* 271–282)

Little wonder that he should merely have admired the "old English dramatists," while feeling that "our" way must differ from "theirs." Little wonder, too, that he early should have inclined toward comedy. "A comedy," he writes, "I take to be the most difficult of compositions, more so than tragedy" (L & J, II,373). As we have observed, from the time of his return to England

---

[43] Evans, *Gothic Drama from Walpole to Shelley,* pp. 232, 237–238.

from the East in 1811, Byron was a constant visitor to the theatre. In the 1813–14 season he held "a box at Covent Garden for the season" (L & J, II,334); and in November of 1813 he began work on a play of his own, a comedy. "This afternoon I have burnt the scenes of my commenced comedy," he writes on November 14 (L & J, II,314); and three days later, "I began a comedy, but burnt it because the scene ran into *reality*;—a novel for the same reason. In rhyme I can keep away from facts" (L & J, II,323), a remark that casts an interesting light on Byron's attitude as an artist about the "autobiographical" nature of his works. Soon thereafter friends were urging him to turn his hand to tragedy, and Byron remarks: "Before I left town Kemble paid me the compliment of desiring me to write a *tragedy*; I wish I could, but I find my scribbling mood subsiding" (L & J, III,16).

Not until the following year was Byron's scribbling mood reawakened. In all probability he was "influenced in his decision to write a play by perusal of the tolerable and intolerable attempts that were submitted to the Committee"[44] of Drury Lane Theatre to which he then belonged. The suicide of Samuel Whitbread, the manager of the theatre, in 1814, led to the formation of a subcommittee of interested parties, one of whom was Lord Byron, to manage the venerable new house. During their tenure they "made experiments and amused themselves at the same time"[45]—with what consequences to superior drama might easily be conjecturable. During this period, in 1815, Byron began work on a tragedy entitled *Werner*, "but Lady Byron's farce put it out of my head for the time of her representation" (L & J, V,391)—the time of her alienation from Byron and their subsequent separation. A fragment until its revision and enlargement in 1822, the only "significance of *Werner* is that it is Byron's one essay in the popular mode, his one effort to meet the stage half way."[46]

---

44 Chew, *Byron*, p. 35.
45 Percy Fitzgerald, *History of the English Stage* (2 vols., London, 1882), II,384.
46 Chew, *Byron*, p. 36.

Unabashedly "romantic" in tenor, the play was written with a story in mind about which Byron says: "I was young (about fourteen, I think) [when] I first read this tale ["The German's Tale, Kruitzner," published in Lee's *Canterbury Tales*][47] which made a deep impression upon me; and may, indeed, be said to contain the germ of much that I have since written" (Preface to *Werner*). But if this is made to sound like a work of significance in the development of Byron's artistic and philosophical beliefs, it should be added that the resulting dramatic product is no less disappointing than the German work from which it was derived. *Werner* is singularly un-Byronic in its lack of humor, in the absence of satiric touches, in the flabbiness of character delineation. In his attempts to be romantic and Gothic, Byron merely demonstrated how little he understood how to fuse these two elements into something that would do for his own age. Given a plot that could not be adapted to conform to requirements based upon "classical simplicity," he allowed his drama to degenerate instead into unconscious burlesque—à la *The Rovers*—of the way in which the most readable of the Gothicizers were constructing their plays of terror "of the soul."[48]

Concurrently a playwright of greater ability in Gothic drama than Byron was working on a play with touches of plot similar to those evident in *Werner*. Through the intercession of Sir Walter Scott, a play by Charles Maturin entitled *Bertram* was submitted to the Drury Lane committee late in 1815, shortly before the arrival of Coleridge's *Zapolya*. The sensation it created, to judge from a letter from John Murray to Scott, dated December 25, 1815, was considerable: "I was with Lord Byron yesterday. He enquired after you, and bid me say how much he was indebted to your introduction of your poor Irish friend Maturin, who had sent him a tragedy, which Lord Byron received late in the evening, and read through without being able

---

[47] *Canterbury Tales* (1797–1805) by Harriet Lee (1757–1851) consists of twelve stories related by travelers who have been thrown together by an unusual circumstance.

[48] "Terror is not of Germany, but of the soul" (Poe, Preface to *Tales of the Grotesque and Arabesque*).

to stop. He was so delighted with it that he sent it immediately to his fellow-manager, the Hon. George Lamb, who, late as it came to him, could not go to bed without finishing it. The result is that they have laid it before the rest of the Committee; they, or rather Lord Byron, feels it his duty to the author to offer it himself to the managers of the Covent Garden."[49]

When produced, on May 9, 1816, Maturin's *Bertram; or, The Castle of St. Aldobrand* was played not at Covent Garden but at Drury Lane. It ran for twenty-two nights in succession. Says Byron: "Maturin sent his *Bertram* and a letter *without* his address, so that at first I could give him no answer. When I at last hit upon his residence, I sent him a favourable answer and something more substantial. His play succeeded, but I was at that time absent from England."[50] As for the personality of this new genius of the theatre, himself a clergyman: "Whilst he was composing Bertram, and living amidst a confused sea of difficulties, a clergyman, high in the church, had called upon him . . . for the purpose of making him an offer of preferment; . . . after the lapse of half an hour, Maturin entered, his hair in dishevelled masses, wrapped in a flowing morning gown, and bearing in one hand a pen, in the other a portion of the manuscript of Bertram, from which he was repeating some highly wrought sentence just completed; he threw himself on the sofa beside his starched visitor, who very soon retreated, leaving the poet to cultivate the muse, in poverty and at leisure."[51]

These eccentricities should not blind us to the realization that Maturin succeeded where the others had failed. A few years later, in 1820, he was again to achieve a first with the publication of his novel of terror, *Melmoth the Wanderer*, possibly the greatest tale in its genre ever written in English. As for *Bertram*, it may well have been the only success of his four

---

[49] Samuel Smiles, *A Publisher and his Friends* (2 vols., London, 1891), I,288.

[50] Thomas Moore, *Life of Lord Byron* (London, 1851), p. 287. Byron "confessed that he had sent him [Maturin] fifty guineas" (Samuel Smiles, *A Publisher and His Friends,* I,288n.).

[51] *Irish Quarterly Review* (1852).

stage plays (the other three being *Manuel, Fredolfo,* and *The Siege of Salerno*). In this work Maturin managed to combine the best, or worst, qualities of the Gothic drama with sentimentality and a kind of blank verse that, if not immortal, at least is eminently readable. The story unfolds with dramatic power and vigor, even if the motives of the villain protagonist forever remain unfathomable. Bertram, who ultimately slays the husband of his beloved Imogine, does so for no better reason than that the author wants him to; he acts, not from inner motivation, but from blind hatred for its own sake. The play offers, in short, a classic example of a motiveless malignity. As a consequence the hero emerges as a figure who in his own personality and character is no more than somewhat mawkishly malign. Neither is there psychological development in the play, nor is more than lip service paid to the concept of a prevailing passion by which the actions of the protagonist can be governed or controlled. Bertram is no more than a villain for the sake of villainy; even in facing death he refuses to repent, and he is not assailed by pangs of remorse. It is the times that have made him unrepentant. In self-justification before he dies he merely declares:

> I died no felon death—
> A warrior's weapon freed a warrior's soul. (V,iii)

The Prior, who has been seeking to wring from him a sense of repentance, is moved to remark on Bertram's emotional plight:

> But terrors move in thee a horrid joy,
> And thou art hardened by habitual danger
> Beyond the sense of aught but pride in death.

Bertram thus is an illustration of resolving problems of motivation by simply ignoring or avoiding them. Not surprisingly, then, the excitement created by *Bertram* "was less due to any of its dramatical qualities than to its performance; the point was made by the admirers as well as by the slanderers of the play, that it was conceived quite 'in the taste of Lord Byron'."[52]

---

[52] N. Idman, *Charles Robert Maturin: His Life and Works* (Helsinfors, 1923), p. 109.

Byron, in 1817, writing to Thomas Moore from Venice, expresses his satisfaction at having been able to assist in producing the "first and well-merited success" of Maturin, whom he calls a "very clever fellow"[53]—a remark that indicates the high esteem in which Byron held this work, he himself being so well on the way toward circumventing motivation by veiling it in mystery and silence. Whether Maturin was of any real influence in prompting Byron to create Satans without satanic justification is a question that need not detain us; even without a Bertram, undoubtedly we would still have with us the shadowy figure of a Manfred wandering upon the heights of the Jungfrau, one who feels, without bothering to understand why, that

> There is a power upon me which withholds,
> And makes it my fatality to live;
> If it be life to wear within myself
> This barrenness of spirit, and to be
> My own soul's sepulchre, for I have ceased
> To justify my deeds unto myself—
> The last infirmity of evil. (I,ii,32–38)

Fortunately, no other dramatists were content to pursue this easy way of Byron and Maturin to avoid facing up to whatever problems the motivations of the characters in their plays might entail. We have seen that "passions of the soul" was one other direction Romantic drama was pursuing in this same period, for example. Byron and Maturin, by selecting the villain as their hero, had added a further element to the basic ingredients, but it was one that when carried to its logical consequences, could only result in an incongruous and banal end product. Not that this direction necessarily was wrong or that the protagonist in drama cannot at the same time be the villain. We have examples enough of that from Elizabethan drama, several of whose villains remarked upon by Byron have been cited earlier, notably Macbeth and Richard III. The difference between the Byronic and the customary approach, to adopt Clarence Boyer's definition of the "villain as hero," is that "a villain

---

[53] Moore, *Byron*, p. 347.

is a man who, for a selfish end, wilfully and deliberately violates standards of morality sanctioned by the audience or ordinary reader."[54] It is "when a character deliberately opposes moral law from wilfulness, and for the purposes of advancing his own interests, *recognizing at the same time the sanction of the law he defies*, [that] we call him a villain."[55] The distinction between the Byron-Maturin villain and the kind of villain who is credible, then, can be ascribed purely to this salient characteristic of Byron's particular concept regarding the "sanction of the law." The Byronic villain recognizes none; he functions in a vacuum of his author's devising, divorced from the strictures —and at the same time from the realities—of the acceptable. The Byronic hero is no more villainous than a figure made out of *papier-mâché*; he is to be distinguished not so much from reality as from the world of common sense. Bertram and Manfred— not to say the rest of Byron's "heroes"—are not even grotesques. What must be present, and what the Byronic hero lacks, is a *raison d'être*. What these villains need is a Shakespearean "cause, it is the cause, my soul." Souls have they none; their motiveless malignity leads merely to the creation of insipid monstrosities. For later dramatists to realize the potentialities of true Romantic drama, drama at once both poetic and credible, some new direction would have to be discovered, certainly a direction attuned to how people live and to how they act as human beings. Turning the Gothic villain into a hero had led merely to the creation of a dramatic dilemma.

As a way out of this impasse, what has been called closet drama seemed to some to offer the ideal solution. This drama of the neo-Elizabethan revival, inaugurated by Charles Lamb's *Specimens* in 1808, was promoted, as we have seen, by an interest in plays written in the grand style for actors like Edmund Kean and Eliza O'Neill. It was these two actors Shelley had in mind for the leading roles in his great drama, *The Cenci*. As Shelley remarks, *The Cenci* was "written without any of the

---

[54] Clarence V. Boyer, *The Villain as Hero in Elizabethan Tragedy* (London and New York, 1914), p. 8.

[55] *Ibid.*, p. 6. The italics are mine.

peculiar feelings and opinions which characterize my other compositions. I have attended simply to the impartial development of such characters as it is probable the persons represented really were, together with the greatest degree of popular effect to be produced by such a development."[56] Thus *The Cenci* is the first conscious attempt by a Romantic playwright to present psychological meaning and characterization within a poetic framework. An interest in the passion of remorse is as evident in *The Cenci* as in *The Borderers* or *Remorse*; the difference lies in Shelley's superior ability to delineate motivation and integrate character traits within the sphere of a coherent and powerful whole. Certainly the end product emerges as one of the finest dramas ever written by an English author; and with *The Cenci*, Romantic drama comes of age.

Says Shelley:

> . . . my principal doubt, as to whether it would succeed as an acting play, hangs entirely on the question as to whether any such a thing as incest in this shape, however treated, would be admitted on the stage. I think, however, it will form no objection: considering, first, that the facts are matter of history; and, secondly, the peculiar delicacy with which I have treated it. I am exceedingly interested in the question of whether this attempt of mine will succeed or no. I am strongly inclined to the affirmative at present, founding my hopes on this, that, as a composition, it is certainly not inferior to any of the modern plays that have been acted, with the exception of "Remorse"; that the interest of the plot is incredibly greater and more real; and that there is nothing beyond what the multitude are contented to believe that they can understand, whether in imagery, opinion, or sentiment.[57]

Yet material assembled by Arthur C. Hicks and R. Milton Clarke on the subsequent career of *The Cenci* shows us far different developments from those so sanguinely anticipated by its author.[58] Despite successful, if not triumphant, stage perform-

---

[56] *Letters of Percy Bysshe Shelley,* ed. Roger Ingpen (2 vols., London, 1909), II,698.

[57] *Ibid.,* pp. 698–699.

[58] *A Stage Version of Shelley's Cenci* (Caldwell, Idaho, 1945).

ances, dating from 1886, critics have stubbornly insisted that the
play is solely a literary (or closet) drama, an argument repeated
with variations by each of the foremost Shelley biographers,
Dowden, Peck, and White.[59] Nor has the matter been allowed
to rest there. K. N. Cameron and Horst Frenz, in their critique,
conclude: "There seems no reason why *The Cenci* should not
take its recognized place as one of the classics of the stage."[60]
Hicks and Clarke believe that "Shelley's tragedy, contrary to the
opinion prevalent among literary and dramatic critics, is not
properly classified as a closet drama unsuited to stage presentation." It "is a great acting drama, one of the very best of its
kind."[61] More recently another critic declares: "Let us not fool
ourselves about Shelley's play: it is a valuable stage piece which
can attain a certain theatrical vitality . . . and become an actable
play. But it will never take a place beside our esteemed stage
classics, beside *Macbeth, Othello, The Masterbuilder, Phaedre,
Oedipus, et al.*, as an acting play of the first rank, one not subject to a peculiar and elusive combination of circumstances
which attend its presentation."[62]

If we have a rather curious collection of contradictory evaluations of Shelley's drama, we have also a play that unabashedly can
take a proud place beside any of the historical dramas of Shakespeare. The wonder is that this work was by an artist then but
twenty-seven years of age, in chronology comparable to when
Shakespeare had hardly begun writing seriously for the theatre.
We must look to *Hamlet* to find anything equal in psychological subtlety, character portrayal, and philosophical profundity to

[59] As an instance, *"The Cenci* can hardly be called a tragedy at
all, in anything like the traditional meaning of the word. In spite of an
intelligent and clever use of the materials, it is obviously defective in
structure, when considered as a play for the stage." (Newman I. White,
Shelley [2 vols., New York, 1940], II,141.) Other negative remarks by
White on *The Cenci* are listed in footnote 63.

[60] "The Stage History of Shelley's *The Cenci,*" *PMLA*, LX (1945),
1105.

[61] *A Stage Version of Shelley's Cenci*, pp. 28; 28–29.

[62] Marcel Kessel and Bert O. States, Jr., *"The Cenci* as a Stage
Play," *PMLA*, LXXV (1960), 149.

Shelley's play.[63] Marlowe's dramas, if more dramatic and more crowded with characters, are inept in comparison with the shades of emotion and fineness of charged effects so evident in Shelley's play. That Shelley was indebted to the Elizabethans as models for *The Cenci* is a matter too well known to dispute.[64] But this does not mitigate against his having made a profound contribution to the drama. Bernard Shaw, one of the many who discuss Shelley's debt to Elizabethan models, possibly has best discovered why *The Cenci* can in the same breath be both a superior drama and a failure. The question is why as "a drama which can, with predictable confidence, be put on the stage in its entirety, or very nearly, without calling attention to bold structural faults —which we can certainly do with our great dramas—*The Cenci* falls far short of success."[65] Shaw says: "*The Cenci*, . . . is a failure in the sense in which we call an experiment with a negative result a failure. But the powers called forth by it were so extraor-

---

[63] Newman I. White, a critic who stands in the opposite camp, in "The English Romantic Writers as Dramatists," *Sewanee Review*, XXX (1922), 206–215, has written: "Shelley's *The Cenci* does indeed have the appearance of great tragedy, but breaks down upon closer analysis. Objective as it seems to be, it does not in reality get beyond the great abstract triangle of Tyrant, Slave and Rebel which robs practically all Shelley's plays and narrative poems of real humanity and makes him the most abstract of all the Romanticists. . . . Wordsworth's *The Borderers*, Scott's *Sensuality and Revenge*, and Coleridge's *Remorse* all belong to a class in which psychological analysis provides the main interest. With Coleridge and Wordsworth at least, this analysis is merely the author's toying with his own mental projections, and is tinged with abnormality." (P. 212.) These comments read like a paraphrase of Nicoll's objections, already quoted in Chapter I above; to them the only remark that can be made is that White wrote these comments before O'Neill had begun *Strange Interlude* and *Mourning Becomes Electra*— not to mention his posthumously produced plays, or the plays of Tennessee Williams.

[64] For a discussion of Elizabethan influences in *The Cenci*, see Ernest S. Bates, *A Study of Shelley's Drama "The Cenci"* (New York, 1908), pp. 54 ff. See also Newman I. White, "Shelley's Dramatic Poems" (unpublished dissertation, Harvard, 1918). For specific reference to Shelly's sources for *The Cenci*, see p. 109.

[65] Kessel and States, p. 148.

dinary that many generations of audiences will probably submit to have the experiment repeated on them, in spite of the incidental tedium. And if the play be ever adequately acted, the experiment will not even be temporarily fatiguing to witness, though it perhaps may prove at one or two points unendurably horrible."[66]

It is true that in *The Cenci* there are moments of "incidental tedium." But about what play cannot the same be said, depending upon individual taste? It is also true that at one or two points *The Cenci* is "unendurably horrible." Yet it is a horror that is unendurable only if we wish to make it so. After the Sybil Thorndike production of 1922, a critic remarked, "If *The Cenci* were produced with garish realism, the physical horror would be overpowering—the superhuman conflict between right and wrong, the interplay of the powers of light and darkness, would be hidden behind a story of incestuous passion and Sadistic oppression."[67] And we may say in paraphrase that if *The Cenci* is received by an audience with closed-mind moral indignation, then the "superhuman conflict between right and wrong, the interplay of the powers of light and darkness" will be hidden behind a mere story of "incestuous passion" and sensationalism for the sake of effect. It is interesting to observe how little we of the present have been willing or able to face up to the problems Shelley raises in *The Cenci*, even going so far as to expunge lines that might appear unseemly to untutored ears. Thus in the notable Bellingham (Washington) production of March, 1940, the last line was omitted in the excerpt that begins:

> . . . Cristofano
> Was stabbed in error by a jealous man,
> Whilst she he loved was sleeping with his rival. (I,iii,61–63) [68]

So far, even in attempts at giving authoritative productions of

---

[66] *Our Corner,* June 1, 1886, pp. 371–372.

[67] Horace Shipp, "Shelley and Chevalier," *English Review,* XXXV (1922), 524.

[68] Hicks and Clarke, p. 75.

our established classics, are we willing to go in order not to vio-
late the dictates of conventional morality!

When it is maintained that *The Cenci* can be successfully
produced only if the text is radically shortened, we can be excused for adopting a questioning attitude. We might grow even
more skeptical after discovering that out of six of nine recent
productions of *The Cenci* that have been compressed for stage
purposes, four (Princeton, Mt. Holyoke, Utah, Oxford) were
given by university groups and a fifth on the radio (BBC).[69]
Surely we do not have to accept college productions of our literary masterpieces as touchstones of their suitability for theatrical presentation!—not unless we are willing to believe that college audiences are superior critics to Broadway audiences. What
is sad is that in not being familiar with *The Cenci* we lose more
than we gain. "Awful are those revelations of the monstrous
heart of the old man [Count Cenci]; tremendous in their hope-
less agony and desolation those staggerings of the mind of
Beatrice from transitory error, that spirit of resignation and immortal love which rises, towards the close of the play, out of
the hell of the earlier parts, and finds its most lovely expression
in the final words. Never did poet more exquisitely show the
triumph of Good over Evil than Shelley has done in that hushed
and sacred ending. It is a voice out of the very depths of the
suffering patience of humanity."[70]

Nor is this tribute overdone. Swinburne, who admired
Shelley only second to the idolized Landor, calls *The Cenci*
"the one great play written in the great manner of Shakespeare's
men that our literature has seen since the time of these."[71]

---

[69] See Bert O. States, Jr., "Addendum: The Stage History of Shelley's
The Cenci," PMLA, LXXII (1957), 633–644. The BBC presented *The
Cenci* twice, in 1947 and 1948. The other three performances were:
Company of Swan, London, 1953; Equity Library Theatre, 1947; Walt
Whitman School, New York, 1950.

[70] *Shelley Memorials,* ed. Lady Shelley (3rd ed., London, 1875),
pp. 117-118.

[71] "Notes on the Text of Shelley," *Bonchurch Edition,* XV,383. But
observe Swinburne's remarks on Wordsworth's *The Borderers,* Chapter
II, footnote 19.

Browning also gave the play unbridled praise, as a youth sending his copy to Kean with the suggestion that it be produced by Covent Garden. Macready, when in retirement, is reported to have offered to return to the stage if he could appear as Count Cenci.[72]

Unfavorable criticism, quite naturally, can readily be found,[73] but let us stay briefly with favorable comments, like those of Swinburne. Swinburne perhaps has put his finger on the greatness of Shelley's play. The verse he of course finds incomparable;[74] but what had preoccupied Shelley, concerned with the play's suitability for production and consequent reception,[75] was the incest theme of Count Cenci's assault on his daughter, Beatrice. In the Preface he even declares guardedly: "The story of the Cenci is indeed eminently fearful and monstrous; anything like a dry exhibition of it on the stage would be insupportable. The person who would treat such a subject must increase the ideal and diminish the actual horror of the events, so that the pleasure which arises from the poetry which exists in these tempestuous sufferings and crimes may mitigate the pain of the contemplation of the moral deformity from which they spring."[76]

Swinburne is not perturbed by *The Cenci*'s theme of incest. He pays high tribute to the depiction of Shelley's Beatrice Cenci; yet he turns with even greater interest to the character of the

---

[72] See Bates, *A Study of Shelley's Drama "The Cenci"*, pp. 26–30, for these and other details.

[73] A typical example of such adverse criticism is the Newman White quotation, footnote 63.

[74] "Et depuis Webster, le confrère et l'héritier de Shakespeare, jamais des vers pareil n'avaient retenti sur la scène anglaise" ("Les Cenci," *Bonchurch Edition*, XV,321).

[75] "It is worthy of note that Mr. Harris of Covent Garden, the first theatrical manager to consider *The Cenci* for production, was so impressed that he requested Shelley to write a tragedy on some other subject, which he would gladly accept, although he considered the theme of incest in *The Cenci* to be so objectionable that he would not even submit the part of Beatrice to Miss O'Neil [*sic*] for reading" (*A Stage Version of Shelley's Cenci*, p. 15).

[76] *Complete Poetical Works of Percy Bysshe Shelley*, Cambridge ed. (Boston and New York, 1901), pp. 209–210.

Count. Possibly he remembered lines from one of Shelley's later poems:

> . . . Man who man would be,
> Must rule the empire of himself; in it
> Must be supreme, establishing his throne
> On vanquished will, quelling the anarchy
> Of hopes and fears, being himself alone.
>
> (Sonnet: "Political Greatness")

For *The Cenci* is peculiarly the drama of a man "qui commande aux autres hommes par le moyen de leur lâcheté et à Dieu par le moyen de son intérêt. Il a Dieu dans son poche et l'humanité sous son talon."[77] He is the reverse side of the coin, the other nature of us all, the man of unmitigated passions and vices who, through wealth and position, is able to give unbridled license to his slightest passion—and who spends his life in consummating his most secret, even if heinous, desires.

After comparing Count Cenci with Cesare Borgia, Napoleon, and Peter the Great, Swinburne goes on to say that "Francesco Cenci, empereur et roi lui aussi à sa façon, peut bien en avoir assez pour le rendre supportable au spectateur qui doit contempler en idée ce colosse eblouissant du crime."[78] We must recall how recently the Napoleonic Wars had taken place: *The Cenci*, dating from 1819, was written four years after Waterloo. In the minds of Englishmen the recollection still was indelibly fresh of the consequences of abuse of power, overweening pride, personal ambition, and private greed. Without exaggeration it can be said that the most important of the Romantic dramas in one way or another were directly concerned with this problem of the unbridled, unprincipled tyrant who must be won back within the fold of common humanity through the awakening of his conscience to the pangs of remorse. Earlier, these moral issues were mentioned relative to the dramas of Wordsworth and Coleridge; in Byron, despite his concern with freedom and liberty, remorse is hidden behind the veil of a mysterious past; in

---

[77] "Les Cenci," *Bonchurch Edition,* XV,324.
[78] *Ibid.*

Shelley, however, remorse becomes subordinate to the disclosure of a monstrous egocentric for whom morality and remorse represent concepts but not realities, all values being instead the playthings of the individual whim. As expressed by Shelley himself, "The highest moral purpose aimed at in the highest species of the drama is the teaching the human heart, through the sympathies and antipathies, the knowledge of itself: in proportion to the possession of which knowledge every human is wise, just, sincere, tolerant and kind."[79]

By getting acquainted with the diabolical character of Count Cenci, we come to know ourselves better. Still, as Shelley wisely notes, the drama is "no fit place for the enforcement" of dogma or cant: "Undoubtedly no person can be truly dishonored by the act of another; and the fit return to make to the most enormous injuries is kindness and forbearance and a resolution to convert the injurer from his dark passions by peace and love. Revenge, retaliation, atonement, are pernicious mistakes. If Beatrice had thought in this manner she would have been wiser and better; but she would never have been a tragic character."[80] In opposition to this position Swinburne declares with some asperity that Shelley in his Preface upholds the inviolability of every human being, even of Francesco Cenci. Remarking on the similarity of Shelley's defense to Victor Hugo's defense of Napoleon, he contemptuously declares: "Pour moi, je dois l'avouer, il me serait aussi facile de croire à l'infaillibilité de Clément VIII et de Pie IX qu'à cette inviolabilité-là."[81] But Swinburne is too astute not to recognize Shelley's purpose in bringing about Count Cenci's downfall and murder: had his daughter Beatrice not acted in bringing about his death, she surely "would never have been a tragic character." Shelley remarks in defense of his theme that despite its concern with incest and retribution, "the deepest and sublimest tragic compositions, *King Lear* and the two plays in which the tale of Oedipus is told, were stories which already existed in tradition, as matters of pop-

---

[79] *Complete Poetical Works of Shelley*, p. 210.
[80] *Ibid.*
[81] "Les Cenci," *Bonchurch Edition*, XV, 326.

ular belief and interest, before Shakespeare and Sophocles made them familiar to the sympathy of all succeeding generations of mankind."[82] A later critic sums up the case for *The Cenci* with admirable sensibility: "In the light of the tremendous tragic force of the play and its high rank as tragic poetry, it should at least be accorded the tolerance which is given without quibble to the Oedipus of old, and allowed to stand upon its own merits."[83] The case is as simple as that.

In Shelley's own day criticism of the play was mixed. Leigh Hunt writes ecstatically: "What a noble book, Shelley, have you given us! What a true, stately, and yet affectionate mixture of poetry, philosophy, and human nature, and horror, and all-redeeming sweetness of intention, for there is an undersong of suggestion through it all, that sings, as it were, after the storm is over, like a brook in April."[84] Keats, more casually acquainted with Shelley, in his famous letter acknowledging a gift copy of the work, is more critical: "You, I am sure, will forgive me for sincerely remarking that you might curb your magnanimity, and be more of an artist, and load every rift of your subject with ore."[85] But Keats's way was not Shelley's in the drama—as had not been Wordsworth's or Coleridge's. It is as if all three poets plagiarized one another: in his way Shelley but repeats in his Preface to *The Cenci* what both Wordsworth and Coleridge had said earlier on the subject of language: "In order to move men to true sympathy we must use the familiar language of men . . ."; "I have avoided with great care in writing this play the introduction of what is commonly called mere poetry, and I imagine there will scarcely be found a detached simile or a

[82] *Complete Poetical Works of Shelley,* p. 209.

[83] Francis C. Mason, *A Study in Shelley Criticism* (Mercersburg, Pa., 1937), pp. 10–11.

[84] *Shelley-Leigh Hunt,* ed. R. Brimley Johnson (2nd ed., London, 1929), pp. 134–135.

[85] *Complete Poetical Works and Letters of John Keats,* Cambridge ed. (Cambridge, Massachusetts, 1890), p. 443. Keats's objective in his own poetry, to present unembellished and compressed description, are possibly nowhere better illustrated than in this quotation. Compare with Shelley's intention for his *Cenci* which follows Keats's objections above.

single isolated description, unless . . ." then going on to mention one suggested to mind "by a most sublime passage in *El Purgatorio de San Patricio*" by Calderon.[86] These poets' interest in the language of drama seems indeed to have been obsessive.

Naturally *The Cenci* would not be particularly pleasing to Lord Byron; the theme, so openly expressed, could hardly have appealed to one of Byron's own unusual experiences. In *Manfred* the confession is made to Astarte:

> . . . Thou lovedst me
> Too much, as I loved thee: we were not made
> To torture thus each other, though it were
> The deadliest sin to love as we have loved. (II,iv,120–123)

But there is no revelation of the promiscuous. Manfred implores:

> . . . but say—
> I reck not what—but let me hear thee once—
> This once—once more! (II,iv,147–149)

And Astarte merely repeats his name. The undisclosable remains undisclosed.

In writing of his reaction to *The Cenci*, Byron avoids mentioning the incest theme. "You also know my high opinion of your own poetry,—because it is of *no* school. I read *Cenci*—but besides that I think the *subject* essentially *un*-dramatic, I am not an admirer of our old dramatists as models. I deny that the English have hitherto had a drama at all. Your *Cenci*, however, was a work of power and poetry" (L & J, V,268). Elsewhere Byron is more forthright in his praise; as recorded by Medwin, he states on one occasion: "The 'Cenci' is . . . perhaps the best tragedy modern times have produced. It is a play,—not a poem, like 'Remorse' and 'Fazio'; and the best proof of its merit is, that people are continually quoting it. What may not be expected from such a beginning?"[87]

Of the great Romantic poets, only Wordsworth and Cole-

---

[86] *Complete Poetical Works of Shelley*, pp. 210–211, 210, 210*n*. See also Salvador Madariaga, *Shelley and Calderon* (New York, 1920).

[87] *Conversations of Lord Byron*, pp. 111–112.

ridge remained silent on *The Cenci*. Probably neither read the play. Or possibly it is because "to Wordsworth, Shelley, like Byron, was a moral suspect, a teacher of dangerous doctrines, made all the more seductively dangerous by the fineness of the art by which they were conveyed."[88] The more tolerant Coleridge boasts that Shelley's "discussions—tending toward Atheism of a certain sort—would not have scared *me*: for *me* it would have been a semi-transparent Larva, soon to be sloughed, and through which I should have seen the true *image*,—the final metamorphosis."[89]

The Cenci is scarcely anti-religious, however. This possible interpretation Shelley took great pains to refute. "Religion co-exists, as it were," he says, "in the mind of an Italian Catholic, with a faith in that of which all men have the most certain knowledge. It is interwoven with the whole fabric of life. . . . It has no necessary connection with any one virtue."[90] At the time critics found the play to be more striking for its obvious mastery of incident. "The mystery of the possession by a mind considered to have been purely visionary of such skill in dramatic realism remained the most astonishing impression,"[91] one commentator observes. A critic in the *Edinburgh Review* even declares that *The Cenci* "is altogether among those miracles of genius, which no philosophy can account for, and no criticism can analyze. . . . That the imaginative faculty usually appears inborn, we know; but how the dramatic talent can be acquired by intuition, is an incomprehensible thing."[92] In his final judgment, as recorded by Trelawny, Shelley himself observes that *"The Cenci* is a work of art; it is not colored by my feelings nor obscured by my metaphysics. I don't think much of it. It gave

[88] David W. Rannie, *Wordsworth and his Circle* (New York and London, 1907), p. 262.

[89] Quoted in Olwen W. Campbell, *Shelley and the Unromantics* (London, 1924), p. 103.

[90] *Complete Poetical Works of Shelley*, p. 210.

[91] *A Study in Shelley Criticism*, p. 42.

[92] American ed., LXIX (1839), pp. 277–278.

me less trouble than anything I have written of the same length."[93] Evidently even to Shelley the circumstances of the composition of *The Cenci* in retrospect had assumed something of the aura of an unfathomable mystery.

In comparison with all the other neo-Elizabethan plays of the Romantic Period we should be inclined to call *The Cenci* something of a miracle. Among the neo-Elizabethans Thomas Lovell Beddoes in particular was one who greatly admired *The Cenci*. In Shelley's play he could see virtues that were missing from his own works. Writing to his friend Kelsall, he explodes: "Why did you send me the Cenci? I open my own page, and see at once what damned trash it all is. No truth or feeling. How the deuce do you, a third and disinterested person, manage to tolerate it?"[94] Elsewhere, in speaking of the "abundant harvest of tragedies" appearing in 1822, Beddoes refers to *The Cenci* as "a tragedy inferior to none in our literature or any other" (D. 542). Otherwise, this "abundant harvest" consists of "two or three with the name but not the spirit of Byron, a Carlos from the Parliamentary Muse of Lord J. Russell, Mr. Croly's Catiline, and a countless litter, equally forgotten, from the Melpomenes of avowed and nameless authors" (D. 542).[95] With deadpan seriousness Beddoes goes on to review a play entitled *Montezuma* by one of these Melpomenes whom he calls "St. John Dorset."

Montezuma is a tragedy rather of the poetical than the dramatic order, it is deficient in action and its principal action is of secondary interest, domestic and little influenced by the political situation of its personae, its poetry is in the modern style, often imitative of Shakespeare and Beaumont and Fletcher among the old writers and of Byron and Cornwall among our contemporaries, but as often and of [necessity] al-

[93] *Last Days of Shelley and Byron,* ed. J. E. Morpurgo (New York, 1952), p. 52.

[94] *Works of Thomas Lovell Beddoes,* ed. H. W. Donner. Hereafter referred to as D. followed by the page number.

[95] The plays of Byron are *Heaven and Earth, Werner,* and *The Deformed Transformed.*

ways more successfully, original, of the right kind, bold, lofty,
magnificent and so comprehensive in its creation as to produce
in one word, and with equal facility, both the Alpine sub-
limity and the weed which blossoms at its feet. (D. 543) [96]

If this succeeds merely in making the play sound impossibly bad,
in Beddoes' method there shines through a genuine concern
with the sorry state of English drama and the factors that had
led to the writing of such lamentable plays. Despite the care
and toil of the effort, Beddoes persisted in the composition of
his own neo-Elizabethan masterpiece, *Death's Jest-Book*. Calling
it the "never-ending Jest-book," he describes how "it lies like a
snow ball and I give it a kick every now and then out of mere
scorn and ill-humour. The 4th act and I may say the 5th are
more than half done, so that at last it will be a perfect mouse:
but such doggrell—ask Procter else whom I lately visited with a
rhyming punishment for his correspondential sins" (D. 616).

In his attempts to improve the quality of his "doggrell,"
Beddoes only shows that he did not understand the limitations
to which a drama must be subject in its construction if it is to
be called a play. Instead, his principal complaint is against
the restrictions writers allow themselves to feel bound by, presumably out of a lack of boldness and imagination. "Chance and
opportunity, the concealed listener, the letter lost, and all the
miracles of the trap-door, all diminish the wide circle of the
drama, deny her the woods and seas, cut out her sky, and draw-
ing away the world from beneath her feet place her on a scaf-
fold; if she must be a muse and not nature, let her be Melpo-
mene, if she must have a prison let it be the Grecian temple"
(D. 544). We could regard this counsel as being merely ironic
were it not that Beddoes took considerable pains to observe it
when writing his own plays—granted that in his first drama, *The
Brides' Tragedy*, shifts in scene are kept within fairly restricted
limits. This play was published in 1822, while Beddoes was an
Oxford undergraduate; he was already convinced that the future

---

[96] The play has been ascribed to either Hugh John Balfour or Rev.
George Stephens. See Donner, p. 726.

of English drama lay in the closet rather than on the stage. Bemoaning the fact that England has become "bespoken and appointed for business and action," he speaks up for those "who like ourselves, do seek not to outstrip the world in the race for gold or glory . . . but delight rather to linger just behind the rolling world, to enjoy its shade and shelter, we would share the pleasure of what we have gleaned in our loitering solitude" (D. 543). If he sounds like an overly literary beatnik of our age, we must remember that Beddoes, Procter, Wells, and the lesser dramatists of the neo-Elizabethan revival possibly were born too late—too late to have shared in the turmoil and excitement of the Napoleonic era, and too late to have been properly able to enjoy, not having worked for them, the fruits of the post-Napoleonic boom. Caught at the end of an age, Beddoes recommends seeking dramatic literature "in the closet, not in their [the drama's] proper home, the populous theatre, . . . our countrymen barely enduring the poetry of Shakspeare as the vehicle of a fashionable song or a gaudy pageant."[97]

Clearly Beddoes places his main emphasis upon the word rather than the action, the spirit of poetry rather than the effect of the words produced. A typical attitude, we might say, of the undergraduate, scarcely one to be adhered to for a lifetime, especially by anyone seeking to write for the theatre "in its present state," as had Coleridge. It is remarkable how consistently these neo-Elizabethans ignored in themselves the faults they were so aware of in their contemporaries. The views of the nineteen-year-old Beddoes written in 1822 coincide so well with subsequent "doggrell" of his *Death's Jest-Book* that it is interesting to note the works he most admired as an undergraduate, when he implores "any unprejudiced person" to "peruse Allan Cunningham's poetical drama, which has won the applause of the highest literary authority of the day; let him dwell upon the energetic grandeur and warlike animation which Croly has so successfully displayed in pourtraying the restless spirit of Catiline;

---

[97] *The Brides' Tragedy,* letter addressed to the Rev. H. Card, Donner, p. 172.

and I think his verdict will place this age not the last among those which have done honour to the British stage."[98]

There is always present in Beddoes' works and in his career such a lurking note of cynical amusement and wry humor that often it is impossible to distinguish the real from the feigned. There are times when the reader is inclined to believe that Beddoes regarded everything, including the theatre, as a monstrous joke. In a letter to his friend Kelsall, written in 1837 from Zurich, he inquires: "What are the votaries of the Muse doing younder? What is Cosmo dei Medici? Paracelsus? Strafford? and Sergeant Talfourd's Ion or John?" (D. 663). Two pages later we read: "You must know that I am an M.D. of the U. of Würzburg and possess a very passable knowledge of anatomy and physiology etc., that I narrowly escaped becoming professor of comparative Anat^y in the U. of Zürich . . . by means of a timely quarrel . . . with several members of the government. . . . Now, being independent . . . sometimes I dissect a beetle, sometimes an oyster, and very often . . . 'peep and botanize' in defiance of W.W." (D. 665). Such was the checkered, and presumably self-amusing, career of Thomas Lovell Beddoes.

It is pertinent that Beddoes was a doctor of medicine. Anatomy and the anatomical pervade his dramatic works almost page for page. The frontispiece to *Death's Jest-Book* depicts a skeleton in contemplative posture examining a skull that rests upon a tomb. The subject matter of his two plays reflects a fascinated, if not morbid, preoccupation with death. *The Brides' Tragedy,* as said, contents itself with remaining earthbound, its scene shifting within fairly restricted limits of Oxford and vicinity. *Death's Jest-Book,* although likewise temporally bound, like Goethe's *Faust* gives the impression, in spirit if not in fact, of roaming over the immeasurable universe. Many of the scenes

---

[98] *Ibid.;* the play in question by Cunningham is *Sir Marmaduke Maxwell,* of which Scott writes in the Introduction to *The Fortunes of Nigel:* "Not a glimpse of probability is there about the plot, but so much animation in particular passages, and such a vein of poetry through the whole, as I dearly wish I could infuse into my Culinary Remains, should I ever be tempted to publish them . . . But never mind . . . honest Allan; you are a credit to Caledonia for all that." See Donner, p. 707.

are of such interminable length that gradually the reader, if not the poet, loses all sense of time; suddenly the scene shifts to a garden, a kitchen, a sepulchre. The incongruous, the banal, the lurid, the grandiloquent, are mingled in dazzling profusion through lugubrious descriptions, elaborate apostrophes, and touches of slapstick comedy. There are passages of exquisite beauty. Unforgettable is Beddoes' description, from *Death's Jest-Book*, of love:

> . . . I never knew before
> The meaning of this love. But one has taught me,
> It is a heaven wandering among men,
> The spirit of gone Eden haunting earth.
> Life's joys, death's pangs are viewless from its bosom,
> Which they who keep are gods; there's no paradise,
> There is no heaven, no angels, no blessed spirits
> No souls, or they have no eternity,
> If this be not a part of them (II,iii,148–156) .

Perhaps we might like to think that this expresses Beddoes' philosophy regarding love and death. But then we begin to doubt: the macabre, the grotesque, are too all-pervasive, the humor too incongruous. A description of alchemy by the court jester, Isbrand, is memorable: "Praised be the secrets of alchemy that can thus embody that subtlety which shall subdue the flesh and all its wickedness in an ounce of hog's lard. But is not this ointment called the fat of the land, with which those who are smeared do hide the hideousness of their souls so often?" (II,i, 163-168). In *The Brides' Tragedy* there is the charming invocation of Olivia addressed to her attendants:

> Henceforth I'll look upon my maiden years
> As lovely pastoral pictures; all of you
> Shall smile again 'neath Memory's wizard pencil;
> The natural beauties that we've marked together
> Will look you back again; the books we've loved
> Will talk to me of your sweet-worded praises,
> The air of our old haunts whisper your voices;
> Trust me, I'll not forget you. (III,iv,60–67)

But for the most part the impression is of an erratic genius unable to separate the ridiculous from the sublime. Too often the reader is forced to feel, in company with Hesperus of *The Brides' Tragedy*, that Beddoes believes:

> . . . In haste
> I've washed, and thought me spotless. Yet I fear
> Mine eye is so familiarized with blood,
> It doth pass o'er and disregard the stains:
> That recks not. (IV,i,20–24)

Like Melville's monomaniac Ahab, from having gazed too long into the hell fires of his own devices, the "wisdom that is woe" in Beddoes' works becomes transmuted into a woe that is madness. The beauties contained in his writings give way for the reader to boredom and disinterest. The absence of a philosophical or esthetic focus leads all too evidently to a dead end, both in timeliness and pertinence. Beddoes' plays are an example of Romantic literature without a *raison d'etre*. And without that, Romantic literature degenerates into emotion merely for the sake of emotion, effect for the sake of effect.[99]

Still, the revival of interest in Elizabethanism must be regarded as important in our story of Romantic drama. As expressed by Shelley in his Preface to *The Cenci*, "our great ancestors the ancient English poets are the writers, a study of whom might incite us to do that for our own age which they have done for theirs."[100] Unfortunately the urge to Elizabethanize, the desire to utter, with Procter,

> . . . a few plain words, honestly told,
> Like those his mightier masters spoke of old.
>
> (Prologue to *Mirandola*)

was, except for Shelley, beyond the capacities of any of them. From the point of view of the theatre the precursor for this movement is Lamb's *John Woodvil* (1802), a play in which an "in-

---

[99] On the macabre and grotesque in Romantic literature and the Romantic temperament, see Mario Praz, *The Romantic Agony*, trans. Angus Davidson (2nd ed., London, 1951).

[100] *Complete Poetical Works of Shelley*, p. 210.

termixture of prose and verse, the use of archaic words and phrases, the lax construction, the employment of types in the *dramatis personae,* are the signs of this Elizabethanism"[101] as it developed in the works of the other revivalists. But from the pens of Beddoes, Procter, Darley, and Wells, the foremost of these other revivalists, stemmed turgid, unwieldy plays, many of which read like parodies of those "mightier masters" of former times rather than original artistic creations that can survive on their own merits. In raising "a ghost to gaze on,"[102] these writers in effect succumbed to the stereotyped and the banal. This is aptly expressed by George Darley in a letter to Mary Mitford: "But the truth is, my mind was born among the rude old dramatists, and has imbibed some of their *ogre* milk, which gave more of its coarseness than strength to my efforts."[103] Of the other dramatists we can say the same: the coarseness is present, the strength fails.

Yet a certain charm is present in the writings of them all. It may be that the plays of these neo-Elizabethans deserve more attention than customarily has been accorded them,[104] but as contributions to literature there is little that remains to be said in their behalf. Only one of the revivalist plays was successfully performed on the stage,[105] Procter's (Barry Cornwall's) *Mirandola,* which was given a run of sixteen performances in 1821. Its success was due not so much to the merits of the play as to the able production lavished upon it by the astute actor-manager William Macready. Procter himself in his "Advertisement" to the play admits: "That the Tragedy has succeeded so well must be ascribed, no doubt in a material degree, to the great exertion

[101] Chew, *Byron,* p. 17.

[102] See *Supra,* p. 50.

[103] Quoted in Introduction (p. xxiii), *The Complete Poetical Works of George Darley,* ed. Ramsay Colles (London, n.d.).

[104] See Chew, *Byron,* pp. 17–19.

[105] The neo-Elizabethan plays of the later John Westland Marston will be discussed in due course. Since they belong in spirit and philosophy to the decade of the liberal 1840's, it is more appropriate to examine them within that context than in conjunction with these more or less pure neo-Elizabethans of an earlier period.

of the performers; and the pleasant task remains . . . of saying
how much I am sensible to the really masterly delineation which
Mr. Macready gave of the varying and difficult character of
Mirandola, and of the high and perfectly admirable portrait
which Mr. C. Kemble embodied of the son." With two such performers, it is difficult to conjecture an unsuccessful run.

As for *Mirandola* itself, it is "an Italian tragedy of passion,
one of the long series from such plays as Webster's tragedies to
Swinburne's *Duke of Gandia*."[106] Such a distinguished line of
dramatic descent is of little help in elevating it above mediocre
competence, however. A mixture of prose and poetry, it is turgid
and often incomprehensible. The blank verse, too, is insipid, of
which the following is typical:

> . . . More wine: fill high!
> Gentlemen! a brave welcome to my son!
> Guido, may discord never, never come
> Between us.—Bring a goblet hither, Sirs,
> And let him taste his welcome. Let the health
> Pass round, and no one slight it. (III, iii)

Or we might cite Procter waxing poetic, with the Shakespearean
influence pathetically transparent:

> Sir, she was fashioned by the self-same hand,
> And with more prodigal beauty than the rose;
> Look at her, she will bear a closer glance.
> 'Tis old Cornelia's child, Camiola—
> You "love a rose"—kiss her, she'll taste as sweet. (III,iii)

The wonder is that the play achieved even a limited popularity. The new school of Shakespearean actors must have labored
valiantly to make it sound well, even for audiences accustomed to
a grand style of acting and to Elizabethan rhetoric. Byron, upon
hearing of Procter's intention to write the play, writes hopefully:
"I just see . . . that there is a new tragedy of great expectation, by
Barry Cornwall. . . . I liked the Dramatic Scenes. . . . I think
him very likely to produce a good tragedy, if he keep to a natural
style, and not play tricks to form Harlequinades for an audience"

---

[106] Chew, *Byron*, p. 18.

(L & J, V,217).[107] But alas, Procter did not "keep to a natural style," so that the disillusioned Byron, upon receiving a copy of *Mirandola* from its author, contents himself by saying: "Barry Cornwall will do better by and bye, I dare say, if he don't get spoilt by green tea and the praises of Pentonville and Paradise Row" (L & J, V,362). It is obvious that Byron, too, by this time recognized one of the central laws applicable to Romantic litera- ture: without a concern for natural language, Romantic drama such as Procter's would find itself doomed to the closet.

In the works of George Darley there is always present an element of fantastic charm. Beddoes, writing to his friend Kelsall in 1825, congratulates him on "awakening to a sense of Darley . . . it will perchance be the first star of a new day" (D. 595). Probably the reference is to tales by Darley published in the *Lon- don Magazine,* one of which, "Lilian of the Vale," provided the germ for a later "lyrical drama" entitled *Sylvia; or, The May Queen,* published in 1827. "Seven long years," Darley writes to Mary Mitford, "did I live on a charitable saying of Coleridge's, that he sometimes liked to take up *Sylvia,*" the same play Eliza- beth Barrett in a letter to Richard Hengist Horne calls "a beau- tiful, tuneful pastoral."[108] With Fletcher's *Faithful Shepherdess* as its model, and containing both Shakespearean and Miltonic overtones, *Sylvia* is, "with the possible exception of Hood's *Plea of the Mid-Summer Fairies,* the best modern effort"[109] to fill the world of literature with Spenserian "fayerye." Unluckily the beauties present in Darley's writings are unremittingly so coyly expressed that the undoubted serious purpose of Darley's poetry becomes blunted. Despite frequent instances of delicacy of treat- ment, the unhappy characteristic is everywhere evident, even in such charming lines as:

> Glutton! glutton! you've been drinking,
> Till your very eyes are winking!

---

[107] For comments on Procter's *Dramatic Scenes,* see Chew, *Byron,* pp. 18–19.

[108] Quoted in Introduction (p. xviii), *Poetical Works of George Darley.*

[109] Chew, *Byron,* p. 20.

Put him to bed in that green tuft.
He should not have a bed so soft!
Let him be toss'd into a thistle!
We'll tease his nose with barley-bristle!
Or paint his face with that ceruse
Which our fine bella-donnas use,
The sweet conserve of maiden-blushes.
Or cage him in a crib of rushes;
There let him lie in verdant jail
Till he out-mourns the nightingale. (IV, v)

"Darley was doomed to disappointment so far as his poetic and dramatic efforts were concerned,"[110] a critic notes. At Tennyson's urging him to collect and publish all his poems, he succinctly replies: "The public don't care for them, and I cannot afford to lose by them,"[111] a judgment with which present-day readers would be inclined to agree. Like Charles Dogdson, Darley by profession was a mathematician, and what recognition he gained in his day was through his works in algebra and geometry; still, few readers alive to beauty in poetry would dissent from the critical evaluation of the *Athenaeum*:

That the attention which Mr. Darley's poems commanded has been unequal to their merits, every true lover of poetry to whom they are familiar will feel: for a true lover . . . will allow for an almost bewildering exuberance of fancies, the offspring of self-indulgent loneliness—for occasional singularities of humour and language . . . —and for a knowledge of passion and insight into character, greater than such experience of life as leads the imaginative creator to prefer what is probable for his subjects and symmetrical in their elaboration. These peculiarities granted . . . , the name of George Darley ought to stand high among the poets of his time.[112]

The fact remains that the works of neither Darley nor (except for *Cenci*) his neo-Elizabethan contemporaries have survived the test of time. Keats's *Otho the Great* and *King Stephen*

---

[110] Introduction (p. xxxii), *Poetical Works of George Darley.*
[111] *Ibid.*, p. xxxiii,
[112] *Ibid.*, p. xxxii,

exist only as fragments. *King Stephen*, though "in versification and imagination of almost Shakespearean richness,"[113] in its extant form is only a couple of hundred lines long. Charles Armitage Brown first outlined *Otho the Great* scene for scene, Keats then writing the text.[114] Neither play, of course, has reached the stage. The other plays of the neo-Elizabethans, *Thomas à Becket* and *Ethelstan* by Darley, *Philip van Artevelde* by Henry Taylor, *Joseph and His Brethren* by Charles Wells, *The City of the Plague* and *The Fall of Jerusalem* by John Wilson, because of their preoccupation with subject matter from English and biblical history, are discussed better elsewhere. Southey's *Wat Tyler* and the dramas of Sir Walter Scott, although written by Romantic writers, are of tangential interest and scarcely important for our present purposes.

Let us, therefore, turn our attention from the dead end into which the Byronic hero and neo-Elizabethanism had led Romantic drama to concurrent, and more crucial, developments. But first let us pause and evaluate the accomplishments of these neo-Elizabethans. Although the following overharsh remarks by Swinburne were intended to apply to Coleridge's *Remorse*, they are even more appropriate to the neo-Elizabethan plays: "There is little worth praise or worth memory [in these plays] . . . except such casual fragments of noble verse as may readily be detached from the loose and friable stuff in which they lie embedded. . . . The characters are flat and shallow; the plot[s] . . . [are] at once languid, violent, and heavy. To touch the string of the spirit, thread the weft of evil and good, feel out the way of the soul through dark places of thought and rough places of action, was not given to . . . [these] sweetest dreamer[s] of [Elizabethan] dreams."[115]

---

[113] Chew, *Byron*, p. 17.

[114] See *The Poems of John Keats*, ed. Ernest de Selincourt (New York, 1909), p. 552.

[115] *Essays and Studies, Bonchurch Edition*, XV,147–148.

CHAPTER IV

Old Precepts Rediscovered and Reapplied

ALTHOUGH neither Byronism nor neo-Elizabethanism offered a way out of the impasse caused by the shift from hero to villain as the central figure of tragic drama, the lesson came hard and proved excessively difficult to learn. Later the obdurate Swinburne would continue where his predecessors had left off; and though we are forced to admire the sincerity and intensity of this Shakespearean and Elizabethan fealty, we become uncomfortably aware of an idolatry approaching the ridiculous when we read:

> For two hundred years at least have students of every kind put forth across the waters of that unsounded sea. From the paltriest fishing-craft to such majestic galleys as were steered by Coleridge and by Goethe, each division of the fleet has done or has essayed its turn of work; some busied in dredging alongshore, some taking surveys of this or that gulf or headland, some putting forth through shine and shadow into the darkness of the great deep. Nor does it seem as if there would sooner be an end to men's labour on this than on the other sea. But here a difference is perceptible. The material ocean has been so far mastered by the wisdom and the heroism of man that we may look for a time to come when the mystery shall be manifest to its furthest north and south, and men resolve the secret of the uttermost parts of the sea: the poles also may find their Columbus. But the limits of that other ocean, the laws of its tides, the motive of its forces, the mystery of its unity and the secret of its change, no seafarer of us may ever think thoroughly to know. No wind-gauge will help us

to the science of its storms, no lead-line sound for us the depth
of its divine and terrible serenity.[1]

These lines of Swinburne's, though justly famous, have no
more to do with the study of Shakespeare than have the closet
plays to do with the mysteries of life and death with which their
authors felt them to be so intimately concerned. It also was of
little avail for the neo-Elizabethans to utilize the prevailing su-
perstructure of Gothicism for their plots and action, since already, if not spent as a force, Gothicism was perceptibly on the
wane by the 1820's, derided, unwept, unhonored, and unsung.
There were, however, cross-currents at play that ultimately
gained the upper hand in English dramaturgy. Thomas Noon
Talfourd, in the Preface to his play *Ion* (1835), writes: "The
tragic drama was about to revive amongst us, and I was not insensible to its progress. Although the tragedies of the last twelve
years are not worthy to be compared with the noblest productions of the great age of our drama, they are with two or three
exceptions, far superior to any which had been written in the
interval. Since the last skirts of the glory of Shakespeare's age
disappeared, we shall search in vain for serious plays of equal
power and beauty with *Virginius, William Tell, Mirandola,
Rienzi*, or the *Merchant of London*."[2] Nor was Talfourd's an
isolated point of view. So let us turn back the calendar and see
what led the author of *Ion* to come to this conclusion; let us examine the course of the mainstream of poetic tragedy subsequent
to the first production in 1813 of Coleridge's *Remorse*. Byronism and neo-Elizabethanism led only to the closet; for successive
playwrights to reach the stage would require the example to be
followed that had been set by Wordsworth and Coleridge.

A recent critic writes:

In 1820 Sheridan Knowles's *Virginius,* as acted by Macready,
accomplished for England what Eugene O'Neill's *Beyond the
Horizon* accomplished for America exactly a century later. It
caught, crudely but measurably, the spirit of the age in many

---

[1] *A Study of Shakespeare, Bonchurch Edition*, XI,3.
[2] *Dramatic Works* (11th ed., London, 1852), p. 8.

of its manifestations. It set forth what was generally taken to be a valid tragic projection of the life and aspirations of its beholders. It was couched in what then seemed a refreshed and vital artistic form. It inspired a considerable flowering of other plays in its wake—initiated a dramatic renaissance which caused deep stirrings and high excitements while it lasted. We have long since rejected Knowles's meaning as limited, naive, and dated, his verse as banal, his structure as shoddy neo-Elizabethanism. But we shall never understand the significance of Knowles and his eager successors unless we accept the enthusiasm of their audiences as quite genuine.[3]

And so at least in some quarters it is agreed that a drama was being written in the early nineteenth century that managed to capture the legendary spirit of the age with which Romantic critics were so taken. It is most certainly true that those writing for the stage in the mainstream of the Romantic tradition did succeed in stating what their readers and their audiences wanted to hear and wanted to believe. The only difficulty is that it would be wrong to attribute this renaissance to a writer of the caliber of Sheridan Knowles. The innovator was William Wordsworth; the pioneer was Samuel Taylor Coleridge; and the first disciple, rather than Knowles, was Richard Lalor Sheil.

First we must turn to another contemporary of Knowles and Sheil, The Rev. Henry Hart Milman. Born in 1791, the same year as Sheil, Milman by right should assume no more than a subsidiary position in our study of poetic drama. His talents are mediocre, his dramatic ability is minor. Nevertheless, this clergyman bears as much importance for our story as Sheil and Knowles. Besides occupying a position midway between what was exemplified by the Byronic hero on the one hand and by the neo-Elizabethans on the other, Milman with his play *Fazio* exhibits many of the tendencies coming to fruition in this period of the mid-teens and early 1820's. Produced three years (in 1818) before Procter's Elizabethan *Mirandola* and a year after Sheil's *The Apostate*, *Fazio* stands as a link between these two

---

[3] Bulwer and Macready: *A Chronicle of the Early Victorian Theatre*, ed. Charles H. Shattuck (Urbana, Ill., 1958), p. 2.

movements that concurrently were heading in diametrically opposite directions, the one into the abyss, the other toward a
genuine renaissance. *Fazio* enables us to catch our breath in as-
sembling the disparate threads that bind Romantic drama together into an explicable entity. For a common bond unites most
of these plays, and *Fazio* is one of the first indications of this
course that Romantic drama will pursue with increasing clarity
and forcefulness in the years to come. Milman's play also gives
us an indication of the thinking of the Romantic playwrights,
bound together in a kind of empathic relationship in their concern with certain issues and vital problems. Finally *Fazio* utilizes
a theme adopted by Byron in his later plays, by Mary Russell
Mitford in her plays of the 1820's, and even by the later Swinburne—Italian independence and liberty.

As Milman declares in his Prefatory Observations to the
play, *Fazio* was written while he was an undergraduate at Oxford, which would have been but two or three years before the
premiere of Coleridge's *Remorse*. "Its first appearance, I believe, was at the Surrey Theatre, where it was brought forward
under the name of 'The Italian Wife,' and it had been acted
some time before I was aware that the piece of that name was
my work." The Surrey Theatre was licensed only for operatic
performances, "but the company contrived to elude this restric-
tion by performing all kinds of Dramas with what they called a
musical accompaniment. Every now and then the string of a
solitary violin was heard, while the actors went on in their parts
without the slightest regard to the said accompaniment, and so
represented any regular drama which might suit their purpose.
It was in this manner that I first saw the performance of
Fazio . . ."⁴ The following month (February 5, 1818), Covent
Garden presented *Fazio* legitimately for fifteen performances,
although this was done by the managers of that theatre "without
even the common courtesy of giving me notice of their intention," Milman notes bitterly.⁵

---

⁴ *Poetical Works of the Rev. H. H. Milman* (3 vols., London, 1839),
III,118.

⁵ *Ibid.*, pp. 118–119.

And so it cannot be said that the one actable play by the man "who kill'd John Keats" (as Byron jestingly chose to believe) was in any way a failure in the theatre; yet it is unfortunately true that as a poet, Byron sneeringly points out, Milman all too frequently is

> That neutralized dull Dorus of the Nine;
> That swarthy Sporus, neither man nor bard;
> That ox of verse, who *ploughs* for every line.
> *(Don Juan,* IV,st. 58)

Genest's remark about Milman's later *Fall of Jerusalem* (1820) —"A dramatic poem such as this is a species of writing which ought not to be encouraged. It is like a mule, neither horse nor ass, but something between both"[6]—would seem eminently justified. And the same can be said for Milman's other "dramas" in verse, *The Martyr of Antioch* (1822), *Belshazzar* (1822), and *Anne Boleyn* (1826). As a clergyman Milman's talents lay more in the direction of his epical *History of the Jews* (1829) than in the field of romantic poetry. But the clergy was becoming an increasingly important element at about this time—not only beyond the footlights, but even upon the stage; Milman is merely another in a long line of descent during the nineteenth century. It will be recalled that Charles Maturin, too, was a clergyman; if he, Professor of Poetry at Oxford and retiring don, is more flamboyant than Milman, an obsession with the wages of sin and an eyebrow-raising interest in promiscuity and adultery are the same in the plays of both. In Milman, in fact, there is far more interest expressed in the love lives of the characters than in putting across a message of virtue and probity. Again, like Procter's *Mirandola,* the play is an Italian "tragedy of Passion," a misspent passion of the hero-villain Fazio for the temptress Aldabella, who endeavors to lure him (and his misgotten fortune) from his faithful wife Bianca. But Fazio is no deep-dyed villain of the Gothic mold, nor is he a Byronic villain without motivation: he has succumbed to the temptation of opportunity, of appropriating the fortune of a usurer murdered by a person un-

---

[6] *Some Account,* X,239.

known. For this theft he must die, his wife Bianca, who has betrayed him out of jealousy of Aldabella, thereafter dying of a
broken heart.

Since it is no more real and no more concerned with current issues than any of the other plays we have thus far encoun-
tered, what has caused us to linger over *Fazio* can scarcely be
said to be its plot. Rather, it is its unconscious relationship to
other dramas of the period that is significant. Since *Fazio* was
written before the performance of *Remorse,* we can hardly
expect to find a correspondence between the two plays philosophically. The theme of remorse is absent, replaced by another
prevailing passion, Fazio's struggle for repentance. Although the
diction of the play is almost mawkish in its attempts to be
Elizabethan, there are detectable conscious efforts on Milman's
part to achieve a Wordsworthian-Coleridgean naturalness of expression in the blank verse. This is the first point that should be
observed about *Fazio*. The effect, if at times incongruous, is
arresting, as:

> The stones whereon I tread do grimly speak
> Forbidding echoes, ay with human voices:
> Unbodied arms pluck at me as I pass,
> And socketless pale eyes look glaring on me.
>
> . . . .
>
> Howbeit, thank God, 'tis safe! Thank God!—for what?
> That a poor honest man's grown a rich villain. (I,ii)

Admittedly, this is not immortal blank verse and would not be
outstanding even for the neo-Elizabethans. The mixture here
of elevation with the commonplace is in fact a good reason why
the mainstream of Romantic drama was veering increasingly
from Shakespearean imitation: Wordsworth and Coleridge were
obviously correct in their contention that, if elevated, the language of the theatre must at the same time be natural. Of all
the neo-Elizabethans, Milman succeeds in this respect the best,
however; another passage might almost be by Coleridge:

> Sir, there's a soil fit for that rank weed flattery
> To trail its poisonous and obscene clusters:

A poet's soul should bear a richer fruitage—
. . . .
'Tis coarse—'tis sickly—'tis as though an eagle
Should spread his sail-broad wings to flap a dunghill;
As though a pale and withering pestilence
Should ride the golden chariot of the sun;
As one should use the language of the Gods
To chatter loose and ribald brothelry. (II,i)

Here it is at the end that Milman falls down in his verse; the beginning is well, even admirably, expressed. It is evident that the grand line of the Elizabethans is alien to Milman; not inborn but learned is the ability to maintain a certain pitch and key and maintain them consistently. Despite a devotion to some, if not all, of the Elizabethan dramatists, in the early nineteenth century such linguistic prowess was a cultivated, not an instinctive, art. That is why, along with Milman's, the plays of the other neo-Elizabethans are forced and stilted: they are exercises learned by rote rather than innate reactions to the handling of words. All too clearly the times were more and more inclining, as Wordsworth prophetically saw, to the "language of real life."

A devotion to Elizabethan precedent, however, continued strong. In the plays of Richard Lalor Sheil this is as noticeable as in the works of Henry Hart Milman. *Evadne; or, The Statue*, his most popular work on the stage, Sheil borrowed from Shirley's tragedy, *The Traytor*; it was given thirty performances at Covent Garden in 1819. Of no special significance dramatically, it owed its success to an all-star cast including Abbott, Macready, Young, Charles Kemble, and Eliza O'Neill. Rather than *Evadne*, the play of Sheil's for our purpose is his first success in London, *The Apostate*, premiered in 1817. And it is the word "apostate" that is relevant, since it points, as does no other expression, to the direction in which the mainstream of Romantic drama will be heading from this time forth. Heralded by Coleridge, now first formalized by Sheil, and more fully developed by later playwrights like Talfourd, Bulwer, and Browning, *The Apostate* is the first sign of the dawning of a Liberal Age, both in politics and on the stage.

The word, although defined as desertion of the faith, principles, or party to which one has heretofore adhered, is a flexible, all-encompassing word that can mean one thing within its own context and another to the listener. Milman quickly adopted it for *Fazio* as his heroine Bianca declares:

> Oh, I am here so wearily miserable,
> That I should welcome my apostate Fazio,
> Though he were fresh from Aldabella's arms. (III,i)

And Procter, in *Mirandola*, as hastily picks up the same expression:

> How fair—how utterly without a peer
> She is! Apostate that I was to doubt:
> And yet I did not: no, no, no . . . (III,iii)

In Sheil's hands the moment comes, more appropriately, as the Moor, Malec, is accusing the hero, Hemaya, of treason against his people. "Traitor! and, if there be a name more foul, Apostate!" (II,i) he cries; and with this single word, Romantic drama gains an immediacy that it had never possessed. With Sheil, Romantic drama first becomes real.

That a barrister should be the initiator, if dimly, of the liberal movement in dramatic literature should not seem especially astonishing. Henry Fielding served as a judge, and Talfourd and Bulwer were members of Parliament. Each of these men, in his politics, acted in accordance with ingrained liberal instincts. In *The Apostate*, however, Sheil is more concerned with Gothic horror and supercharged suffering than he is with the cause of liberalism. The plot he borrowed from Calderon's tragedy *Love After Death; or, The Mountains of Grenada,* a play based upon a Moorish revolt against Philip II. In his Preface, Sheil takes great care to cover his tracks, to "relieve himself," as he says, "from the imputation of having sought the illegitimate assistance of political allusion." But at this point he immediately shifts ground from "political allusion" to the Inquisition, always a good whipping boy, after which he declares: "It would be hard, indeed, to write a play upon *any* event in the reign of Philip the

Second, without inveighing against the persecutor and the tyrant. It would be impossible in the *present* instance. . . . It would be a very strange delicacy, indeed, were the author to spare the guilt, the ferocity, and the baseness of Philip, out of *respect* for such a man as the present King of Spain!"

Byron would not have been so reticent. But then Byron purportedly did not write his plays with a view to having them produced. And Byron also was to write at a somewhat later date:

> . . . I grant him all the kindest can accord;
> And this was well for him, but not for those
> Millions who found him what oppression chose.
> (Vision of Judgment, st. 46) [7]

Or, more explicitly,

> He ever warr'd with freedom and the free:
> Nations as men, home subjects, foreign foes,
> So that they utter'd the word "Liberty!"
> Found George the Third their first opponent. Whose
> History was ever stain'd as his will be
> With national and individual woes? (st. 45)

The verse may not be immortal, but the point is put across with deadly clarity: George III, the Hanoverian, is as much a "persecutor and tyrant" as Philip II ever was; a Sheil may not desire to express this view publicly in so many words, a Byron has no such compunction.

To be sure, by this time Byron was safely on the Continent, out of harm's way. His fellow dramatists had to cope with the rigors of censorship and a Licensing Act. Although undoubtedly no reproach was intended and Sheil could scarcely have been in a position to have Byron in mind while writing *The Apostate*, certain lines from the play are appropriate to the literary situation in England: Wordsworth becoming increasingly conservative, Byron and Shelley in exile, Coleridge turning to religious issues, Leigh Hunt imprisoned.

---

[7] We have already seen how Byron used the word "apostate" in his condemnation of Wordsworth. See *supra,* p. 80.

Renounce the faith   ..
That suffering had endeared, when twenty thousand
Of his brave countrymen are leagued together,
To break the bonds of Philip's tyranny!
When freedom's flame from yonder mountain tops
Will blaze through Spain's wide realm, he basely falls
Before the tyrant's edict, and obeys! (II,i)

In other respects *The Apostate* bears several resemblances to Coleridge's *Remorse*. Lip service is paid to the word itself in Hemaya's lines:

Open my heart, and stab; drive in more deep
The arrow of remorse; (II,i)

and their close similarities in plot and locale—Moors being the central figures in Sheil's play—are equally striking. In one scene Florinda, the heroine, visits her imprisoned lover, Hemaya, in much the same manner as does Doña Teresa in Coleridge's play. And there are even reminiscences of Beethoven's opera *Fidelio* in this and other scenes.[8] Obviously in the Romantic Period the cry for liberty was limited neither to one country nor to one artistic genre. Increasingly even playwrights were beginning to take seriously Shelley's dictum that poets should be "the unacknowledged legislators of the world."

As interesting, if less pertinent, to a study of English Romantic drama is the fact that Sheil wrote all his plays with Eliza O'Neill expressly in mind for the heroines. His first play, *Adelaide* (1814), provided her with a role appropriate to her talents while she was still playing in Dublin; Florinda was the first original part in which she appeared on the London stage. A commentator remarks about *The Apostate*: "As usual with Shiel [sic], his heroine is, perhaps unduly prominent," although he at once adds that "the powerfully drawn character of Pescara, as played by Macready, and subsequently . . . by Booth, leaves an impression upon an audience fully equal to that produced by

---

[8] For a similar resemblance to Beethoven's *Fidelio,* See Byron's *Two Foscari,* III,i.

the woes and suffering of *Florinda*."[9] This reminds us that Macready achieved his first decided success with London audiences in the role of Pescara.

But let us return briefly to Milman's *Fazio*. Concern with liberty and freedom was bringing in its wake an interest in the sorry political conditions prevailing both in Italy and in Greece. Milman declaims dramatically:

> Sad and sunken Italy!
>   The plunderer's common prey!
>   When saw the eye of day
> So very a slave as thee?
> Long, long, a bloody stage
>   For petty kinglings tame,
>   Their miserable game
> Of puny war to wage.
> Or from the northern star
>   Come haughty despots down,
> With iron hand to share
>   Thy bruised and broken crown. (II,i)

Under the circumstances this opinion about foreign perfidy may well have been an oversimplification by Milman of conditions in English politics, or so at least we might assume, judging by Byron's acid remarks in his *Vision of Judgment*. In expressing his convictions concerning the English in society, political or otherwise, Byron declares feelingly: "*Don Juan* will be known by and bye, for what it is intended,—a *Satire* on *abuses* on the present states of Society and not an eulogy of vice: it may be now and then voluptuous: I can't help that" (L & J, VI,155).[10] Wordsworth had sensed much the same prevalence of abuses in society in 1802:

Milton! thou shouldst be living at this hour:

---

[9] Editorial Introduction (p. iv), *French's Standard Drama*, No. LVII: *The Apostate, by Richard Lalor Shiel* [*sic*] (New York, n.d.).

[10] The blue-stocking Lady Blessington comments: "Byron sees not, that much of what he calls the usages of cant and hypocrisy are the fences that protect propriety. . . ." (*Conversations of Lord Byron* [Philadelphia, 1836], pp. 134–135.)

England hath need of thee: she is a fen
Of stagnant waters: altar, sword, and pen,
Fireside, the heroic wealth of hall and bower,
Have forfeited their ancient English dower
Of inward happiness. We are selfish men;   (*London, 1802*)

and in one of the best contemporary appreciations of Wordsworth's poetry, it is made evident this very sense of ordinary humanity was primary among the characteristics of the Wordsworthian style that captured the hearts and imaginations of his
readers. The lines are noteworthy as well, for what they indicate
by indirection was needed by the theatre before there could in
any sense truly be a poetic renaissance. As Procter writes:

> As you read the verse of Wordsworth, his words frequently
> have a wonderful influence in assimilating your thoughts to
> his. You see the bare moors, round which the winds sweep—
> the hills over which the sheep move like a cloud—the sheaves,
> and sheets of snow—the poor cottager and the wandering ped-
> lar—and all that comes to peasant life—its loves and hopes
> broken down by sickness and old age. The beggar chirps
> querulously; the shepherd toils wearily up the mountains. All
> that is cast upon the world by poverty comes forth, to live,
> and toil, and die. There are no crownings of kings; nor march
> of conquerors; no bevies of ladies or courtiers, who laugh and
> lie, who rise and flourish, and fall like the leaves in autumn;
> but common human nature pines and fades away, and leaves
> a sigh in the reader's breast, which it is long before he can
> forget.[11]

The theatre desperately needed poetic plays in which there
would be "no crownings of kings; nor march of conquerors."
Procter declares mournfully: "The toil of placing a tragedy or
comedy on the stage (apart from the trouble of writing it), is
sufficient to daunt most men from repeating the experiment"[12]—
sentiments uttered somewhat earlier by Coleridge. And still the
fates were destined to be kind to the cause of poetic tragedy: the

---

[11] Bryan Waller Procter, *An Autobiographical Fragment and Biographical Notes* (Boston, 1877), p. 142.
[12] *Ibid.*, p. 44.

appearance of William Macready provided the means by which many a successive poetic tragedy would reach production. With his help even the crownings of kings and the march of conquerors would be rendered less intrusive. English drama began to take on new life. The man who achieved his first success in *The Apostate* slowly evolved from an adapter, a father confessor, and a leading apologist to—ultimately—the *doyen* of poetic tragedy. From now on, with increasing frequency, we shall read that the success of this or that play has been due to Macready's acting the leading role. If Romantic drama was born with Wordsworth and Coleridge, after 1820 it was William Macready who kept it alive.

Not that the period lacked dramatists: what was happening was that actors and actor-managers were rapidly gaining the upper hand. The star system was coming into full force, with all its advantages and limitations. Edmund Kean had a great fondness for subjects from Roman history; his suggestion led to Sheridan Knowles's earliest play, *Gaius Gracchus*, based on Plutarch, acted in Belfast in 1815.[13] Later Kean commissioned J. H. Payne to write *Brutus* (fifty-two performances at Drury Lane in the 1818–19 season) and Knowles, *Virginius*.[14] William Macready, besides acting in six of Knowles's plays, employed Knowles as collaborator in an adaptation of *The Maid's Tragedy*, entitled *The Bridal*. He helped Procter write *Mirandola*, and performed the title role. He acted in Mary Mitford's *Julian* and assisted her in the composition of *The Foscari* and *Rienzi*. He staged Byron's plays *Werner, Sardanapalus, The Two Foscari*, and *Marino Faliero*. He adapted and played in all three of Talfourd's tragedies. Macready collaborated with Edward Bulwer; he performed Browning's *Strafford* and offered advice during the writing of *A Blot on the 'Scutcheon*. He was responsible for preparing and performing in a stage version Henry Taylor's dramatic poem *Philip van Artevelde*.[15]

---

[13] Cf. Leslie H. Meeks, *Sheridan Knowles and the Theatre of His Time* (Bloomington, Ind., 1933), p. 139.

[14] B. W. Procter, *Life of Edmund Kean* (New York, 1835), p. 59.

[15] Shattuck, *Bulwer and Macready*, p. 5.

This indicates clearly the extent to which Romantic drama was growing dependent upon and indebted to a new generation of actor-managers rising to prominence in the second decade of the nineteenth century. With a singular degree of truth we can say that almost all Romantic poetic plays staged after 1820, except those of Sheridan Knowles, owe their success more or less to outside assistance, either advice or adaptation. From this point our story will become a dispiriting and somewhat embarrassing catalogue of playwrights who have been given an assist in writing their poetic masterpieces—at their side a silent (if at times outspoken) collaborator to offer counsel and instruction in the rudiments of making something that would "do for the Theatre in its present state." Cold comfort to discover that of the plays lauded by Talfourd as surpassing in "power and beauty" anything written in English drama since the days of Shakespeare, only one was not suggested by an actor-manager or did not require collaboration to reach the stage! In his list Talfourd mentions *Virginius* (suggested to Knowles by Kean), *William Tell* (suggested to Knowles by Macready), *Mirandola* (written by Procter with Macready's assistance), *Rienzi* (by Mary Mitford with Macready's collaboration), and *The Merchant of London* by T. J. Serle. Alas, only the last lies at least partly beyond the pale—and more because it is not a poetic tragedy than because Macready did not have a deft hand in its production. In truth, those who would heap ridicule upon any idea of "power and beauty" (and originality) in Romantic tragedy have in their favor more than the bare essentials for formulating an almost incontestable law: not only is Romantic drama unreal, without outside help it is unperformable!

But then, eyewitness testimony to the contrary, the same has been written often enough about Shelley's *Cenci*. And in the Romantic age itself many a theatregoer honestly believed that certain plays, Shakespeare's in particular, were better if not performed altogether. Coleridge once said: " 'It was natural that Shakespeare should avail himself of all that imagination afforded. If he had lived in the present day and had seen one of his plays represented, he would the first moment have felt the shifting of the scenes. Now, there is so much to please the senses in the performance and so much to offend them in the play, that he would have constructed them no doubt on a different model. We are grateful,' said Coleridge, 'that he did not, since there can be no comparative pleasure between having a great man in our closet and on the stage . . .' "[16] In his famous essay *On the Tragedies of Shakspeare*, Lamb unreservedly declares: "It may seem a paradox, but I cannot help being of opinion that the plays of Shakspeare are less calculated for performance on a stage, than those of almost any other dramatists whatever. Their distinguishing excellence is a reason that they should be so. There is so much in them, which comes not under the province of acting, with which eye, and tone, and gesture, have nothing to do."[17]

Autres temps, autres moeurs. If we of today find these views inexplicable, possibly as incomprehensible as Hazlitt's opinion that his own age was "undramatic," how many times, about Romantic drama (or Romantic anything), must we read "criticism" to the effect that "The literary geniuses [of the Romantic Period], refusing to make the practical study of the theatre that Shaw and O'Neill have made today, left their dramatic pieces largely unacted. The art of the stage, in which Shakespeare served a long and serious apprenticeship, they thought beneath them"![18] To clinch his point, the same critic continues by quoting Hazlitt: "The age we live in is critical, didactic, paradoxical, romantic, but it is not dramatic."[19]

Drama is as drama does. Possibly the age seemed undramatic to Hazlitt; but in retrospect it appears to have been something more than that—turbulent, dynamic, challenging, and constantly in flux. The events taking place upon the contemporary stage in the early nineteenth century mirrored conditions that existed in the political as in the economic arenas of English cultural life.

Let us, therefore, resist the desire of Allardyce Nicoll to take

---

[16] From a report by J. Tomalin of a lecture given by Coleridge, 1811–1812; quoted in *Coleridge's Writings on Shakespeare,* ed. Terence Hawkes (New York, 1959), p. 104.

[17] *Works,* ed. E. V. Lucas, I,115.

[18] Meeks, p. 20.

[19] *Works,* ed. P. P. Howe, XVIII,302.

the Romantic playwrights over our knees and spank them for
being the "thin-skinned, spoilt children of our literature." Let
us remember that it is the works of Coleridge, Wordsworth,
Bulwer, Browning, Talfourd, Mitford, and Knowles that we
read and remember—the contributions made by Kean and Macready to their plays are acknowledged, if at all, as footnotes in
histories. This of course does not minimize the fact that in the
Romantic age collaboration between author and actor actively
existed; yet it is the author's work that continues to live, the
actor long ago having made his last bows upon the stage. Although we must pay credit where credit is due, we must not
throw overboard plain fact in favor of prejudice and circumstan-
tial evidence. Let us reserve judgment for a time: despite Macready's "assistance" to the aspiring playwright, we shall soon
discover that often such assistance was more a curse than a boon.
Browning used the theatre as a springboard to immortality,
whereas his collaborator, Macready, merely went on to act in
other authors' plays.[20]

For the time being, we must admit that there is more than
a grain of truth to charges of collaboration, not to mention
mediocrity. That such an allegation does not hold for Coleridge,
Wordsworth, Shelley, and Maturin has been shown earlier; but
Talfourd, Milman, Mitford, Bulwer, Browning—the list of those
who required collaboration for their plays to be stageworthy is
almost inexhaustible. This phenomenon developed about the
year 1820, about the time of Sheridan Knowles's first success.
What explanation, then, can be advanced for this rather remarkable development—a development that coincided almost exactly with the accession of the Prince Regent as George IV? Are
there pertinent reasons behind the correspondence between the
occurrences, or is the astute remark of one of Knowles's biographers that "for several decades English theatre-goers enjoyed
their favorite actors in the rôle of the Roman father"[21] merely
to be taken as an inexplicable reflection of English taste?

---

[20] To be sure, Macready was a playwright in his own right, although the point is that he was a very minor one.

[21] Meeks, p. 83.

In *King of the Sandwich Islands,* W. M. Praed depicts George IV as devoting his time to

> ... building carriages and boats
> And streets and chapels and pavilions,
> And regulating all the coats
>   And all the principles of millions,
> And drinking homilies and gin,
>   And chewing pork and adulation,
> And looking backward upon sin,
>   And looking forward to salvation.[22]

It is not surprising, considering this monarch's dissoluteness and ineptitude, that Edmund Kean should have hit upon the idea of Virginius, the Roman Father, as a subject for a successful play. The story goes that he assured Knowles it would be a sure hit in London and that he himself would guarantee its success by assuming the title role.[23] "This promise," writes Knowles's biographer, "fired Knowles with hope. . . . He glimpsed bread for his bairns and fame for himself. Using a school-boy's slate, which his wife proudly preserved, he wrote feverishly. Incredibly enough, the play was finished and ready for the stage trial in three months."[24] Knowles was a teacher (in addition to being an actor); an Irishman transferred to Scotland; and poor. What, then, could Knowles have to contribute to a London audience's knowledge of Virginius, the Roman Father, other than a knowledge gained from books?

"I have no patience," growls Byron,

> with the sort of trash you send me out by way of books; except Scott's novels, and three or four other things, I never saw such work or works. Campbell is lecturing, Moore idling, Southey twaddling, Wordsworth driveling, Coleridge muddling, Joanna Baillie piddling, Bowles quibbling, squabbling, and sniveling. . . . The pity of these men is, that they never lived either in *high life,* nor in *solitude:* there is no medium

---

[22] Quoted by Charles William Previté-Orton, *Political Satire in English Poetry* (Cambridge, 1910), p. 174.

[23] Cf. Meeks, p. 59.

[24] *Ibid.,* pp. 59–60.

for the knowledge of the *busy* or the *still* world. If admitted into high life for a season, it is merely as *spectators*—they form no part of the Mechanism thereof. Now Moore and I, the one by circumstances, and the other by birth, happened to be free of the corporation, and to have entered into its pulses and passions, *quartum partes fuimus.* Both of us have learnt by this much which nothing else would have taught us. (L & J, V,362–363)

Or are we to reject this analysis of the quality of the works of his contemporaries on the grounds that, in Nicoll's words, Byron was too "thin-skinned"? Growing restive under Murray's frequent requests for advice on the merits of various writers, he once retorts: "Why do you ask me for opinions of your ragamuffins? You see what you get by it; but recollect, I never give opinions till required" (L & J, V,84). It is not that Byron's opinions are so intrusive by their frequency as that often they are so invaluable. In this instance Byron's judgment appears to be extraordinarily percipient: the playwrights of the 1820's, fired with visions of a new and better world, were merely spectators of the actions they depicted; they formed "no part of the Mechanism thereof."

We begin to perceive the relevance of Byron's observation when we examine the careers of Sheridan Knowles and his contemporaries. Author, actor, teacher, and Baptist minister, Knowles brought a singular combination of talents to the stage in composing plays that have best been described as "perhaps one part genius and three parts sheer twaddle."[25] On May 17, 1820, his career was launched in London with *Virginius*, Macready acting the title role. Afterward Macready writes:

Its early scenes were not unattended with danger, Charles Kemble being so hoarse that not one word, spoken in the loudest whisper, could be heard; but the action of the scene told its story with sufficient distinctness to keep alive its interest. This grew as the play advanced, and in the third act, in Icilius's great scene, Kemble's voice came out in all its natural strength, and brought down thunders of applause.

[25] *Ibid.*, p. 58.

With the progress of the play the rapt attention of the audience gradually kindled into enthusiasm. Long-continued cheers followed, involuntary ejaculations burst forth when the fatal blow was struck to the daughter's heart, and the curtain fell amidst the most deafening applause of a highly excited auditory.[26]

The success of *Virginius* was assured. Naturally, dissident voices were raised; but of the laudatory comments that poured out, the sentiments of T. N. Talfourd, as well as any, reveal those qualities in the play that presumably attracted contemporary fancy the most. Writing in the *Retrospective Review,* Talfourd declares:

> Though the dramatic works of Sheil, Maturin, Coleridge, and Milman are not so grand and harmonious as the talent of their authors would lead us to desire, they are far superior to the tragedies of Hill, Southern [*sic*], Murphy, Johnson, Philipps, Thomson, Young, Addison, and Rowe. Otway's *Venice Preserved* alone—and that only in the structure of its plot— is superior to the *Remorse,* to *Bertram, Fazio,* and *Evadne.* And then, more pure, more dramatic, more gentle than all these is the tragedy of *Virginius,* a piece of simple yet beautiful humanity, in which the most exquisite succession of classic groups is animated with young life and connected by the finest links of interest.[27]

It is the appeal to the emotions, the aura of sentimentality, the "simple yet beautiful humanity," the "most exquisite succession" of tableaux "animated with young life" that captured the sensibilities of Knowles's audience. Dissenting voices would not agree that "this tragedy deserves to be considered as nothing less than the commencement of a new and splendid era in the dramatic art, or the revival of the old era of Elizabeth."[28] But Knowles's close friend, Hazlitt, some five years later merely echoes Talfourd's earlier views of the playwright's merits by

---

[26] William Charles Macready, *Reminiscences,* ed. Sir Frederick Pollock (New York, 1875), p. 159.

[27] 1820, Part II, Vol. II, p. 205.

[28] *Blackwood's Magazine,* VII (1820), 307.

saying: "The most unconscious, the most unpretending, the most artless of mortals, he instinctively obeys the impulses of natural feeling, and produces a perfect work of art. . . . By thinking of nothing but his subject, he rivets the attention of the audience to it. All his dialogue tends to action, all his situations form classic groups. There is no doubt *Virginius* is the best acting tragedy on the modern stage. . . . Mr. Knowles is the first tragic writer of the age."[29]

Yet again we may be excused for doubting Hazlitt's judgment as a critic. This is particularly true in light of his statement that whereas Knowles's dialogue "tends to action," his "situations form classic groups." For these two characteristics are mutually exclusive, not complementary. We must remember that Hazlitt and Leigh Hunt were the first "professional" English critics to write about the theatre. Critical judgments, aside from appreciative or condemnatory comments, obviously had far to go before they could be of any practical value in correcting a play's faults of structure and organization. The question has frequently been asked why writers like Byron, Coleridge, and Lamb, each of whom at one time or another was an ardent theatregoer, should themselves have been unable to write plays of equal merit to the Elizabethan specimens they witnessed. Evidently the answer to this question again is tied up with the point of view of the age as a whole, its attitude toward reality and its attitude toward life. Despite successive conjectures as to what the Romantic age was really seeking in its drama, the conclusion remains close at hand that what the Romantic age wanted in its drama is what it got: effusions of emotionality, a Gothic aura of unreality, static groupings of actors in grandiloquent poses, and a depiction of a dreamlike if sometimes beautiful world of make-believe. The poetic dramatists, like their contemporaries in other fields, were hoist by their own petard. Out of the conviction that the spirit of their age demanded a representation of the "might be," not the "is," they merely demonstrated in their dramas, as in their poetry, this escape into the "far." As a critic notes with some asperity, "Had Shakespeare

---

[29] *Spirit of the Age, Works,* ed. P. P. Howe, XI,184.

himself come back to earth to resume his career where he had left off, he would have written but little better than Coleridge and Sheridan Knowles, and would have been no more highly esteemed by the theatrical public."[30]

Let us not make the blanket statement that this attitude is necessarily wrong. Rather, the Romantic age was looking in its drama for values that to us seem banal and trivial; then, however, such values were found to be of worth. Nor was it thought that the drama being written was divorced from life. Through its concern with language, its interest in emotions, and its increasing involvement with liberal developments, Romantic drama managed to reflect as adequately the problems of its age and the spirit of the times as does the theatre of our own day. From the modern point of view it is often difficult to detect in Romantic literature any purpose or meaning behind the façade of an Elizabethan diction and behind themes persistently devoted to liberty and to the retributive passion of remorse. Yet it is there, if we remember that the spirit of idealism must be substituted for what we might prefer to call a realistic attitude.

In returning to Sheridan Knowles, let us keep in mind Byron's objection to his contemporaries' forming "no part of the Mechanism" of the "*busy* or the *still* world." A commentator says:

> In a former Introduction, it has been erroneously stated, that, like Burns, Mr. Knowles was an uneducated man. In his youth he had read several of the Latin prose and poetic classics, only occasionally assisted by some friend or acquaintance. It is true, that with the classics of his own country he was little acquainted, as, from the moment that he became ambitious of authorship, he designedly abstained from reading them, lest he should be guilty of plagiarism. His intimacy with certain of our dramatists may be dated from the period when he became connected with the stage, as an actor. His turn for dramatic composition was first developed on the oc-

---

[30] W. E. McNeill, "A History of the English Drama from 1788 to 1832" (unpublished dissertation, Harvard, 1909), pp. 464–465. See also Coleridge's remarks, *supra*, p. 42.

casion of his taking a part in some juvenile private theatricals.[31]

Such was the man called by Hazlitt "the first tragic writer of the age." Crabb Robinson gives us possibly the most succinct estimate of Knowles in an excerpt from his diary of April 29, 1825: "I called at Lamb's, with whom I found Knowles. . . . A very Irishman in manners, though of the better kind. Seemingly a warm-hearted man. No marks of talent in his conversation, but a bold, decisive tone. He spoke of William Hazlitt as his friend, and this does not speak for his discretion or moral feeling."[32]

Granted, Hazlitt's *Liber Amoris* had appeared in print but two years previously; yet Robinson's estimate, if snobbish in tone, is probably just. Even Hazlitt's tribute to his longtime friend is little more than a backhanded compliment when he says: "We are glad to find an old and early friend unaltered in sentiment as he is unspoiled by success; the same boy-poet after a lapse of years as when we first knew him, unconscious of the wreath he has woven around his brow; laughing and talking of his play as if it had been written by anyone else; and as simple-minded, downright, and honest as the unblemished work he has produced."[33]

It is not so much that Knowles was especially simple-minded (in our sense) as that he lacked *savoir-faire*. He was stage-struck to the extent of naming his son in honor of Richard Brinsley Sheridan,[34] but all in all he scarcely deserved the critical encomiums heaped upon him by his contemporaries. Lamb's injunction

---

[31] Introduction (p. v), *The Dramatic Works of James Sheridan Knowles* (London, 1859).

[32] Quoted in E. V. Lucas, *Life of Charles Lamb*, (2 vols., London, 1905), II,209.

[33] Quoted in Richard Brinsley Knowles, *The Life of James Sheridan Knowles* (London, 1872), p. 152.

[34] Macready also was inclined to name his children in honor of playwrights. Two of his sons were named Henry Frederick Bulwer and Walter Francis Sheil; Macready's close friend, John Forster, provided the name for a third of Macready's ten children, Jonathan Forster Christian.

Proceed, old friend; and, as the year returns,
Still snatch some old new story from the urns
Of long dead virtue.
(To J. S. Knowles, Esq. On His Tragedy of Virginius)

offers more a pious hope for the future than commendation for
what Knowles attained in actuality. In his comedy *The Hunch-
back* and in his adaptation of Schiller's *Wilhelm Tell*, works he
snatched from the musty records of antiquity, along with the
rest of his some fourteen other plays, in addition to five
adaptations, all too frequently "only our surface emotions [are
stirred], leaving our desire for something deeper and finer entirely unsatisfied."[35] What Knowles, Mitford, and Milman all
lacked was an Arnoldian ability to see life steadily and see it
whole, even within the framework of poetic tragedy.

Nonetheless, like *The Borderers* and Shelley's *Cenci*,
Knowles's *Virginius* is another landmark in our story of Romantic drama. Of the first two plays, both are concerned primarily
with reconciling tangled psychological motivations to the exigencies of a morality based upon the guiding emotion of remorse
so that the protagonist may be led to repent his state of wickedness. In *Cenci*, moreover, Shelley is intrigued by motivation inflated to Byronic proportions of inhuman egocentricity, whose
crushing entails the destruction of the guilty as well as of the
innocent. All three plays exhibit Shakespearean and Elizabethan
influences, a Gothic frame of reference, tinges of sentimentality,
and an all-pervasive concern with the problem of language, most
particularly with a form of expression that will at the same time
be both elevated and natural. The difference between the approach of Wordsworth and Shelley and the approach of Knowles
is that whereas Wordsworth and Shelley—and Coleridge—were
consciously seeking to develop these concepts within a dramatic
framework and were endeavoring with equal intentness to create
something that could be produced upon the stage as well,
Knowles was writing with this second consideration kept fully
in mind, but not the first. What Knowles's plays lack is a philo-

---

[35] Meeks, pp. 144–145.

sophical core; they were written for the day, not for all time.
And even were their topicality to be questioned, it cannot be
denied that the vaguely democratic devotion to liberalism that
pervades them is by itself hardly enough to ensure their survival
as documents in the history of ideas. Of Knowles as a literary
artist, little more can be said than that "when melodrama, scenic
extravaganza, and crude foreign borrowings were threatening
to submerge plays of an artistic nature, he strove to preserve the
high traditions of the English stage."[36]

The remarkable part is that when it was produced, because
of its political overtones *Virginius* caused something of a furor.
As a dramatist Knowles's faults can easily be surmised from a review of *William Tell* in *Fraser's Magazine*: "He suffers not his
peasants to wear their native plainness, but they must speak
sentiment and talk love, whether married or single. His hero
must apostrophize clouds and rocks and boast of freedom and
talk politics, regardless of the fact that to a mountain people
rocks and clouds are things familiar, and excite no wonderment,
no passionate appeals. . . . Knowles's treatment is, in all these respects, the mere antipodes of the philosophic Schiller. Yet is the
play a meritorious production, though not an extraordinary one
like the German's, and deserved the success and favor which it
found."[37] And although *Virginius* is not quite such a Wordsworthian pastiche as this statement would imply, its faults are
similar to those of *William Tell*, its sentiments mawkish, its expression frequently banal. Its main virtue is the effort it shows
"to combine the qualities of the closet drama and acting
drama," in which endeavor what emerges is "decidedly a play
for the stage."[38] In itself this is meritorious—but it is not enough.
Even Sheil's *Apostate* reads as though it would stage better than
Virginius.

Knowles not only attempted to ride too many hobbyhorses
at the same time, he sought to straddle too many political fences.
Ironically, despite his efforts to cater to all tastes in his handling

---

[36] *Ibid.,* p. 181.
[37] XIII (1836), p. 459.
[38] Meeks, pp. 82–83.

of the dangerous themes in *Virginius* of tyranny and rejection
of established authority, he merely succeeded in making enemies.
"The conservatives naturally hated his warm defense of the common people; the king even ordered some lines censored as dis-
respectful to authority. To men of this opinion, Shakespeare's
attitude towards the mob was much more acceptable. They liked
the pictures of the rabble in *Coriolanus* and *Julius Caesar*, but
they could not brook the democratic ideals of Virginius."[39] Thus
poor Knowles was left to champion a liberalism still aborning,
not as yet a thriving, popular cause. When we reflect what must
be done with a scene to make it seem real, we should be able
to sympathize with the plight of Knowles, however; a party
writer trying to conform to the current political line, after all,
would be faced with the same sort of problem, realistically, with
which the aspiring dramatist was confronted in his attempts to
satisfy all political directions that existed in early nineteenth century England.

And so, if not outstanding as drama, even as historical drama,
Virginius is the second step (*The Apostate* the first) in the direction being taken by poetic tragedy toward a concern with
contemporary political issues, a cry for independence and liberty. This theme is central, too, to *Gaius Gracchus*, written in
1815, and to *William Tell*. The difficulty is that in his efforts
to soften the warmth of his liberal convictions, Knowles all too
often merely succeeds in tainting the sublime with the commonplace. At one point in *Virginius*, Icilius, in defending his be-
trothed, Virginius's daughter, Virginia, from the blandishments
of the tyrannous decemvir, Appius, waxes eloquent in verse that
at first rings with sincere conviction:

> Is't not enough you have deprived us, Appius,
> Of the two strongest bulwarks to our liberties,
> Our tribunes and our privilege of appeal
> To the assembly of the people? (III,iii)

Coming a year after the infamous Peterloo Massacre at Man-

---

[39] *Ibid.*, pp. 78–79. For a defense of Knowles's liberalism in *Virginius*, see Hazlitt's review in the *London Magazine*, July, 1820 (*Works*,
ed. P. P. Howe, XVIII,345–348).

chester, the inspiration for Shelley's *Masque of Anarchy*, this scarcely could have failed to produce a profound effect upon the audience. No wonder that at *Virginius*'s first performance Charles Kemble here rose dramatically to the occasion. But what comes next? Instantly the language shifts from the impassioned to the pedestrian:

> . . . Cannot
> The honour of the Roman maids be safe?
> Know, then, this virgin is betroth'd to me,
> Wife of my hope—Thou shalt not dross my hope
> And I retain my life—Attempt it not!

This habit of darting from the elevated to the trivial, the grand to the ineffectual, is a characteristic of Knowles even at his best. The noble and the ignoble are mingled together in haphazard profusion. Wordsworthism, Byronism, liberalism, sentimental-ism—everything is there; lacking are conviction and philosophy. Stirring indeed, when heard upon the stage, must have been the lines from *William Tell*:

> Ye crags and peaks, I'm with you once again!
> I hold to you the hands you first beheld,
> To show they still are free. Methinks I hear
> A spirit in your echoes answer me,
> And bid your tenant welcome to his home
> Again! O sacred forms, how proud you look!
> How high you lift your heads into the sky!
> How huge you are! How mighty and how free!
> How do you look, for all your bared brows,
> More gorgenously majestical than kings
> Whose loaded coronets exhaust the mine!
> Ye are the things that tower, that shine, whose smile
> Makes glad, whose frown is terrible, whose forms,
> Robed or unrobed, do all the impress wear
> Of awe divine, whose subject never kneels
> In mockery, because it is your boast
> To keep him free! Ye guards of liberty,
> I'm with you once again! (I,ii)

Yet we are forced to wonder what it is supposed to mean. Full of sound and fury, Sheridan Knowles's plays signify, if not exactly nothing, very little. Although an able craftsman in the theatre, Knowles did not possess the ability to construct more than literary makeshifts that instruct the intellect as seldom as they move the emotions. No, to find writers capable of enlightened and ennobling expression within the framework of Romantic drama, we must turn from Sheridan Knowles; we must turn to Byron, and to one of his lesser rivals, Mary Russell Mitford, two authors deeply interested in the cause of freedom and especially Italian liberty.

The times, auspicious for the cause of freedom and independence, seemed to foreshadow freedom for the individual and independence for both the city and for the State. Age-old tradition, the glories of past heroism, historical precedent, and data both literary and legendary evoked in the minds of Englishmen everywhere a picture of a brilliant and glittering age of change and innovation in the Italian cultural scene at the time of the Renaissance to complement contemporaneous political and economic conditions, a bygone Italy dominated by Florence and Venice, with the power of Rome existing concomitantly as a force of reaction and decadence. As with Byron, so with Mary Mitford—conjured up by the name Italy was a country of teeming contrasts, energetic vitality, impassioned convictions, beauty, brutality. Venice in particular, fascinated these writers: "Everything about Venice is, or was, extraordinary—her aspect is like a dream, and her history is like a romance" (Preface, *Marino Faliero*). The scene in both *Marino Faliero* and *The Two Foscari* takes place in periods when Venice was at the height of her power and prestige. The same is true for Miss Mitford's *Foscari*. In the Preface to this play it is erroneously stated that her version was performed at Covent Garden (in 1820) before Lord Byron's work on the same subject reached publication, repeated in the Prologue as:

> . . . Deem not of it worse
> That 'tis a theme made sacred by his [Byron's] verse.
> Ere his bold Tragedy burst into day,
> Her trembling hand had closed this woman's play.

Byron's play was published on the same day that Miss Mitford
sent her work to the management of Covent Garden, a coinci-
dence that caused her considerable chagrin. "I am distressed at
the idea of competition," she writes, "not merely with his lordship's talents, but with his great name . . . I have written to Mr.
Talfourd requesting him to consult another friend on the propriety of entirely suppressing my play."[40] Luckily Miss Mitford
was unaware of Byron's judgment of women who attempt to
write plays; "Women (saving Joanna Baillie) cannot write
tragedy: they have not seen enough nor felt enough of life for it.
I think Semiramis or Catherine II. might have written (could
they have been unqueened) a rare play" (L & J, III,197). And
again, there is Byron's laconic remark: "Voltaire has asked *why*
no woman has ever written even a tolerable tragedy. 'Ah (said
the Patriarch) the composition of a tragedy requires *** (a
man).' If this be true, Lord knows what Joanna Baillie does"
(L & J, IV,92). After the first performance of Miss Mitford's
Julian in 1823, a critic of the *London Magazine* unconsciously concurs in Byron's judgment: "The truth is . . . no
lady has ever yet succeeded in tragedy: and, from the powers
which are absolutely necessary for a grand success, we shall be
pretty safe in asserting, that no lady ever will be splendidly triumphant."[41] But Mary Russell Mitford was of a different mind.
After she read *The Two Foscari*, she but felt renewed confidence
in her own play at discovering that Byron had "taken up the
business just where I left it off, so that his play does not at all
clash with mine. The Doge is well executed, I think; but young
Foscari notwithstanding good speeches, is utterly imbecile—an
ultra-sentimentalist, who clings, no one knows why or where-
fore, with a love-like dotage, to the country which has disgraced
and exiled and tortured, and finishes by killing him; and his
wife, Marina, is a mere scold."[42]

---

[40] Quoted by Vera Watson, *Mary Russell Mitford*, (London, 1950),
p. 147. For the full story of the *Foscari—Two Foscari* relationship, see
the above pp. 147–148.

[41] April, 1823.

[42] Quoted by Vera Watson, p. 148.

There is much to be said for both sides. *Marino Faliero* is the greater of Byron's plays on Venetian subjects, since here there is more substance to the background material from which he derived his plot. The story of *The Two Foscari* depends entirely upon the motive of revenge, revenge by the Patrician, Loredano, for the purported murder by the doge, Foscari, of his father and uncle. Loredano is the Byronic hero; his motiveless malignity all too patently is the single peg upon which the action hinges; psychologically Loredano is a cardboard figure rather than flesh and blood. Yet another of Byron's villains without a cause, nothing moves him, not even remorse, "Go too," he says to a confederate,

> . . . you're a child,
> Infirm of feeling as of purpose, blown
> About by every breath, shook by a sigh,
> And melted by a tear. (I,i)

What impels this Byronic creation onward is not so much conviction or belief—and this despite Byron's continual reiteration of the words freedom and liberty—as the consummation of the project that lies at hand, be it for good or be it for ill. The Byronic hero, whether a Manfred or a Marino Faliero, is always a compulsive figure anyway, someone headed for disaster by design, caught up in an unfathomable web of fate he disdains to circumvent. Ruled by fortune, his touchstone is success, his goal is the unachievable, his end inevitably failure. His code is honor, the honor of family and high birth, but his ideals are warped, his conscience is stunted. When contemplating treason against his country, betrayal of his own class, the Doge Faliero intones fulsome words about his family honor:

> . . . I will redeem it
> By sweet revenge on all that's base in Venice,
> And freedom to the rest, or leave it black
> To all the growing calumnies of time,
> Which never spare the fame of him who fails,
> But try the Caesar, or the Catiline,
> By the true touchstone of desert—success. (I,i)

This remains the true tragedy of the Byronic drama: the breadth and sweep of great poetry are present, obeisance is made to high ideals, but there is no correspondence between the idealism and the actuality. Noble and grandiloquent as they undoubtedly seemed to Byron himself, to a later age the sentiments of his heroes read like the distortions we have come to expect from political and economic propagandists and apologists. The case against *Marino Faliero* is succinctly stated by a representative of those accusing the Doge of high treason; this same accusation can be leveled against Byron's heroes in general: they claim to stand above and beyond the laws they have been given to uphold and to which nominally they themselves subscribe. Speaking for his fellow patricians, a juror exclaims in wonderment:

> . . . the Doge, who should protect the law
> Seeking to abrogate all law, can claim
> No punishment of others by the statutes
> Which he himself denies and violates! (V,i)

This fact Faliero neither sees nor recognizes. To him all values are absolutes; one either fails utterly or succeeds overwhelmingly —there is no in-between:

> . . . you oppress'd the prince and people;
> I would have freed both, and have fail'd in both:
> The price of such success would have been glory,
> Vengeance, and victory, and such a name
> As would have made Venetian history
>
> . . . .
>
> Failing, I know the penalty of failure
> Is present infamy and death. (V,i)

Given the blindness of the heroes, it is left to the lesser, secondary figures of Byronic tragedy to experience qualms or second thoughts about the course that those exalted above them have adopted. What Loredano cannot feel is felt by his close friend and confederate, Barbarigo. And it is Barbarigo who links Byronic drama with its Wordsworthian-Coleridgean forebears in a concern for rehabilitating the villain into society through the operation of his own conscience and his feelings of remorse.

To us this fact may seem confirming evidence of an impossible naïveté of the Romantic mind, although to writers of a Romantic sensibility and temperament such a process not only seemed possible and explicable, it also seemed real. The philosophy of a Rousseau, an appeal to "natural" man and his "pure" emotions, was a factor that obviously had continued to be of tremendous importance in the Romantic attitude both toward society and toward the role within this social structure of the more than ordinarily gifted individual. The problem of how to deal with a Napoleon, after all, was still of pertinent concern to everyone.

Of course, to the anti-romantic such an attitude appears little short of banal, a "corruption of conscience, the transformation of conscience from an inner check into an expansive emotion." Yet the anti-romanticist, after his fashion, has merely succeeded in distorting Romantic beliefs into private convictions that do not necessarily correspond to actual fact, either. Taking leave for a moment of Byron's Barbarigo, let us turn to opinions expressed by Irving Babbitt. To Babbitt, "nothing is in itself romantic, it is only imagining that makes it so. Romanticism is the pursuit of the element of illusion in things for its own sake; it is in short the cherishing of glamour."[43] If this is so, what cannot be said of realism but exactly the same thing, substituting "non-glamour" for "glamour" at the end of the definition? Surely it is an oversimplification, wrought by the worst of the anti-romanticists, to believe that "partial evil we are told is universal good; or else evil is only good in the making. For a Rousseau or a Shelley it is something mysteriously imposed from without on a spotless human nature; for a Wordsworth it is something one may escape by contemplating the speargrass on the wall."[44] No, the immanence of evil, the villainous nature of man, the problem of his redemption and of his remorse, are too all-encompassing, in their dramas as in their poetry, for us to be able to brush aside the Romanticists as easily as all that. An element

---

[43] Irving Babbitt, *Rousseau and Romanticism* (3rd ed., New York, 1957), pp. 198, 203.

[44] *Ibid.*, pp. 200–201.

of illusion assuredly is present in their plays, along with sentimentality and a devotion to Elizabethan precedent. But in their
concern with universal and human problems, the plays of the
Romanticists, if fantasy, are real. To deny this would be to deny
all opposing evidence.

But again let us return to Barbarigo and to remorse. "Follow
thee!" exclaims Barbarigo,

> . . . I have follow'd long
> Thy path of desolation, as the wave
> Sweeps after that before it,
>
> . . . .
> . . . but this son and sire
> Might move the elements to pause, and yet
> Must I on hardily like them—Oh! would
> I could as blindly and remorselessly! (I,i)

It is merely the meaning of "remorse" that has changed from
Coleridge's use of it, remorse being here not a pang of conscience
to exact repentance but a goad to drive man on to greater
heights. What these heights are, by extension, no longer can be
said to be the emotional torment of the individual blinded by his
misdeeds. Instead, in his later Italian plays Byron becomes interested primarily in the magic word "liberty." In *Werner*, however, begun in 1815 and completed in 1822, "remorse" is still
used in a Wordsworthian-Coleridgean sense of repentance, as the
Prior exclaims to Werner in granting absolution:

> . . . in the general orison of thanks
> For bloodshed stopt, let blood, you shed not, rise
> A cloud upon your thoughts. This were to be
> Too sensitive. Take comfort, and forget
> Such things, and leave remorse unto the guilty. (IV,i)

And still the "man of feeling" conception of a Mackenzie, it
is clear, plays no role in the Byronic scheme of things: if remorse
is not necessary, why worry about it? To do so one would be too
"sensitive." By the same token, Byron has become more concerned with the feelings and emotions of the individual, or let us
say, of the individual who is least able to affect the course of

events in his plays! The convention of an age in expecting sentiment in its drama is satisfied without sentiment's actually being
present. We have both ends playing against the middle. Yet, as
with his other plays until Macready took them in hand, *Werner,*
declares Byron, "is neither intended, nor in any shape adapted,
for the stage" (Preface). Little wonder: in the villain Ulric's
point of view there is neither sentiment nor sentimentality.
Ulric's "sentiments" read remarkably like those of Wordsworth's
villain, Oswald. The difference is that Ulric has no guileless fool,
no Marmaduke, upon whom to impress his peculiar philosophy;
he is clearly a Byronic villain-hero in its purest guise, his motives
obscure, his actions inexplicable. His credo?

> . . . *Who* proclaim'd to me
> That *there were crimes* made venial by the occasion?
> That passion was our nature? that the goods
> Of heaven waited on the goods of fortune?
> Who show'd me his humanity secured
> By his *nerves* only? *Who* deprived me of
> All power to vindicate myself and race
> In open day? By his disgrace which stamp'd
> (It might be) bastardy on me, and on
> Himself—a *felon's* brand!
>
> . . . .
> . . . Is it strange
> That I should act what you could *think?* We have done
> With right and wrong, and now must only ponder
> Upon effects, not causes.
>
> . . . .
> . . . *You* kindled first
> The torch—*you* show'd the path: now trace me that
> Of safety—or let me! (V,ii)

The "you" and the "who" here are, of course, Werner,
Ulric's hard-put-upon father, who, after this outburst, understandably can only utter the broken sentence: "I have done with
life!" Nor does Ulric suffer death for his misdeeds: he merely
"exits," to his wife's heartbroken cry:

> . . . Oh, great God!
> And I have loved this man! (V,ii)

No more than with his Manfred has Byron here been able to make villainy credible—or even meaningful. Miss Mitford may, in fact, be excused for having taken somewhat of a patronizing attitude in comparing her own *Foscari* "not merely with his lordship's talents, but with his great name . . ."

It must be admitted that Mary Mitford is never able to achieve Byron's poetic heights. There are times when he is writing lyrically that Byron can be very good indeed. Memorable is Jacopo Foscari's apostrophe to Venice:

> . . . Ah! you never yet
> Were far away from Venice, never saw
> Her beautiful towers in the receding distance,
> While every furrow of the vessel's track
> Seem'd ploughing deep into your heart; you never
> Saw day go down upon your native spires
> So calmly with its gold and crimson glory,
> And after dreaming a disturbed vision
> Of them and theirs, awoke and found them not. (III,i)

And in *The Two Foscari* there are even lines on the art of swimming, as Jacopo exclaims:

> . . . exulting,
> With a far-dashing stroke, and drawing deep
> The long-suspended breath, again I spurn'd
> The foam which broke around me, and pursued
> My track like a sea-bird. (I,i)

None of this poetic talent is apparent in Mary Mitford. Although sincerity shines through almost every line, her expression is usually forced and labored. In *Julian*, as a critic wisely points out, it is the plot that is "the worst thing Miss Mitford has to answer for; and, indeed, its unnatural and improbable exaggeration goes very near to the distraction of several of the leading characters towards the end of the play. They have difficulty to keep their senses in the situations."[45] Part of this may be accounted for by the strained "poetic" language Miss Mitford employs, which often misses fire exactly because it is unpoetic, as when the Doge Foscari declares:

---

[45] *London Magazine*, April, 1823.

> . . . That I have made
> Liberty common as the common air,
> The sun-light, or the rippling waves that wash
> Our walls; that every citizen hath been
> Free as a Senator; that I have ruled
> In our fair Venice, as a father rules
> In his dear household, nothing intermitting
> Of needful discipline, but quenching fear
> In an indulgent kindness; these ye call
> My crimes. (II,i)

It is Miss Mitford, the well-bred lady, speaking here, not the Doge of Venice. More often the most impassioned expressions seem merely trite; from *Rienzi*:

> . . . Gods! what tyranny
> Men will endure in freedom's name. (III,i)

However true this is, it is a statement that makes little more than contradictory sense, detrimental not only to the author's purpose but to the reader's credulity: attention has been paid to formulating a catchy maxim, but it is a maxim that is scarcely original. A critic observes that in all Miss Mitford's plays "there is strong vigorous writing,—masculine in the free unshackled use of language, but wholly womanly in its purity from coarseness or license, and in the intermixture of those incidental touches of softest feeling and finest observation, which are peculiar to the gentler sex."[46] This describes her as a stylist all too well. Fortunately Miss Mitford's verse is rarely intrusive; we can sympathize with her plight as a woman writer when she writes: "Since I have become a professed authoress, woe is me! A washerwoman hath a better trade."[47]

Despite Miss Mitford's lapses in style, strong, vigorous writing is there, as well as a strong, vigorous mind to match. More prescient than Byron, her plays penetrate much deeper into the problem of the hero unjustly accused, the latter-day Othello

---

[46] "Biographical Sketch of Mary Russell Mitford," *The Works of Mary Russell Mitford, Prose and Verse* (Philadelphia, 1888), p. 3.

[47] *Life of Mary R. Mitford*, ed. A. G. K. L'Estrange (2 vols., New York, 1870), II,17.

helplessly entangled in the web fashioned for him by his enemies. If the great man grown vainglorious is a problem to society, we can hear Miss Mitford say, then the problem of the great man in the toils of his adversaries must also be relevant. In *The Two Foscari*, Byron takes up the thread of the story where she leaves off; and there are many parallels in theme between their two plays. In each a villain endeavors to wreak revenge upon the Foscari by accusing them of complicity in actions treasonous to the state: in Miss Mitford's play the villain, Erizzo, bribes a friend to kill an enemy of the Foscari, suspicion of the deed falling upon the younger Foscari, the Doge's son; in Byron's play the villain, Loredano, incites the Venetian patricians to exile Foscari's son and depose the Doge. In both plays the words freedom and liberty are given considerable prominence. But Miss Mitford's play, in spite of its ever-present appeal to sentiment as regards its villain, reads vital and alive, whereas Byron's play sounds staged and contrived. In *The Two Foscari* motive is used to excuse villainy, not explain it; in the *Foscari* of Miss Mitford, with Shakespeare's Iago as her model, Erizzo, if no more motivated in his hatred, does not have to contend with a pseudo-philosophical basis for his actions. Like Maturin's Bertram he is a free agent of villainy and so sounds more fresh and vigorous. A harking back to the pure Gothic villain, he almost wins the reader's sympathy as he cries triumphantly:

> . . . The insect that is born
> And dies within an hour would not change lives
> With Foscari. I am content. For thee
> I have a tenfold curse. Long be thy reign,
> Great Doge of Venice! (V,ii)

This still does not resolve the problem of what to do about villainy. Either the villain is a free agent, unfettered, or he ultimately receives his just deserts—or he is redeemed by remorse. But he is present, and he is a problem; like the tyrant-hero, he exists. To Miss Mitford, as to Wordsworth and Coleridge, his rehabilitation finds, if not a ready solution, at least a challenge—a challenge with which Byron is little concerned. Marino Faliero dies unrepentant, as does Miss Mitford's Erizzo, but with a difference: Faliero should have been the heroic father of his country, but he is not; he is the central figure of the action, and nevertheless he turns villainous; moreover, he finds

> . . . a comfort in
> The thought that these things are the work of Fate;
> For I would rather yield to gods than men,
> Or cling to any creed of destiny,
> Rather than deem these mortals, most of whom
> I know to be as worthless as the dust,
> And weak as worthless, more than instruments
> Of an o'er-ruling power; they in themselves
> Were all incapable—they could not be
> Victors of him who oft had conquer'd for them! (V,ii)

Stiff-necked and haughty to the end, Faliero denounces the spirit of the Byronic creed of liberty and freedom by his very words. Arrogance is substituted for tolerance and understanding, vainglory for prudence and respect. The dilemma imposed by the Byronic concept of heroism remains unresolved.

A surer presentation of the dangers inherent in a situation in which the great man gradually becomes villainous is offered by a hero of the stature of Miss Mitford's Rienzi. Like Coriolanus, Rienzi is trusted by his people, he rises to dizzy heights of power, he grows contemptuous of those whom presumably he has best meant to serve, and, like Faliero, through arrogance and short-sightedness he ultimately falls. Instead of stubborn pride, however, his final speeches reveal insights that pierce to the heart of the issues of liberalism, freedom, and liberty which the dramatists of the 1820's from Knowles to Mitford were raising and attempting to resolve. Basically the problem is not the form of liberty but its essence; not how to prevent treason from arising but how to cope with it once it has arisen; not how to unmask villainy at its source but how to uproot it after it has become entrenched. Too late Rienzi realizes that he has become as evil and despicable as any of his enemies; and with him, as with the enlightened liberals of Miss Mitford's time, the question has now arisen: what next? what can be done?

. . . Oh, had I laid
All earthly passion, pride, and pomp, and power,
And high ambition, and hot lust of rule,
And sacrificial fruits, upon the altar
Of Liberty, divinest Liberty—
Then—but the dream that filled my soul was vast
As is his whose mad ambition thinned the ranks
Of the Seraphim, and peopled hell. These slaves!
Base crawling reptiles—may the curse of chains
Cling to them ever. (V,i)

Obviously liberty itself is not at fault; it is Rienzi's attitude toward the people for whose benefit this liberty should have been directed that has gone off course. As with contemporary liberalism, so with contemporary drama; and it is Miss Mitford, not the usually percipient Byron, who puts her finger on the nub of the problem at its source: what is to be done with the liberal who loves liberty but hates people, the liberal who worships freedom but despises the slaves in whose name the word is being uttered, in whose behalf the maxim of its dispersion is being preached? Rienzi, possibly along with many a contemporary of Miss Mitford, woefully declares:

. . . For liberty! Go seek
Earth's loftiest heights, and ocean's deepest caves,
Go where the sea-snake and the eagle dwell,
'Midst mighty elements—where nature is,
And man is not, and ye may see afar,
Impalpable as a rainbow on the clouds,
The glorious vision! Liberty! I dream'd
Of such a goddess once; dream'd that you slaves
Were Romans, such as ruled the world, and I
Their Tribune. (V,ii)

A far cry this from Byron's Shelley-like ecstasy at the vision of an intangible freedom in *Marino Faliero* as one of Faliero's fellow conspirators in treason declaims:

. . . They never fail who die
In a great cause: .   .   .   .   .
   .   .   .   .

> . . . Though years
> Elapse, and others share as dark a doom,
> They but augment the deep and sweeping thoughts
> Which o'erpower all others, and conduct
> The world at last to freedom. (II,ii)

Miss Mitford here is more perceptive than the otherwise clear-headed and cynical Byron. Having sensed the course that Romantic drama and the cause of liberalism would henceforth pursue—investigation, psychologically, of the hero-villain's motivations and the raising of second thoughts about the cause of freedom and liberty—she is among the first to express these views in a play for the stage. Characteristically, as always, if romantic in tendency, her *Rienzi* manages to remain completely real.

Of the other historical plays of the 1820's less need be said. Lord Byron's admiration of John Wilson's *The City of the Plague* is understandable more for its pervasive atmosphere of imminent doom and catastrophe than for its literary qualities. The dialogue is stilted, the tone didactic, the relationships among the characters are rigidly proscribed by a code of morality that is both unnatural and ridiculous. To modern ears this is partly because of the play's diction, which is inflated rather than elevating:

> . . . The soul oft feels
> Mysterious presence of realities
> Coming we know not whence, yet banishing
> With power omnipotent all misgiving fears.
> So feel I at this moment—she is living. (I,i)

Soon such dialogue, continued over more than one hundred fifty pages, becomes wearisome. Emotionality is substituted for emotion, sentimentality for sentiment. In many early-nineteenth-century authors this tendency is so altogether noticeable that frequently it sounds overwrought or rings insincere. Thomas Campbell, the author of *Gertrude of Wyoming*, a writer who exemplifies this attitude as well as any of his contemporaries, remarks in his correspondence:

A poor sweep, who had that day stockings without feet on his little legs—a child of eight years old—going towards Penge Common, was overtaken in a drift, at four in the morning, where he had been sent along with another boy of ten, to sweep a chimney at Dulwich. The Coroner's inquest sat on his body. The survivor said, that on the way his companion said, "Jack, I'm ill; go home, and tell somebody to come and carry me." The lad tried to lift him, but he struggled a little and fell down. Instead of venturing to knock at a neighboring door, the other boy went literally home—and when the master arrived, their poor little sweep was dead! He had lain for hours; but it was discovered—by the confession of the brute himself, who had passed him on the road—that a carter had come up to him and said, "Why don't you get up?" and passed on. The poor child—as this wretch acknowledged—raised up his head without speaking, and lay down again! Included in the slave-trade, the sweep-trade should have been abolished, or at least examined. A child of eight years old, on such a day without feet to his stockings.[48]

To this we can only say that this pre-Dickensian mood of righteous indignation, with its misplaced emphasis upon stockings rather than economic conditions, is not unique to Campbell—or to Wilson. Like his audience the English author was but beginning to grapple with the problem of developing a social conscience. As a consequence the drama, too, was forced to labor under the banner of a misdirected idealism, a mawkish diction, and a distorted philosophical focus—the patent weaknesses of Wilson's plays.[49]

Darley's historical dramas, *Thomas à Becket* and *Ethelstan,* like Procter's *Dramatic Scenes,* point more to the later historical plays of Tennyson than to new directions in the early-nineteenth-century English theatre.[50] They are unnecessarily long and static,

---

[48] *Life and Letters of Thomas Campbell,* ed. William Beattie (2 vols., New York, 1850), I,489–490.

[49] Wilson's other play, *The Fall of Jerusalem,* is of even less consequence than *The City of the Plague* for a study of poetic tragedy.

[50] Ramsay Colles, editor of Darley's works, has owned a copy of *Thomas à Becket* given by Darley to Tennyson. Any indebtedness to this play in Tennyson's *Becket,* however, must be regarded as more theoretical than real.

and they are concerned more with historicity than with plot or character development. Miss Mitford's *Charles the First* shows similar weaknesses in its concern with (in her words) "minute and apparently trifling touches which might serve to realize the scene, and supply, by a vivid impression of the people and the time, the usual sources of dramatic attraction, the interest of story and suspense" (Preface). As Miss Mitford and George Darley apparently did not realize, the "usual sources of dramatic attraction" can be supplied only by the genius of the author; any "minute and apparently trifling touches" are but means to this end, and then only if interestingly interwoven into the plot. Unfortunately, in the hands of early-nineteenth-century playwrights historical drama as often as not leads us not so much to form any vivid impression as to tread the bypaths of tedium and monotony.

The same is even truer of Henry Taylor's *Philip van Artevelde*. In the lengthy Preface Taylor examines the Byronic hero under the microscope and finds that as a group they "exhibit rather passions personified than persons impassioned," heroes who are "creatures abandoned to their passions, and essentially, therefore, weak of mind." "Strip them," he writes, "of the veil of mystery and the trappings of poetry, revolve them into their plain realities, and they are such beings as, in the eyes of a reader of masculine judgment, would certainly excite no sentiment of admiration, even if they did not provoke contempt."[51] Much as we can only admire Taylor's astute disclosure of the inherent fallacy in the Byronic hero concept, what solution does he himself advocate for creating heroes who are not weak of mind? Alas, to Taylor intellectuality is all: "no man can be a very great poet who is not also a great philosopher," he believes[52]—thereupon writing an endlessly involved and for the most part highly unintellectual play to prove his point. The story is based upon Flem-

---

[51] *Philip van Artevelde* (London, 1883), p. xi.

[52] *Ibid.*, p. ix. Compare Taylor's with Coleridge's statement: "No man was ever yet a great poet, without being at the same time a profound philosopher" *(Biographia Literaria,* ed. Shawcross, II,19). Yet it will be observed that Coleridge shifts from the intellectual to the mystical and figurative in the immediately succeeding sentence: "For poetry is the blossom and the fragrancy of all human knowledge, human thoughts, human passions, emotions, language."

ish history; there are the usual cries for liberty and freedom; the noble hero ultimately becomes tyrannical; the love scenes are stilted and forced. No. Taylor's formula for philosophical drama was scarcely the answer to the issues that liberalism and the question of political integrity were presenting to the English dramatist. And Taylor's cry that "from . . . unbounded indulgence in the mere luxuries of poetry, has there not ensued a want of adequate appreciation for its intellectual and immortal part?"[53] can best be answered by saying that, "intellectual and immortal part" aside, his own verse is generally mawkish and inept.

Others writing in the mainstream of the Romantic tradition also knew that an "unbounded indulgence in the mere luxuries of poetry" alone was insufficient. Yet to them it was also clear that a concern with linguistic niceties, the "natural" language of men, perforce would forever have to remain of supreme relevance in Romantic literature. Nor by itself could philosophy suffice to make poetic drama timely and pertinent—of that Macready, Browning, and Bulwer were well aware. What the Romantic playwright needed was a way in which to veil references to contemporary issues behind the smoke screen of historical fact, "real" if fictionalized. The Romantic playwright somehow had to be able to delve ever deeper, historically, into his past. Sheil, Knowles, Milman, Mitford—each had explored new avenues of approach; clear-cut problems had begun to arise. For the further course of Romantic drama Shelley had unconsciously supplied a motto:

> Nor happiness, nor majesty, nor fame,
> Nor peace, nor strength, nor skill in arms or arts,
> Shepherd those herds whom tyranny makes tame;
> Verse echoes not one beating of their hearts,
> History is but the shadow of their shame.
>
> (Sonnet: "Political Greatness")

And in the dawning decade of the liberal 1830's new playwrights were eagerly at work to test the validity of this idea upon the stage.

---

[53] *Van Artevelde,* p. vii.

CHAPTER V

The Liberal 1830's

ON THE EVENING of May 26, 1836, the premiere of Thomas Noon Talfourd's drama *Ion* at Covent Garden Theatre was followed by a dinner party given at the home of the author, at 56 Russell Square. Mary Russell Mitford, a house guest of the Talfourds' at the time, was subsequently to refer to this evening, as were Crabb Robinson and William Macready, two others present at the gathering.[1] Although Macready is most concerned in his diary entry with his own recently completed performance in the title role of *Ion,* its weaknesses and its strength, he carefully records the fact of having been seated at this party "very happily . . . between Wordsworth and Landor, with Browning opposite, and Mrs. Talfourd next but one—Talfourd within two." And Macready also punctiliously mentions an exchange in his evening's conversation with the sage of Rydal Mount. Writing on a note of evident pride, he recalls that "Wordsworth seemed pleased when I pointed out the passage in *Ion,* of a 'devious fancy,' etc., as having been suggested by the lines *he* had once quoted to me from a MS. tragedy of his; he smiled and said, 'Yes, I noticed them,' and then he went on—

> 'Action is transitory—a step—a blow,
> The motion of a muscle—this way or that—
> 'Tis done; and in the after vacancy
> We wonder at ourselves like men betrayed.' "[2]

---

[1] *Life of Mary Russell Mitford,* ed. A. G. K. L'Estrange, II, 173–174; *Diary, Reminiscences, and Correspondence of Henry Crabb Robinson,* ed. Thomas Sadler (2 vols., 3rd ed., London and New York, 1872), II,176; *The Diaries of William Charles Macready,* ed. William Toynbee (2 vols., New York, 1912), I,318–320.

[2] *Diaries of Macready,* I, 319—hereafter cited at M. I, etc., followed by the page number.

Otherwise, concerning drama, we only know the effect this evening was to exert upon the playwrighting career of Robert Browning.[3] But what has come down to us is enough. Thanks to this tantalizing record preserved from the conversation of that memorable night, we perceive that poetic tragedy has reached a full circle. Once again we find ourselves at its point of origin.

It is open to conjecture how significant these offhand comments seemed to the speakers. Wordsworth could scarcely have attached any great importance to such a trifling bit of plagiarism as this; whereas for Macready the incident in all probability merely provided a moment of passing recognition in the self-effacing task of behind-the-scenes revision for his latest dramatic discovery, Talfourd. Macready makes no other reference in his personal diary to this collaboration. The question arises whether other guests might have overheard the exchange. Probably Landor was not listening, for between Landor and Wordsworth a quarrel already was brewing that transformed them from mutual admirers into the bitterest of enemies.[4] Henry Hart Milman, Sheridan Knowles, and Barry Procter, who also were present, could have overheard Macready and Wordsworth in conversation. If they did, were they aware that through these few remarks a symbolic laying on of hands was taking place? No, probably only Coleridge would have realized the significance of the remarks, and the appropriateness of this extraordinary assemblage of poetic dramatists at the dinner table of T. N. Talfourd, their author-host. But for Coleridge no place had been set in the festively lighted dining room, nor had a chair been drawn up for Byron, or Shelley, or Keats. Sheil, Maturin, possibly Wilson, Bulwer and Richard Hengist Horne most certainly—these writers, too, were noticeably absent. Otherwise the conclave was complete: at the Talfourd residence had gathered all of the principal figures in our study of English poetic tragedy.

-----

[3] See pp. 193–194.
[4] See David W. Rannie, *Wordsworth and His Circle,* p. 305, for a detailed account of this Wordsworth-Landor quarrel.

The occasion was memorable for another reason: on this May 26 Talfourd was celebrating his forty-first birthday.[5] Not only could the author of the newest successfully produced poetic tragedy look back upon a notable career of public service; now he could look forward to recognition as a leading figure in the literary scene. But alas, Talfourd was destined never to rise above the heights of his first poetic tragedy.[6] For his vicissitudes with *Ion*, they had begun somewhat more than a year earlier, in 1835. Macready, upon learning of Talfourd's literary ambitions, confides to his diary: "Forster told me of Talfourd having completed a tragedy called *Ion*. What an extraordinary, what an indefatigable man!" (M. I,219). But later that same year, after Talfourd entrusted *Ion* to his personal care, Macready grew somewhat dubious of the play's stageability. "Then sat down to read over attentively," he writes, "and endeavour to reduce into an acting form and dimensions, Talfourd's sweet tragic poem of *Ion,* which I accomplished, although it occupied more time than I anticipated. I expect to find him refractory on some points —and where some of the most poetical passages are omitted, it is difficult to persuade an author that the effect of the whole is improved; but imagery and sentiment will not supply the place of action." (M. I,246.)

But this new breed of poetic dramatists, more compliant than their predecessors, readily fell in with the dictates of a William Macready. For Macready, action would have to be the primary interest in any play; poetry, sweet and tragic as it might be, would have to take a back seat. Only Browning refused to subordinate his poetic principles to the dictates of England's leading actor-manager. But Talfourd was eagerly prepared to accept the advice and recommendations of the virtual poetic dictator of the theatre. In the Preface to *Ion,* Talfourd congratulates him-

---

[5] Talfourd is the youngest of the poetic dramatists born in the eighteenth century. Bulwer, Browning, Horne, and Marston were all born in the early part of the 1800's.

[6] Talfourd's other two plays are *The Athenian Captive* (1838) and *Glencoe* (1840).

self on his good fortune in being able to enjoy "the friendship of the delightful artist to whom all have by turns been indebted for the realization of their noblest conceptions, and . . . to enjoy with more exquisite relish the home-born affection with which those were endued, and the poetical grain breathed around them, by finding the same influences shed by Mr. Macready over the sphere of his social and domestic life."[7] The Victorian Age is closing in upon the literary artist's subjective attitude: Macready is a fine person, he leads an exemplary domestic life; therefore he must be a great man and, by extension, a genius in the theatre.

As for the theatre itself, "To Covent Garden Theatre the sternest moralist may now conduct those whose moral nurture he regards as his most anxious and most delightful duty, without fear lest their minds should be diverted from the blameless gaieties or noble passion of the scene by intrusive suggestions of vice, which he would screen, as far as possible from their thoughts."[8] At last children, too, can safely be taken to the theatre. We may ask, for what purpose? Here again we find ourselves confronted by the question of taste: the early Victorian gentleman wanted his children to gain all the advantages of every accepted cultural milieu; children, therefore, must be acquainted with their Shakespeare "live." But children are essentially delicate flowers of nature, innocent and pure; they must be protected. Shakespeare and the theatre in general, then, must be cleaned up, made socially acceptable, made decent, made nice. Thus one more obstacle has been placed in the path of creative expression for the author aspiring to reach the stage.[9]

---

[7] T. N. Talfourd, *Tragedies* (New York and Boston, 1846), p. 21.

[8] *Ibid.*, p. 27.

[9] In defense of Talfourd's apparently prudish attitude concerning "intrusive suggestions of vice" it must be remembered that the theatre in this period was a major operating ground for prostitutes and panderers. See Dewey Ganzel, "Patent Wrongs and Patent Theatres: Drama and the Law in the Early Nineteenth Century," *PMLA*, LXXVI (1961), 384–396. "John Forbes [part owner of Covent Garden, in testifying before the Parliamentary Select Committee on Dramatic Literature presided over by Edward Bulwer in 1832] admitted, under persistent

"It must be remembered in extenuation of Macready's foibles of temper," writes his biographer, "that the best hours of his life were given up to a task which is notoriously trying to the most angelic disposition—that of drilling careless, inefficient, and over-worked actors in country theatres." Macready has also been described as "the affectionate if somewhat over-scrupulous and exacting husband and father, the urbane and even formally courteous gentleman, the man of sane and liberal instincts, just to himself, generous towards others." For Macready's biographer it is his "inability to conceal the perpetual struggle between the Jekyll and Hyde in his composition" that is of particular interest; Browning's appraisal is but a trifle less barbed: "I found Macready as I left him—and happily, after a long interval, resumed him, so to speak—one of the most admirable and, indeed, fascinating characters I have ever known; somewhat too sensitive for his own happiness, and much too impulsive for invariable consistency with his nobler moods." To this "Macready in a nutshell!"[10] his biographer exclaims—about the man upon whom Romantic tragedy would have to depend for its very existence in the few years that yet remained before it would vanish from the English stage.

It had been back in June, 1823, some thirteen years before the premiere of *Ion,* that Macready first met Wordsworth face to face. Wordsworth read aloud those lines from *The Borderers* Macready was to remember well enough to use as a "suggestion" for adding lines to Talfourd's "sweet tragic poem." At the time Macready noted in his diary that he had been moved by these lines;[11] and thirteen years later they were as relevant to the lib-

questioning, that Covent Garden owned a house not immediately attached to the theatre but 'up the passage in Princes-street, next the box-office.' Although he finally agreed that anyone might reside there, he indignantly denied that this was a brothel." (P. 391.)

[10] William Archer, *William Charles Macready* (London, 1890), pp. 209, 208, 207, 214, 214.

[11] *Reminiscences,* ed. Pollock, pp. 216–217. Wordsworth liked these lines from *The Borderers* so well that he used them as the motto for *The White Doe of Rylestone.* See *Poetical Works,* ed. de Selincourt, III,548–549.

eral-political situation as they had been earlier. The difference between Wordsworth's lines and Talfourd's is that by 1836 liberalism had become somewhat more the proper thing, somewhat more acceptable than in 1823—or 1796. Possibly for that reason the derivative lines from *Ion* are pallid in comparison with those of Wordsworth's *Borderers;* indeed, except so far as they are inspired by Wordsworthian philosophy, they are scarcely worthy of serious attention. We would hardly recognize this verse as having been suggested by lines from Wordsworth's play:

> A devious fancy, and a muscle raised
> Obedient to its impulse! Dost thou think
> The tracings of a thousand kindnesses,
> Which taught me all I guessed of brotherhood,
> Are in the rashness of a moment lost? (IV,iii)

But Wordsworth's influence in general is quite another matter. Talfourd was the first of the leading critics to appreciate Wordsworth's genius—and in 1820 it must have required courage to state one's case so baldly and directly, "On the Genius and Writings of Wordsworth," from the title itself on. Talfourd goes even further: "Wordsworth's persons are not invested with antique robes," he writes, "nor clad in the symbols of worldly pomp, but they are 'apparelled in celestial light.' By his power 'the bare earth and mountains bare' are covered with an imaginative radiance more holy than that which old Greek poets shed over Olympus. The world, as consecrated by his poetic wisdom, is an enchanted scene—redolent with sweet humanity, and vocal with 'echoes from beyond the grave.' "[12]

Sweetness has become the keynote of critical appreciation, whether the figure is Knowles's Virginius, the poet Wordsworth, or Talfourd's own creation, the Grecian Ion. Macready expresses the same idea, in the same words, when he calls *Ion* a "sweet tragic poem." And it is this word that best characterizes the di-

[12] *Critical and Miscellaneous Writings of T. Noon Talfourd* (3rd American ed., New York, 1864), p. 49. For other writings by Talfourd on Wordsworth in the same period see William S. Ward, "An Early Champion of Wordsworth: Talfourd," *PMLA,* LXVIII (1953), 992–1000.

rection being followed by the new spirit of this liberal age. A precursor to Arnold's concept of sweetness and light, the attitude is a mixture of optimistic hardheadedness with a considerable portion of sentimental credulity. At times such sentimentally optimistic sweetness grows a trifle cloying, as in the characterization Talfourd's Ion gives of himself:

> I am a lone stray thing, whose little life
> By strangers' bounty cherish'd, like a wave
> That from a summer sea a wanton breeze
> Lifts for a moment's sparkle, will subside
> Light as it rose, nor leave a sigh in breaking. (I,i)

Ion's vis-à-vis may rightfully be excused for expostulating: "Ion, no sigh!"—so different is this "new" (age-old) sentimental attitude from the unashamed, yet hardly lily-drooping-on-the-stalk, Byronic sentiments of a Manfred, or from the worst outbursts of a sentimental Wordsworthian Marmaduke; while the speeches of Coleridge's Don Alvar, by comparison, ring with a double portion of sincerity and manly eloquence. Without calling him insipid, we cannot accept Ion as someone who is quite real. Possibly he is real ideally, yet he is scarcely true to actual life. This figure of Talfourd's creation is but a forerunner of those many goody-goody Victorian heroes who thread their way so monotonously through the novels of even the best of the nineteenth-century prose masters. When we read on in the Preface to *Ion,* we are not surprised to learn that Talfourd, who had been prevented "by the conscientious scruples of friends an early acquaintance with plays, . . . derived from Mrs. [Hannah] More's 'Sacred Dramas' my first sense of that peculiar enjoyment which the idea of dramatic action, however imperfectly conveyed, gives." To this should be added his afterthought of how "stiff and cumbrous . . . they now seem," although in its way this provides but small comfort, since Talfourd immediately mentions "that debt of gratitude" he feels is due the author of the *Sacred Dramas* "which others may perhaps share with me, who have first looked on the world of literature through the net-work of [the] most sincere but exclusive opinions"[13] expressed in Mrs. More's works.

Of principal interest in Talfourd's *Ion* is the question of motivation. What hideous misdeeds Ion and Adrastus, his father, must atone for in this play remains forever hidden. The attentive reader is led to suspect that the play's obscurity can be attributed to a murkiness in Talfourd's own mind. Not that Talfourd seems to be seeking intentionally to spare his audience's sensibilities; rather, he seems not to be consciously aware that there should be valid reasons for occasioning the wrath of his Grecian gods. The title for *Ion* he borrowed from Euripides, although he adds: "otherwise there is no resemblance between this imperfect sketch and that exquisite picture."[14] What this imperfect sketch does present, at least for us, is a picture of a mild-mannered and well-intentioned early Victorian liberal who is struggling for the causes of freedom and liberty. In his attempts to obtain justice, however, Ion ironically discovers too late that he has been fighting against his own best interests. Ion the hero has made a solemn vow to murder Adrastus the tyrant; but at the last possible moment the hero finds that what he has been on the verge of committing would in itself have been an act of parricide. The spell of the word liberty is dissipated by the stronger bond of self-interest and the ties of blood. Tyranny and fatherhood, as represented by Adrastus, are discovered to be one and the same. At this crucial moment of discovery Talfourd's play immediately loses whatever vestiges of credibility it has possessed. The mind guiding the pen is not perceptive enough to grasp the drift the action so suddenly has taken. Shakespeare, perhaps yes—but left to the fumbling care of T. N. Talfourd and William Macready what might have been the stirring disclosure of the dichotomy that faces any liberal when confronted by the difference between

---

[13] Talfourd, *Tragedies,* p. 19. Probably Talfourd was merely being charitable in referring to Mrs. More's "exclusive opinions." Since she was accused by many Anglicans of being a Methodist because of her philanthropic activities, we might substitute in our own minds "eccentric opinions" for the term Talfourd employs.

[14] *Ibid.,* p. 17.

theory and reality—the chasm between the ideal and the real—
self-interest and selfless disinterestedness—these problems are
never presented with any clarity. What might have provided a
memorable casebook for the later liberal ends as it began—a
sweet tragic poem, and little more.

It is possible that it was Talfourd's conscious intention to
remain inscrutably ambiguous. But there is no internal evidence
to suggest that the conflict presented in *Ion* was designed for anything more than a conventionally theatrical effect. Talfourd
mourns the fact that "the composition of dramatic blank verse
[was] even more difficult now that I had present to me the
ease and vividness of my friends, than when I had been contented to emulate the ponderous lines of the dramatists of Garrick's age,"[15] a complaint other contemporary playwrights might
well have echoed from time to time! Nevertheless, as it stands,
Talfourd's verse is not inordinately bad. If not memorable, it
rarely descends to the platitudinizing level of a Barry Procter or
a John Wilson. There are times when the effect is suggestive of
Wilson at his worst:

> . . . Thrill me not
> With words that, in their agony, suggest
> A hope too ravishing—or my head will swim,
> And my heart faint within me. (I,ii)

But such are fairly infrequent. More typical of Talfourd's verse
is a distinct effort to achieve a Wordsworthian phraseology:

> . . . We must look *within*
> For that which makes us slaves:—on sympathies
> Which find no kindred objects in the plain
> Of common life—affections that aspire
> In air too thin—and fancy's dewy film
> Floating to rest . . . (II,iii)

Or rather, Talfourd's Wordsworthian kind of diction emerges
with distinct Shakespearean overtones. Assuredly he had read
his *Julius Caesar* beforehand, and probably his Pope.

---

[15] *Ibid.,* p. 22.

> . . . No Cyrthes!—in ourselves,
> In our own honest hearts and chainless hands
> Will be our safeguard:—while we seek no use
> Of arms, we would not have our children blend
> With their first innocent wishes; while the love
> Of Argos and of justice shall be one
> To their young reason; while their sinews grow
> Firm 'midst the gladness of heroic sports . . . (V,iii)

The Byronic influence is seen to exert its apparently never-ending fascination.

> . . . To the mountains
> I fled, and on their pinnacles of snow
> Breasted the icy wind, in hope to cool
> My spirit's fever—struggled with the oak
> In search of weariness, and learn't to rive
> Its stubborn boughs, till limbs lightly stung
> Might mate in cordage with its infant stems . . . (II,i)

Although this passage may make Ion's father Adrastus sound somewhat like a precursor to Longfellow's Hiawatha, at least on the whole Talfourd comes up with frequent imitations of the great masters of English prosody. Naturally there are the by now customary effusions on freedom and liberty:

> . . . not such words as flash
> From the fierce demagogue's unthinking rage,
> To madden for a moment and expire,—
> . . . .
> But words which bear the spirits of great deeds
> Wing'd for the Future; which the dying breath
> Of Freedom's martyr shapes as it exhales . . . (I,i)

Nor is the theme of remorse absent. Initially this remorse appears in the guise of pity and despair as Ion muses: "I know that we should pity—" to which Adrastus, whose relationship to his son has not as yet been disclosed, replies scornfully:

> . . . Pity! dare
> To speak that word again, and torture waits thee! (II,i)

But later in the action the ever-hopeful Ion implores Adrastus's
enemies:

> . . . should ye find him touch'd
> With penitence, as happily ye may,
> O give allowance to his soften'd nature! (II,ii)

Once again a common chord has been found that ties *Ion* in
with its forerunners in poetic literature. Another gentle hero
has set out to woo villainy to repentance by appealing to the
voices of conscience and remorse.

We have not lingered over Talfourd's *Ion* because it is in
any way a monument in the history of poetic drama. Except
possibly for the superior quality of its verse, *Ion* is no more
memorable or significant than Knowles's earlier *Virginius*. In
its own day *Virginius* was considered something of a milestone
in the adaptation of blank verse for theatrical (and liberal) purposes; and now, fifteen years later, critics and commentators were
making the same fulsome comments about Talfourd's first poetic
play. The years that had elapsed saw an ample number of other
poetic tragedies staged, had contemporary critics bothered to
study them attentively, to offset any claim of Talfourd's having
achieved a liberal first. But undeniably it does not injure an
author to have a wide circle of friends. When a first play is being premiered, it does no damage to one's reputation to invite
some of them to the theatre, especially if one's birthday happens
to fall on that day. And so, *Ion* seems by accident to solidify in
the theatre a concern with a new liberal age that actually had
been established years earlier with the plays of Sheil and
Knowles.

What, then, has caused us to linger over *Ion?* And why have
we looked forward to *Ion* in this study for so long? The answer
is clear. In *Rienzi*, Mary Mitford had clearly foreseen the problem faced by the liberal hero when confronted by sober reality:
ideals, persuasions, convictions—these are of no pertinence when
one is tried by the actual event—the gullibility of men, the weaknesses in human nature, vice and greed. The sweeter child of
nature, Ion, is never compelled to curry favor with such plebs

as plague a Rienzi or a Faliero. On the contrary Ion is left to die in expiation for a father's, rather than a nation's, crime, yet a crime that is forever as shadowy and obscure to others as it is to him. The emphasis in *Ion* in fact has been shifted—shifted from one's duties and responsibilities to others—where the emphasis should have rested—to one's duty to some undisclosed ideal; and in the process the potentialities inherent in the conflict between the self and the state, the individual and the family, the family and society, have been ignored. Alas, rather than a profound liberal statement, *Ion* seems in retrospect a bungle of confused ideas and fumbled opportunities. It is a venture into a pseudo-Wordsworthian world of make-believe ideality rather than into the world of actual fact. *Ion* fails as a play because it holds a mirror up to fantasy and not to truth. *Ion* is more fanciful in its way than any of the pure fantasies of Coleridge.

    This fact brings us back to the problem of Macready. How significant after all was Macready's contribution to this later development of poetic drama in the theatre? Without him the plays of Talfourd, Bulwer, and Browning would hardly have reached the stage; with Macready functioning as guide and mentor, however, the emphasis in Romantic tragedy is beginning to undergo a perceptible change. From the poetic language of real life it is moving on to other considerations: plot development, action, smooth transitional passages, and more dramatic entrances and exits for the actors. Technically the influence of Macready is salutary in that poetic tragedy is becoming more dramatic, more forceful, more dynamic. But the question remains to what extent this drama of the Liberal 1830's has been able to maintain the vitality of its origins and adhere to its former direction as established by Wordsworth and Coleridge in their more labored and less skillfully constructed dramas. More skill is becoming evident; what is lacking is the heart, the conviction, to keep poetic drama at its former strength! Huzzas are still given to those ideals of old, but they do not ring with the old defiance, nor do they re-echo with the same idealistic fervor. Ironically, the more influential liberalism becomes, the weaker grows the voice of Romantic drama that had been one of liberalism's strongest advocates. The more tangibly this new liberal age emerges—this early period of Queen Victoria—the more noticeably Romantic drama commences first to languish and then to die. By the decade of Victorian consolidation, in the early 1840's, for all intents and purposes Romantic tragedy becomes but one more victim of this consolidation, its justification undermined, its future already lying in the past. And by 1843, poetic tragedy is no longer even a salable commodity on the stage.

Macready, ever the shrewd prognosticator of theatrical taste, had become aware of this change as early as 1838. By now Edward Bulwer had emerged as his latest property, an author hailed by his admirers as the successor to Scott, damned by critics for his ultraliberal tendencies, envied for his prestige and wealth, scornfully abused by Macready himself (in his private diary) for playing the dilettante. Still, when Macready learned that Bulwer was dedicating his first play, *The Duchess de la Vallière,* to him, he who otherwise permitted himself but the most reserved admiration for anyone in any way connected with the theatre felt genuinely moved. "In associating my name with your own you graced me with a lasting honour," he writes to Bulwer in response, "and rendered me an important service. I was already sufficiently indebted to you to be conscious of my own inability ever to requite your kindness:—what then am I now to say to you?"[16] Bulwer shows the side of his personality that was to typify the many years of his friendship with Macready by answering: "Many thanks . . . for your most kind and generous letter—which pays me a thousandfold for all my good intentions, and small exertions."[17]

Bulwer's exertions, both for the theatre and in Macready's behalf, were scarcely small. Their first social contact, dating from 1834 in Dublin, had been quite to the liking of them both. Both men by instinct and inclination were passionately liberal, and both were committed to supporting liberal positions wherever found. On May 31, 1832, Bulwer had introduced into Parliament a motion to create a select committee to investigate the

[16] Quoted by Shattuck in *Bulwer and Macready,* p. 77.
[17] *Ibid.*

parlous state of English drama. This "committee was to make an 'inquiry' into the decline of the drama, but under Bulwer's direction it was not to be a forum for airing the grievances of the patent theatres, whose 'monopoly' was continually violated. Its purpose was to display to Parliament and to the country at large the inadequacies of the legal status quo."[18] So by the time of his first meeting with Macready, under Bulwer's direction all the ramifications of the notorious Licensing Act had been thoroughly investigated; theatre managers and the public alike now knew, from a legal point of view, the status of monopoly in the theatre. Not until 1843 would the Licensing Act be revoked, but by the time of the Bulwer-Macready theatrical collaboration beginning in 1836, one thing was widely known: the monopoly of the patent houses had been broken, *de facto* if not *de jure*. In their attempts to contravene the statute permitting legimate dramas to be played only by the two patent houses, Covent Garden and Drury Lane, other theatres had, besides presenting the ever popular melodrama, adopted the expedient of performing burlettas, an entertainment of a lighter sort entailing song and recitation. As the popularity of these burlettas increased, attendance in the legitimate houses fell off, and these houses were soon forced to introduce burlettas into their programs and to hire inordinate numbers of actors who specialized in their own particular *genre*.[19] As the patent houses rushed into the fray to stem the decline in their receipts resulting from the competition of melodrama, burletta, and their assorted variations, the lesser houses began to dispense altogether with the burletta's musical camouflage. By the time the parliamentary committee was formed, by 1832, "the distinction between a 'burletta' and a 'play' no longer existed."[20]

---

[18] Ganzel, "Patent Wrongs and Patent Theatres," p. 384.

[19] Ganzel mentions that "John Forbes, proprietor of Covent Garden, set the number of persons dependent on Covent Garden Theatre at 2,000 with 1,000 'constantly employed.'" "Osbaldiston, proprietor of the Surrey Theatre, said that he employed roughly four hundred persons, only one-fifth to one-fourth the number retained by Covent Garden, although his theatre held twenty-three hundred, more than two-thirds the capacity of the patent theatre" (p. 390).

[20] Ganzel, p. 387.

Most theatres by this time were performing previously forbidden legitimate drama, the music in the performed version having been openly dispensed with, "although it was still retained as a legal dodge in the copy of the play licensed by the Lord Chamberlain."[21] The patent theatres could do little more than helplessly observe the continuing decline in their own box-office revenues.[22]

As recognition of these new conditions spread, it grew apparent that the monopoly of the patent theatres had become a dead issue overnight: "Henceforth, even without the legal sanction which came only in 1843, the serious playwright could, without professional jeopardy, give his dramas to any theatre in London."[23] At this point, some four years later, the Bulwer–Macready collaboration begins—its significance, its initial impulse, and its relevance for us stemming for both artists from this mutual recognition of the current theatrical situation.

Other and ulterior considerations were to motivate their association. No longer is theirs primarily an attitude of fabricating something that would "do for the Theatre in its present state"; instead, the Bulwer–Macready relationship concerned itself with one overriding consideration: to create not only plays that would be poetic, but plays that would be sure-fire hits, plays that most emphatically would sell.

At once a new element has been injected into poetic tragedy —a conscious appeal to popular taste as well as popular sentiments. The writer of poetic tragedy is beginning to abandon his attempts to use the language of real life. Now he begins to focus his attention on satisfying the dictates of an emerging middle class. But this middle class has been veering from the poetic creed of freedom and liberty into the backwashes of a pallid

---

[21] *Ibid.*

[22] "Unpatented theatres in London and its environs could and did produce the regular drama and there was, evidently, nothing the patent theatres could do about it" (Ganzel, p. 388). It will be recalled the circumstances under which Milman first saw a performance of his play *Fazio* at the Surrey Theatre in 1818. See *supra,* p. 125.

[23] Ganzel, p. 392.

liberalism.[24] This liberalism, moreover, is so distinctly mild as to be little distinguishable from what might otherwise be termed conservatism. By the time of the Bulwer–Macready collaboration it is not Wordsworth alone who is no longer even mildly apostate: an entire generation has been growing conservative. Ironically the same conditions now prevail as existed in the years of Wordsworth's experimental *Borderers;* the godfather of poetic tragedy and this his godchild's most recent manifestation are finding that they are able to live together side by side—if uneasily at times, at least without a sense of mutual embarrassment. Only one element in this picture has radically changed; comparing the conditions of the 1830's and those of 1796, one truth is sadly evident: as with Wordsworth, so with poetic tragedy—both with the passing years have become increasingly less liberal.

The end would not be reached until the next decade, the 1840's. And in 1836 it still seemed to many that the destiny of poetic drama lay as before in the future rather than in the past. In retrospect it is obvious that the responsibility for the demise of Romantic tragedy can be charged to Bulwer and Macready as much as to anyone. In itself such a charge is hardly a fair representation of the inherent problems of the theatre of their time, nor does it take into consideration the weight of other factors that might as easily have led to Romantic drama's ultimate stagnation. Nonetheless, the presumed reforms with which Bulwer and Macready were both so ardently concerned indicate the path for us all too clearly, so it is that much easier to force them into the roles of villains rather than of the innocent-minded reformers for Romantic tragedy they believed themselves to be. During their earliest intimacy, in the course of the agonizing weeks of preparing *The Duchess de la Vallière* for production, both artists labored to piece together an acceptable play, a play that not only would conform to the liberal inclinations of the theatre-

---

[24] We would not go far wrong in defining liberalism as understood by the typical nineteenth-century English middle-class gentleman as complacent confidence in the ultimate solution of all thorny economic and political issues superimposed upon a benevolent, if condescending, concern for the social welfare of the plebs.

going public but would earn a tidy profit. Unfortunately in the
process we find ourselves seemingly once again at the beginning
of our story rather than near a terminal point. Time seems to
have stopped. No sense of progression is evident. The creative
mind, with dogged determination, is again at work in seeking to
create, à la Coleridge, something that would "do for the Theatre
in its present state" "by a better subordination of the characters,
by avoiding the duplicity of interest, by a greater clearness of the
Plot, and by a deeper Pathos . . . "[25] In effect Romantic drama
is reverting to those very instruments that were so utterly unable
to offer it presentable solutions in the past.

There were mitigating circumstances. Macready was nearing
the end of an engagement, under Alfred Bunn's management, at
Drury Lane. The conditions under which he worked seemed to
him intolerable.[26] At this juncture Bulwer informed him of
planning to turn to the drama with a play entitled *The Duchess
de la Vallière*.[27] Concerning their meeting Macready remarks:
"Called on Bulwer, whom I found in very handsome chambers
in the Albany, dressed, or rather *déshabillé*, in the most lamentable style of foppery—a hookah in his mouth, his hair, whiskers,
tuft, etc., all grievously cared for. I felt deep regret to see a man
of such noble and profound thought yield for a moment to
pettiness so unworthy of him. His manner was frank, manly, and
cordial in the extreme—so contradictory of his appearance"
(M. I,278). But Macready's impression of Bulwer's foppery did
not affect his impression of the play itself. "What talent he possesses!" he exclaims excitedly (M. I,279).[28] And the die was cast:
an author-manager collaboration was formed between the two
men, an association that led to the writing and production of
The Duchess de la Vallière, The Lady of Lyons, and *Richelieu,*
Bulwer's so-called French trilogy.

---

[25] See *supra,* p. 75.

[26] See Shattuck, *Bulwer and Macready,* pp. 30–31, on the Bunn–
Macready episode.

[27] *Eugene Aram,* converted into a novel in 1832, had originally
been written by Bulwer as a drama.

[28] The history of this and the succeeding Bulwer–Macready collaboration is described by Shattuck in detail.

Of the three *The Duchess de la Vallière,* premiered on January 4, 1837, is undeniably the weakest. Not only is it the weakest, it was criticized the most severely by the press. The *Times* of January 5 declares: "No man but one whose vanity has been flattered . . . would have ventured to produce a drama, the subject of which is the heartless debaucheries of a profligate monarch and his equally profligate courtiers. It is in the worst taste of the worst school, the school of the modern French romance. . . . This may pass in Paris, where jaded roués and faded demireps require the stimulus of blasphemy to rouse their exhausted passions; but in England the public mind is, thank God, yet too healthy to demand such abominable incentives."[29] Undoubtedly Bulwer's avowed liberal politics played a role in the vituperativeness of this and similar lashings from critics—but the truth is that Bulwer "bowed to the inevitable, faced the facts, and cut" the play, choosing to adopt the policy, if not of political, at least of pecuniary expediency.[30]

Lines from the Prologue that speak of an endeavor in *The Duchess de la Vallière* to

> . . . point the proper goal,
> And make the Affections preachers to the Soul

must be regarded therefore as the expression of an effort to reconcile a possible purpose with an existing circumstance. For Bulwer's main interest in this first play and in its successors is historical veracity rather than beautiful poetry. What poetry is present in *The Duchess* is of mediocre quality at best. In the Preface of 1835 Bulwer congratulates himself upon having placed Louis XIV, the Duchess's lover in the play, "in the very position most favorable to his external graces, his felicity of phrase, his magnificence of taste, his softness of feeling disguising

---

[29] Quoted by Shattuck, p. 51.

[30] *Ibid.* Expressions in *The Duchess* such as "Heaven" and "O Father, bless her" seemed to have aroused the most indignation among contemporary critics. See Shattuck, p. 51. One that escaped pruning is:

> . . . Lord of Hosts, for this
> Hast thou preserved me from the foeman's sword. (II,ii)

his want of heart, and that peculiar royalty of thought and sentiment, which had the twofold advantage of rendering homely and
plebeian those who rejected, bombastic and ridiculous those who
adopted, the imitation."[31] But when we read on in the play itself, we discover that Louis is described by the Duchess in terms
that are no more than a strained and somewhat pathetic attempt
at imitating Elizabethan diction:

> Nay, ev'n the very presence of his greatness
> Exalts the heart from each more low temptation.
> He seems to walk the earth as if to raise
> And purify our wandering thoughts, by fixing
> Thought on himself;—and she who thinks on Louis
> Shuts out the world, and scorns the name of love! (I,v)

Not alone in this new liberal age was the ear for an Elizabethan tone irrevocably past; more exactly, Bulwer's ear for
poetic diction, like that of many of his contemporary poetic
dramatists, is distinctly bad. Another character in the play declares:

> Pleasant! This comes, now, of one's condescending
> To talk with men who cannot understand
> The tone of good society. Poor fellow! (II,i)

And the sound, the rhythm, the cadence, in *The Duchess,* more
often than not, are of this very kind—slanted, awry, offkey. Nor
do recurrent melodramatic effects, to say nothing of the blasphemy contemporary critics found so objectionable, contribute
as they should to a unified poetic synthesis, as for example when
the Duchess exclaims:

> Let me not hear him, Heaven!—Strike all my senses!
> Make—make me dumb, deaf, blind,—but keep me honest!
>   (II,iv)

At this time Bulwer forthrightly acknowledges himself as
belonging "with the Neophytes of that great class of writers
whose rights, some years ago, when he little thought he should

---

[31] *The Duchess de la Vallière* (2nd ed., New York and London,
1837).

ever be one of so illustrious a fraternity, it was his fortune to
protect and to extend" (advertisement to *The Duchess,* 1836).
And neophyte he most certainly is here in a play that portrays
the unintentional fall to the level of courtesan and the ultimate
redemption of a warmhearted if puritanically minded heroine,
more Victorian than French.

Even aside from the mediocrity of the poetry, there is little to
justify the author's cavalier belief in at last being a member of
an illustrious fraternity of liberal playwrights. Liberalism is more
apparent by inference in *The Duchess* than in fact. "People,"
exclaims the villain Lauzun;

> . . . what's the *People?*
> I never heard that word at court! The *People!* (II,i)

and his vis-à-vis drily responds:

> I doubt not, duke. The People, like the Air,
> Is rarely heard, save when it speaks in thunder.

Although the effect upon the audience may no doubt have been
pronounced when the French Revolution is foreshadowed in a
speech by Bragelone, the Duchess's protector and stalwart admirer, the historicity that Bulwer in his details and in his prefatory remarks so consciously has been seeking to emphasize is
called in question by such editorializing. It is a threadbare and
artificial device that strains credulity, as when Bragelone exhorts
the king:

> . . . Awake!—awake!
> Great though thou art, awake thee from the dream
> That earth was made for kings—mankind for slaughter—
> Woman for lust—the people for the palace!
> Dark warnings have gone forth; along the air
> Lingers the crash of the first Charles's throne!
>
> . . . .
>
> Lord of the silver lilies, canst thou tell
> If the same fate await not thy descendant! (IV,iv)

The king in an address to the Duchess is "Accurst" by Bragelone,
yet it is not for his social misdeeds against the "People"; when

the Duchess replies in consternation: "Hold!—thou malign'st thy king!" (II,iii), the response comes: "He spared not thee," and the emphasis is restored to the king not as a political figure but as a lover and a despoiler of innocent virtue. Louis XIV is

> . . . the king who has betray'd his trust—
> Beggar'd a nation but to bloat a court,
> Seen in men's lives the pastime to ambition,
> Look'd but on virtue as the boy for vice;   (IV,iv)

but attention throughout the play has been focused not upon liberal problems but upon the repentant profligate, the dashing lover rather than the reactionary autocrat. Evidently Bulwer felt compelled to interject liberal republicanism into the picture somehow; but in his maiden effort his devices are too mechanical and too transparent. His play needs subtlety.

This problem of Bulwer's in formulating dramatic action was one he resolved to circumvent in his next play by writing more in prose and less in blank verse. Again, the second play, *The Lady of Lyons*, is placed against a French background. Because of his interest in things French and his familiarity with the French language and French customs, presumably Bulwer would in any case have tended to turn toward France for his source material. But within the realm of poetic drama itself he did not lack precedent for employing the more recent French past as inspiration. Classical antiquity was suitable enough for playwrights like Knowles or Talfourd, and an Italian background for writers whose interests were concerned with Italian independence and liberty; yet there was *The Fall of Robespierre* by Southey and Coleridge as an example of the use of a French locale; and Sheil, too, had used French history in *The Huguenot*, one of his lesser plays. Each of these poetic dramatists merely utilized whatever background material seemed most suitable for his purposes and conformed most nearly to his personal interests—not that this fact necessarily makes the results more immediate, more contemporary, or more true to life.

Where Bulwer differs from his contemporaries is in a trait of style that emerges vaguely in the *Duchess de la Vallière*, but

is much more evident in *The Lady of Lyons*. This is an ability
to write natural-sounding dialogue instead of the declamations
so characteristic of the other poetic dramatists. Poor as he is with
poetry, Bulwer is good with prose. Through his experience in
writing novels he had gained a facility for constructing good
dialogue. Forced to express themselves in Elizabethan diction
and phraseology, naturally the figures of the other poetic playwrights will be speaking more or less poetically, no matter how
limited the talents of the authors in other respects. But Bulwer,
in his latest experiment, discards all such laborious artificiality:
The Lady of Lyons is a poetic tragedy in prose.

This is not to say that poetry is altogether absent. In the
romantic passages between Pauline Deschappelles, the lady of the
title, and her rustic lover, Claude Melnotte, the dialogue is in
blank verse. Bulwer says in his Preface: "It was in the development of the plot and the arrangement of the incidents that I directed my chief attention;—and I sought to throw whatever be-
longs to poetry less into the diction and the 'felicity of words'
than into the construction of the story, the creation of the
characters, and the spirit of the pervading sentiment." Or, we
might say, the plot has been poetically designed but not the
dialogue. Bulwer simply threw poetry overboard in favor of an
aura of romantic sentimentality. The play was hastily put together, yet in spite of its defects, the debut of *The Lady*, on
February 15, 1838, was a complete success. Even the dubious
Macready reports to Bulwer: "I hope you were satisfied with
last night:—I heard nothing but expressions of delight—and was
myself indeed delighted at the feeling of the audience."[32] And
a recent critic remarks: "If the author could have supplanted
the dialogue verbiage with true verse or firm prose, and the
banality with wit, we might enjoy it still today."[33]

A drawback in the play, at least for the time of its production,
is its number of asides. In the vastness of Covent Garden, with
the actors forced to bawl out their lines anyway, this device must

---

[32] Shattuck, p. 71.

[33] *Ibid.* For the source and background of *The Lady of Lyons,* see
Dewey Ganzel, "Bulwer and His *Lady*," *MP*, LVIII (1960), 41–52

have seemed pathetically threadbare, even to audiences accustomed to it in their Shakespeare. But here Bulwer was not yet completely at his ease in handling the problems entailed in staging and stage techniques.

By his next play, *Richelieu*, however, he had grown conversant with any problem that might confront him—and in this final play of his French trilogy the experiment of asides is not repeated. Something else is very nearly abandoned by Bulwer in this latter play, too—the theme of remorse. In *Richelieu* remorse arrives somewhat late, almost as an afterthought,[34] and in no way does it influence the course of events: by now, in 1839, remorse had become no more than a traditional prop, required by the very fact of a play's being a poetic tragedy, even though hardly significant for the development of the plot as a whole. In *The Duchess* remorse is superfluous, since the Duchess has already begun repenting for having fallen in love with the king before the arrival of Bragelone upon the scene to upbraid her for this crime. As she weeps, he wonders (in an aside):

> Are these the tokens of remorse? No matter!
> I loved her well! And love is pride, not love,
> If it forsake ev'n guilt amidst its sorrows! (II,ii)

Such remorse has come to have a frivolous, worldly meaning—not a feeling that can redeem villainy from its evil course but merely one that prevents virtue from veering from the path of decorous probity. And somewhat later when the Duchess declares:

> . . . But the blow was sudden;
> How can the heart play courtier with remorse? (III,ii)

she is bemoaning the purported death of this same Bragelone, who assuredly is no villain but if anything the hero. Here is the basic point: Romantic drama has lost its element of tragedy;

---

[34] There is but a single reference, when Richelieu declares:

> . . . To thy knees, and crawl
> For pardon; or, I tell thee, thou shalt live
> For such remorse, that, did I hate thee, I
> Would bid thee strike, that I might be avenged! (III,ii)

no one dies in any of these three plays; there is no longer a villain to redeem. Remorse has become an appendage, maintained
for tradition's sake. Bulwer's talents anyway inclined toward the
comic rather than the tragic—and with neither remorse nor
blank verse worthy of the name, his plays themselves hardly
merit the title of poetic tragedy, except nominally.

Bulwer was too astute not to realize that fact. Again, rather
than the author, it is Macready who seems to be to blame. Bulwer
originally wrote *Richelieu* in prose, "but Macready with an eye
on 'literature' must have insisted on its being poeticized," a
task that "took nearly three weeks."[35] At its first reading as
poetry the faithful John Forster, friend to them both, promptly
fell asleep. This deadly criticism caused Bulwer to examine his
play minutely from the beginning, and he discovered that although "I knew I had written a Poem, . . . by some alchemy—
the poetry was subtracted"[36]—which indeed is true. In addition
Bulwer offers several revealing comments on his own personal
attitudes toward the play, attitudes Macready apparently was
not already aware of: "the Dialogue of the retained parts should
be rewritten and the business part rendered poetical. A fearful
vice in composition (according to my conception of Art), but
which I suppose is nevertheless essential—since I now see why
more experienced Dramatists—Knowles and Talfourd—have
studiously sought it—I say when a Door is to be shut, 'Shut the
Door.' Knowles would say, as I think he has said somewhere,
'Let the room be airless.' Probably he is right. . . . I doubt if
I can do it at all."[37]

It becomes evident that Bulwer was not the person Macready sought—at least not for poetic and dramatic reform on
the stage. All the while his latest playwright had been struggling
to fit himself into a mold for which his talents were not suited.
Had John Forster been a writer of plays, possibly Macready

[35] Shattuck, p. 91.

[36] *Ibid.,* p. 96.

[37] *Ibid.* For the sources and background of *Richelieu,* see C. B.
Qualia, "French Dramatic Sources of Bulwer–Lytton's *Richelieu.*"
PMLA, XLII (1927), 177–184.

would have found in him someone who represented an approach closer to his own. It is difficult to know what Forster does mean in a letter to Bulwer during the composition of *The Duchess,* in 1836:

> One thing, I think, should never be lost sight of in Dramatic Writing. All that is *material* is there actually present to the Eye. All that is *Ethereal,* therefore, should be absolutely discharged from the task of setting forth what is already visible, or ought to be visible. Now the passions of a scene, the progress of it, the results of it,—all these are visible and existing things, and should as little as possible be described with words. Words, in fact, flow at once from the existence of these things, and are never needed to assure us that they do exist. Virtually indeed they assure us of it, and in the highest degree, but (words as they are beside a passion!) they are there because of the passion, not the passion because of them. Now this *Effluence* of words, in my mind, as a pure effect of passion, constitutes the true dramatic writing; and it is . . . comparatively unintelligible to all but to those who are capable of supplying from their own imagination those materials.[38]

To Bulwer the matter presumably was equally unintelligible; in his response he merely says: "Many thanks for your most kind letter . . . ,"[39] before turning to mechanical problems in the construction of a still-born play entitled *Cromwell.* Nevertheless, one thing was clear to Forster if not to Bulwer: words must lend expression to some passion, and these words in themselves must be motivated through the inner workings of whatever the passion entails; words are designed to produce a cumulative effect, emotionally, for emphasis: they are not auxiliaries, they are present to move, to sway, to motivate.

Bulwer, who labored long in Macready's cause, could never grasp the subtle ramifications of such a plan, a fabric woven in one piece with words employed for their cumulative meaning, their varied nuances. Nor, with the frequent revisions required

[38] Shattuck, p. 38.
[39] *Ibid.,* p. 39.

by structural alterations as they occurred, would he in all probability have been able to achieve such an ideal even with the best of intentions. The ending of *The Duchess*, for example, he wished to devote to spectacle and pageantry; Macready's insistence on Louis' making a last despairing attempt to wrest the Duchess from a convent, he rejected as improbable, eventually, however, capitulating on this point.[40] Again, as concerns poetry, Macready forced Bulwer to write in a style for which his talents were scarcely fitted. Interestingly, it is with the play *Money* that Bulwer for the first (and only) time hit his real stride—and *Money* was written while Bulwer was in Germany, away from Macready's surveillance! In short, in the trilogy we cannot avoid the conclusion that for Bulwer poetic tragedy was little more than an unnecessarily prolonged aberration from his natural and intuitively sensed métier, which was of course social comedy.

As for liberalism, after their composition Bulwer took pains to envelop his trilogy with an aura of liberal opinion by careful suggestion if not stated inference. In the Introduction to the 1841 edition of the three plays (and *Money*), he asks the reader to compare the ages these dramas represent with the progression from "one man" (in *Richelieu*) to the "multiform people" (in *The Lady of Lyons*).

In the time of Richelieu the people, in its own person awed and sullen, recedes from the stage, as the minister and the noble play their desperate game for power. In that of Louis XIV, effeminate and corrupted, the people stand, not invisible indeed, but in silence and shadow, behind the gorgeous throne which the victorious minister bequeathed to the successor of the monarch he ruled and humbled. In the time

---

[40] "Macready strove hard to help improve the play. . . . His most valuable contribution was to insist inexorably that Louis should pursue Louise [the Duchess] the second time, to the very end of the play. Bulwer resisted this action in the name of 'probability,' naively wanting to depend upon pageant and spectacle to bring off the finale. But he capitulated. This is but the first of many instances of his taking instructions from Macready in the manipulation of stage actions." (Shattuck, p. 20.)

of the French Republic noble and king, coronet and crown, are alike gone; and the people reappears for a brief time in the character of a second youth, impetuous and ardent, capable of doing all things for glory, unwise to accomplish anything for self-government, resisting a world for the defence of freedom, and tendering freedom to the first warrior who dazzled its imagination and flattered its self-love.[41]

By this time it may well have seemed to Bulwer that in his poetic trilogy he had been doing no more than recounting France's thorny road from absolutism to republicanism—and from there into the arms of Napoleon. To us, in retrospect, these, his first three staged plays, represent a deviation from his natural and instinctive dramatic development. It is in social criticism that his talents lay, in an ability to perceive the incongruous in individual idiosyncrasy and individual variation from the social norm. His attempts to present a panoramic view of French history within the framework of theatrical conventions, with all of the paraphernalia of poor wit and even poorer blank verse, do not reveal to us Bulwer at his best.

One element in Bulwer's dramas forcibly reminds us of the changing climate of the times, the shift in attitude from a concern with the great man as a figure for rehabilitation to an interest in the leader as a personage of interest in his own right as an innovator, an institutor of state principles, a director of the tide of human events, a shaper of history. In the plays of Mary Russell Mitford, even in the works of Sheil and Milman, this tendency has already been evident. And in Henry Taylor's play, *Philip van Artevelde*, this direction is perceptibly more focused upon a concern with the leader who is not so much a pawn in the hands of some inexplicable, amorphous, despised entity, an entity that for lack of a better word is called the people, as one who himself is actively the initiator, the determinator, who sets the direction history will pursue in its groping search for those intangibles, freedom and liberty. If earlier we have been following the ramifications of the last stages of an older age ex-

---

[41] Reprinted in The Earl of Lytton, *The Life of Edward Bulwer* (2 vols., London, 1913) , I,555.

emplified by the dictates of Rousseau, the period of revolution, the epoch of the rights of man, now we begin to enter an era in which these impulses are being consolidated by an entire class. Not that these impulses have been dying out; rather they are now finding fulfillment by the bourgeoisie. Revolutionary impulses on the Continent had not stopped altogether—but for England after 1830 the most immediate dangers were receding into the past. Chartist uprisings, Irish revolts, mass meetings, inflammatory speeches at Hyde Park Corner—but not revolution: these were the substitutes on English soil for the upheavals on the Continent.

In England, at least in theory, this early stabilization on the political scene permitted ample leeway for the introduction of new attitudes, new methods of experiment. By the same token this experimentation forever is being relegated to the realm of make-believe rather than applied to the sphere of the applicable; the theorist, in taking new positions toward the governing of world affairs, offers to his reader the picture of how the future must appear *if*, although how this same future will be governed *after* remains intangible. In the world of economic politics the political thinker obsessed with theory deserts fact. If today we find ourselves heir to the disasters resulting from the need to be able to put certain nineteenth-century theories into practice, now that some of them have become accepted as our collective attitudes, possibly it is easier to comprehend how disturbing and how intoxicating these ideas must have looked to the early-nineteenth-century English intellectual—when, for example, he first read the theory of the "Divine Idea" and the reinterpretation by Carlyle of German and existentialist Romantic philosophy—new and seemingly ultraliberal ideas.

On Heroes, Hero-Worship, and the Heroic in History was delivered as a lecture in 1840 and published in 1841. But by then the tenets of this Carlylean philosophy were not totally new. In fact, the previous decade, the age in which Bulwer, Talfourd, and Browning were writing their plays, as well as the decade of the 1840's itself, might be termed collectively the "Age of Carlyle." In the drama the ground had been well prepared by Wordsworth's and Coleridge's concern with the individual; the almost accidental shift, through Edmund Kean's and William Macready's personal interests, to history for subject matter in the plays of Knowles and his contemporaries had provided Romantic drama with a new and vital focus; gradually the dawn of a new liberal age armed playwrights with devious methods for adapting their historical subject matter to fit contemporary interests; with Bulwer historical drama is growing increasingly topical in point of time; and Romantic drama the while has been evolving into a form to suit the spirit of this new age, an age "which looked on history in the main as the achievement of great individuals."[42]

A critic states the case: "Even if the adjective 'realistic' may not be applicable to the plays [of the early nineteenth century], the theory that 19th-century dramatists were impotent because they were always retreating into the past will not hold water. Often they read the present into the past, but they were none the less reading the present. Especially in two things, Browning was timely. He 'studied' heroes and hero-worship, learning not to hope too much of any heroic 'liberator.' "[43]

Let us look at the career of Robert Browning, dramatist, about whose work as a playwright the customary attitude may perhaps best be indicated in the following terms: "An analysis of the plays reveals that Browning's basic interest as a poet precluded successful drama, for his interests were not in the objective representation of character and event in such a way as to reveal the development of character, but rather he presented in his plays a study of character under the strain of incident or event solely to analyze the conditions of the soul in relation to event . . . they are essentially character studies in the guise of plays."[44] We may say in short that Browning is a typical Ro-

---

[42] H. B. Charlton, "Browning as Dramatist," *Bulletin of the John Rylands Library*, XXIII (1939),46.

[43] Arthur E. DuBois, "Robert Browning, Dramatist," *SP*, XXXIII (1936), 654.

[44] Charles E. Johnson, Jr., "The Dramatic Career of Robert Browning: A Survey and Analysis," *Dissertation Abstracts* (Ann Arbor, Michigan, 1959), XIX, 2601.

mantic playwright. Yet, as with Shelley, Browning's claim to be an *effective* dramatist has been disputed as much as any possible pretension of his to be a *Romantic* one. One critic denies him the title of Romanticist altogether: "Browning never wrote . . . 'romantic drama' although he was sometimes 'romantic.' Comparing his *Pauline* with Shelley's *Alastor* one would guess that Browning never would write 'romantic' drama."[45] And this critic, in an attempt to determine what exactly Browning was if he was not Romantic, comes up with the word "ironical"[46] to characterize Browning as a *littérateur*.

What Browning himself aspired to be as a playwright is clear: he regarded himself as an arch-Romanticist. We have no need to pursue the course of the later Browning, the philosopher and religious thinker, the sentimental optimist, the expounder of a doctrine that finds succor in the spiritual value of failure, the advocate of a "paradox that comforts while it mocks." For us it is the younger Browning, the visionary optimist, the author of the confusing *Paracelsus* and the bewildering *Sordello*, the incoherent dramas and the early poetry, who is of interest. When we encounter Browning for the first time, it is on the evening of Talfourd's famous dinner party of 1836. Browning had already met Macready at a dinner on November 27, 1835, a meeting mentioned by Macready in his diary.[47] And soon thereafter Browning's thoughts began to turn to writing for the theatre.

"Forster and Browning called," Macready writes, "and talked over the plot of a tragedy, which Browning had begun to think of: the subject, Narses. He said that I had *bit* him by my performance of Othello, and I told him I hoped I should make the blood come. It would indeed be some recompense for the miseries, the humiliations, the heart-sickening disgusts which I have endured in my profession, if, by its exercise, I had awakened a spirit of poetry whose influence would elevate, ennoble, and adorn our degraded drama. May it be!" (M. I,277). The idea of a play on the theme of Narses was abandoned.

---

[45] DuBois, "Robert Browning, Dramatist," p. 627.
[46] *Ibid.*, p. 626 ff.
[47] See M. I,264.

Browning needed some other, more relevant and timely, idea. After the dinner party at Talfourd's, Macready overtook Browning with the jesting remark, "Write a play, Browning, and keep me from going to America." To this Browning replied, "Shall it be historical and English: what do you say to a drama on Strafford?"[48] The idea pleased them both. And Browning at the time was helping his friend John Forster with a Life of Strafford for the "Lives of Eminent British Statesmen" in Lardner's *Cyclopedia,* so that this theme tied in well with his other work. As for the result, Browning declares his being "not without apprehension that my eagerness to freshen a jaded mind by diverting it to the healthy natures of a grand epoch, may have operated unfavorably on the represented play, which is one of Action in Character, rather than Character in Action. . . . While a trifling success would much gratify, failure will not wholly discourage me from another effort: experience is to come; and earnest endeavor may yet remove many disadvantages."[49]

Again we have a writer who is conscientiously laboring to perfect his style and his technique in an effort to make something that would "do for the Theatre in its present state." So we can scarcely number Browning among the "thin-skinned, spoilt children of our literature." Indeed, Browning was most attentive in his efforts to improve his plays and render them suitable for the stage.[50] That he was not especially successful is obvious. Still, the fault does not lie altogether on Browning's side. Other factors must be taken into consideration in evaluating Browning's contribution to Romantic drama and dramatic literature. As late as 1844, at a time when Browning's career as a playwright was in effect already past, Talfourd, in the Preface to his tragedies, remarks hopefully: "If the Stage, in spite of its

---

48 Mrs. Sutherland Orr, *Life and Letters of Robert Browning* (2 vols., New York and Boston, 1892), I,125.

49 Preface to the first edition of *Strafford.*

50 The Browning–Macready relationship is discussed by Joseph W. Reed, Jr., "Browning and Macready: The Final Quarrel," *PMLA,* LXXV (1960), 597–603; see also the sections on Browning's plays in Park Honan, *Browning's Characters* (New Haven, Conn., 1961), pp. 41–103.

emancipation, shall fall to decay, I shall deplore it—if it be only
for what we shall lose in [Mr. Horne] and in the younger genius
of Robert Browning—a genius only yet dimly perceived, but
deeply felt, and which requires and deserves the noble discipline
of dramatic conditions."[51]

Of course, the emancipation to which Talfourd refers was
the repeal of the Licensing Act, in 1843. Strangely, in that same
year Romantic tragedy had reached its terminal point. Without
exaggeration it can be said that with "the failure of Browning's
Blot on the 'Scutcheon in 1843 the revival of romantic tragedy
came to an end."[52] Talfourd, without realizing it, was uttering
a prophecy about a condition that already had become unattain-
able. What was it, after all, that Talfourd and his contemporaries
writing in the field of Romantic drama—among whom can be
numbered Browning himself—were attempting to achieve? Possibly the answer is best expressed in Talfourd's own words, in a
review entitled "On Maturin" (1816): "The vast majority of
readers, in an age like ours, have neither leisure nor taste to seek
and ponder over the effusions of holiest genius. They must be
awakened into admiration by something new and strange and
surprising; and the more remote from their daily thoughts and
habits—the more fantastical and daring—the effort, the more it
will please, because the more it will rouse them. Thus a man
who will exhibit some impossible combination of heroism and
meanness—of virtue and of vice—of heavenly love and infernal
malignity and baseness—will receive their wonder and their
praise."[53]

But alas, this review had been written in the first faint beginning of the Liberal Age, in the period of the plays of Coleridge, Shelley, and Knowles. In the interim the tenor of the
times had changed. And we find this new attitude expressed unconsciously by Browning himself as he strove so valiantly to bring
before his audience those scenes "the more remote from their
daily thoughts" of which Talfourd speaks. We see the new at-

---

[51] *Tragedies,* p. viii.
[52] Chew, *Byron,* p. 13.
[53] *Critical and Miscellaneous Writings,* pp. 19–20.

titude reflected in his preoccupation with psychology, "Action in Character, rather than Character in Action," and in his fruitless attempts to achieve those dramatic effects so desired by Macready. The problem of reconciling this new realism with the romanticism of the past causes Browning to declare: "There is *action* in it [*A Blot on the 'Scutcheon*], drabbing, stabbing, et autres gentillesses,—who knows but the Gods may make me good even yet?"[54] The playwright, in coming into contact with an increasing interest in literal fact and less in imaginative fancy, is discovering that Romanticism no longer can cope with the requisite drabbing and stabbing. Whereas Bulwer found difficulty in expressing "shut the door" in poetic terms, Browning is now discovering that the theatre is rapidly shearing Pegasus's wings: the involvements, the obsession, of the author with the problems of the soul so dear to Joanna Baillie, Wordsworth, and Coleridge are in this new liberal, practical, hero-worshipping age no longer acceptable. What audiences are demanding is more action, coupled with rather than divorced from the depicted event. A playwright confronted by such an attitude soon will find that the static picture, the static groups, that permit poetic dialogue are no longer feasible. And where there is no longer leeway for poetic dialogue, there can not be poetic plays.

It is action, then, that the early Victorian public seems to want. The influence of melodrama or other attendant causes to the side, circumstances have changed. About Browning's first play, *Strafford*, the critic of *John Bull* declares: "Now, unfavourable as is our judgment on the tragedy, it has been given in no intolerant spirit. . . . It is for the promise which the effort betokens that we speak. . . . The very faults of the drama are proofs of talent. . . . The very plainness of the language, too, evinces strength, and is a good augury for the future. . . . In his next attempt, let him bring on the scene character in action, and we will answer for it that he triumphs."[55] There are statements, too, by those in the opposite camp; and when we read

---

54 *Letters of Robert Browning, Collected by T. J. Wise* (New Haven, Conn., 1933), p. 5.

55 Quoted by H. W. Griffin and H. C. Minchin, *Life of Robert Browning* (3rd ed., rev., London, 1938), p. 111.

Dickens's ardent defense of Browning's second and last play to be presented under Macready's aegis, *A Blot on the 'Scutcheon*, it is almost like turning back the clock to Hazlitt's appraisal of *Virginius* by Knowles: "To say that there is anything in its subject save what is lovely, true, deeply affecting, full of the best emotion, the most earnest feeling, and the most true and tender source of interest, is to say that there is no light in the sun, and no heat in the blood. It is full of genius, natural and great thoughts, profound and yet simple and beautiful in its vigour. . . . And I swear it is a tragedy that *must* be played: and must be played, moreover, by Macready."[56]

So there is evidence for both sides, the old and the new. Which side to adopt when writing his plays must have presented the aspiring playwright with thorny and not easily circumventable problems. We see these problems constantly coming to the fore in the brief period of collaboration between Browning the author and Macready the actor-manager. Apparently Browning took in good stead whatever suggestions for alteration Macready proposed for *Strafford*;[57] but *A Blot on the 'Scutcheon* developed somewhat differently. Between these two plays stand *King Victor and King Charles* and *The Return of the Druses*, neither of which greatly impressed Macready; he called the latter play (in his diary) "a *great mistake*" (M. II,23). Certainly both plays are confused, jumbled, and disjointed in their construction, although disturbing for dimly indicated perceptions on the part of leaders supposedly in charge of governing historical events, yet who themselves are prey to motiveless passions, misguided convictions, and vaguely grasped ideals. In *King Victor* there is carried to an even greater extent the concern with psychological subtlety as developed in *Strafford*; as compensation for the fact that next to nothing happens in this play, whatever does occur is expressed through lengthy monologues that indicate in detail the doubts and inner motivations of King Victor and his son, King Charles. Also disturbing from Macready's point of

---

[56] John Forster, *The Life of Charles Dickens* (3 vols., London, 1872–1874), II,25.

[57] See Reed, p. 597.

view may have been Browning's indifference to paying even cursory lip service to the guiding key word of Romantic drama, "remorse." To be sure, in both plays the problem of repentance is an underlying theme, but this repentance is the expression of a personal sense of guilt for conscious tyranny and baseness against others rather than a gradual redemption of the villain whose misguided passions have led him to revolt against mankind. Browning's way was obviously not the safe way to which Macready had become accustomed through his long association with Romantic drama and Romantic dramatists. And about *The Return of the Druses,* a play in which Browning handled a theme of Moorish vengeance and retribution in much the same fashion as Coleridge had done in *Remorse,* Macready, with his own conception of dramatic action, was so disturbed as to sorrowfully declare: "Read Browning's play, and with the deepest concern I yield to the belief that he will *never write again* —to any purpose. I fear his intellect is not quite clear" (M. II,72).

But it is not Browning's intellect that was not quite clear. If anything, the problem of having to adjust himself to Macready's dictates was what served as the stumbling block to his success. Although little exists as proof in the way of written evidence, it is probable that in the writing of *The Return of the Druses,* "Macready did not actually collaborate, but Browning kept the actor and his dramatic standards uppermost in his mind as he wrote. He attempted to write a 'really good play' by bearing in mind what Macready's practical objections might be: a play stood or fell on the actor's word alone."[58] In short, here Browning sought to write a play for actors rather than for an audience. And if this appears to place a reinterpretation upon Browning's true purposes, unjustly shifting the blame for his lack of success upon Macready's shoulders, we have the conviction of one critic to the effect that Macready "was the only audience that Browning even began to understand."[59] Unfortunately, however, this attitude does not easily explain why *A Blot on the*

[58] *Ibid.,* p. 598.
[59] *Ibid.*

'*Scutcheon*, as Browning later reports, was "a play . . . deprived of every advantage, in the way of scenery, dresses, and rehearsing—[that] proved—what Macready himself declared it to be—'a complete success.' "[60] In justification Browning writes: "If 'applause' means success, the play thus maimed [*A Blot*] and maltreated was successful enough: it 'made way' for Macready's own Benefit, and the theatre closed a fortnight after."[61] The shabby treatment given Browning's play by Macready and Macready's colleagues led to a rupture between the two men that was never fully healed.[62] Despite his chagrin Browning continued to write plays. Afterward he maintained that he had not; but the theatre was in his blood.[63] By 1884 possibly Browning felt that he had indeed stopped writing plays as he declares about the composition of *A Blot on the 'Scutcheon*: "In fine, I wrote it for a friend's [Macready's] sake, and the friend's vanity got the better of his friendliness and customary fairness to boot:— the shock to me was considerable and interrupted a friendship hitherto unfailing: it was of minor importance that I conceived a disgust for play-writing and never attempted it again."[64]

We have, nevertheless, three further plays, *Colombe's Birthday, A Soul's Tragedy*, and *Luria*. *A Blot on the 'Scutcheon* is his major attempt to compromise his artistic convictions with practical reality; thereafter, he wrote as he saw fit. Significantly, only in *A Blot* is mention made of the word "remorse," patently an attempt to reconcile convention with the Romantic inclina-

[60] Orr, *Life and Letters of Robert Browning,* I,179.

[61] *Ibid.,* p. 175.

[62] For details, see Orr, I,168–184. After their rupture the two men did not meet again until "Browning had returned, a widower, from Italy. Mr. Macready, too, had recently lost his wife; and Mr. Browning could only start forward, grasp the hand of his old friend and in a voice choked with emotion say, 'O Macready!' " (P. 181.)

[63] Byron, too, doggedly continued to write plays despite his many disclaimers, and his resolutions never to compose dramas "seeing how much everybody that did write for the stage was obliged to subject themselves to the players and the town" (L & J V,223).

[64] Quoted by Reed, p. 602,*n.* 22, from a ms. in the Yale University Library.

tions of Browning's own temperament. Mertoun, caught and
fatally stabbed by his mistress's brother, declares:

> . . . say, I saw him die
> As he breathed this, "I love her"—you don't know
> What those three small words mean! Say, loving her
> Lowers me down the bloody slope to death
> With memories . . . I speak to her, not you,
> Who had no pity, will have no remorse,
> Perchance intend her . . . (III,i)

But this is a far cry from remorse for past misdeeds or crimes;
instead it is remorse for witlessly slaying an honorable lover, one
who understands "what those three small words mean!" We have
penetrated into a realm other than the impersonality of preced-
ing Romantic dramatists who have been concerned solely with
redemption and liberty. In *A Blot* we are presented with personal questions and issues, questions that affect the individual
and not society or the state. Little wonder that Browning was
incredulous at Macready's suggestion that Tresham, the villain,
be shown planning to take refuge in the arms of the church at the
end of the play,[65] instead of murmuring as he dies: "Vengeance
is God's, not man's! Remember me!" (III,ii). Macready's substitution

> Within a convent's shade in stranger lands
> Penance and prayer shall wear my life away

evokes Browning's rejoinder: "The above, in Macready's hand-
writing, was the substitution for [what] he found written: this
to avoid giving the piece the dignity of Tragedy . . ."[66] It may
well be true that "Tresham's death is consistent with neither his
character nor the dramatic situation; perhaps it makes the play
more pathetic, but scarcely anything more";[67] yet surely this is
not the point of Browning's argument. The issue is brought out
more clearly in *Colombe's Birthday* (printed in 1844 as No. IV

---

[65] See Reed, p. 601.
[66] *Ibid.*
[67] *Ibid.,* p. 602.

of *Bells and Pomegranates*), Browning's next play, in which the Duchess asks: "And is love then the sole reward of love?" (V), to which Browning himself would have answered ardently, "Yes." To him love is something sacred and inviolate.

This problem is one that scarcely lends itself to exposition upon the stage—particularly when Macready, mindful of similar difficulties that had attended the production of Bulwer's plays, endeavors to excise anything smacking of the indelicate.[68] And so, in effect, Browning did make his exit from the theatre with *A Blot on the 'Scutcheon*, his last play to be produced under Macready's tutelage.[69] Henceforth, although we may not have great drama, we do have great blank verse. In the twilight of its life, through Browning, in its verse Romantic tragedy rises to unparalleled heights of grandeur. Seldom is Browning's poetry less than magnificent. It is colloquial yet undistracting, never labored for effect, always pure and at the same time ringing with the cadences of the language of real life. With Browning, although it is dying as an artistic form, poetic drama has come of age. When we compare almost any of Browning's plays with what has come before, with Sheil, Mitford, Milman, Knowles, the difference at once becomes apparent. We are dealing here with a master craftsman, a poet who knows instinctively how to handle words.

> . . . Here Cleves!
> Whose haggard craftsmen rose to starve this day,
> Starve now, and will lie down at night to starve,
> Sure of a like to-morrow—but as sure
> Of a most unlike morrow-after-that,

---

[68] See Reed, pp. 600–601, for excisions in *A Blot*. "Wherever possible, he [Macready] changed Browning's use of the word 'God' to 'Heaven' throughout the play" (p. 601). See *supra,* pp. 181–182, for similar difficulties with Bulwer's plays.

[69] *Colombe's Birthday* was successfully produced in 1853 at the Haymarket Theatre and again for the Browning Society in 1885; *A Blot* has been revived by the Browning Society and in Washington, D.C. by Lawrence Barrett; *Colombe's Birthday* was produced in Boston at about the same time of its production at the Haymarket, "in 1853 or 1854" (Orr, I,184).

Since end things must, end howsoe'er things may.
What curbs the brute-force instinct in its hour?
What makes—instead of rising, all as one,
And teaching fingers, so expert to wield
Their tool, the broadsword's play or carbine's trick,
. . . .
And swords lie rusting and myself stand here?
There is a vision in the heart of each
Of justice, mercy, wisdom, tenderness
To wrong and pain, and knowledge of its cure:
And these embodied in a woman's form
That best transmits them, pure as first received
From God above her, to mankind below.

> (*Colombe's Birthday,* II)

Shakespearean, perhaps? Scarcely that. Browning has developed the ability to express in poetry the idiom of the age, free from the restrictions of a merely imitative, archaic Elizabethanism. With Browning the efforts instituted by Wordsworth, Coleridge, and Shelley to utter effortlessly and poetically the expressions of the colloquial conversation of the age have been fully realized. And it cannot be denied that through his dramas Browning was steadfastly perfecting the form of the dramatic monologue.

New feeling fresh from God, which, could we know
O' the instant, where had been our need of it?
—Whose life re-teaches us what life should be,
What faith is, loyalty and simpleness,
All, once revealed but taught us so long since
That, having mere tradition of the fact,—
Truth copied falteringly from copies faint,
The early traits all dropped away,—we said
On sight of faith like yours, "So looks not faith
We understand, described, and praised before."

> (*Luria,* V)

Yet we would oversimplify Browning's contribution as a dramatist were we to relegate his plays to the level of exercises that were merely aids to him in developing the monologue. Unfortunately the usual attitude is to do just that. As a critic says:

"What if the [Browning-Macready] quarrel had not taken place. . . . Probably Browning would not have turned from the drama so soon. If he had continued would he have created a milestone to mark the desert of dramatic history which stretches from Sheridan to Ibsen? Or would he have become another Bulwer-Lytton? . . . Given the circumstances, the theatres, the actors, the audiences, and the literary environment of the early Victorian Age, it is very likely that the drama would not have been much changed. Of course, the literature might have lost an important poet."[70] But then, it is questionable what effect the experience Shakespeare gained from writing his sonnets had in helping him to write *Hamlet*, for example; or how much the composition of *Osorio* aided Coleridge in piecing together *Kubla Khan* or *The Ancient Mariner*, both of which belong to that same artistic period; or to what extent Wordsworth was helped in *The Prelude* by the insights gained from work on *The Borderers*. An artist working in one genre is almost necessarily assisted by insights gained from working in another; it does not follow that work on his dramas significantly contributed to Browning's development of the dramatic monologue. The evidence from *Paracelsus* and *Sordello* is clear that Browning would have inclined toward that medium, no matter what had been his apprehensions gained from a more purely dramatic technique. Regarded in this light, the drama was but an offshoot from Browning's logically projected artistic development rather than the consequences from which his poetry would later stem.

And still, after the successful failure of *A Blot on the 'Scutcheon* and after having written three more plays, why did Browning irrevocably turn his back upon the stage? *Strafford* he dedicated to Macready, *Colombe's Birthday* to Barry Procter, *Pippa Passes* to T. N. Talfourd, and *Luria* to Landor. It can hardly be said, then, that he disdained dramatic immortality. In the dedication to *Luria* he employs a phrase ("Wishing what I write may be read by his light") which, as he points out, once had been applied to Shakespeare—for it is evident that no less than any of his contemporaries Browning felt himself to be an

[70] Reed, p. 603.

inheritor and perpetuator of a venerable dramatic tradition. And there were other writers in this same period, chief among them John Westland Marston and Richard Hengist Horne, who burned with the desire to further the development of Romantic tragedy. But Browning knew that poetic tragedy as an active artistic medium was dead. The question, of course, is, Why? The answer is intimately connected with words from *A Soul's Tragedy* (1846): "I desire to be able, with a quickened eyesight, to descry beauty in corruption where others see foulness only; but I hope I shall also continue to see a redoubled beauty in the higher forms of matter, where already everybody sees no foulness at all. I must retain, too, my old power of selection, and choice of appropriation, to apply to such new gifts; else they only dazzle instead of enlightening me" (II).[71] Browning clearly realized that henceforth in order to be heard the poetic dramatist would have to abandon the theatre and turn his talents to some other—some more financially profitable—genre.

---

[71] Act I of *A Soul's Tragedy* is in blank verse; Act II is in prose.

CHAPTER VI

Aftermath

AND SO WE SEE that for the poetic dramatist the hope of a Liberal Age by the early 1840's proved to be delusive. Instead of contributing to the glorious rebirth of a new age as Talfourd and, possibly through him, Wordsworth and Macready so fondly had hoped, these artists found in retrospect that what they had believed to be but the beginning was in reality the end; a dusk rather than a dawn. Even as Talfourd was writing his plays twilight was falling and by the time of Browning's poetic contributions to the stage night had come. The year after the premiere of *A Blot on the 'Scutcheon* a book appeared by Richard Hengist Horne entitled *A New Spirit of the Age* (1844), but what it heralded had already taken place; and from this period forth poetic drama for all practical purposes ceased to occupy even that tenuously sanctioned position that it once held through Coleridge's *Remorse*.

In a way the sentiments expressed by Horne in this critical work, this hopeful appendix to Hazlitt's earlier *Spirit of the Age*, sound much like those expressed by Emerson in his essay "The Poet," an excerpt from which we have used earlier.[1] "The new order of dramatists, both acted and unacted, only await the man, come when he may, who, having the material means in his power, shall mould a form congenial to the present spirit of the age; and this once done, the abundant existing dramatic genius will gather round it, and the Drama again become popular."[2] Both Emerson and Horne were waiting expectantly for the appearance of a poet, Emerson for someone to dramatize

---

[1] See *supra,* p. 21.

[2] "Sheridan Knowles and Macready," *A New Spirit of the Age* (London, 1844), pp. 260–261.

the story of American life, Horne for a savior to redeem and purify the English stage. But Horne does not believe that this task is possible for an artist of the caliber of Macready or Sheridan Knowles: "Mr. Macready, throughout his whole career, has produced on the stage no great or standard work of dramatic genius: or, if 'Ion' or 'Virginius' be regarded as exceptions, who will name a third?—and he has wasted the time of more men of genius and talent than any other individual on record."[3]

Obviously Horne is an extremist in his views. But from what we have seen of Macready's artistic "assistance" to his poetic playwrights, we should be able to muster a measure of sympathy for Horne's attitude. Macready did not contribute anything of profound significance to the efforts of his dramatists; indeed, in the process of creativity he often showed himself to be more of a stumbling block than a courageous mentor and spiritual guide in the handling of their idiosyncrasies. It is not surprising, then, that Horne was never to be numbered among Macready's personal discoveries; nor have any of Horne's plays subsequently reached the stage. This is another way of saying that Horne disagreed even more violently with Macready's philosophical concept of the relative value of poetry and action than did Robert Browning—or Horne is more outspoken in unburdening himself. To him the principles of action, of realism, as advocated by Macready are "*not* the true representative of the age; it is not understood much better than the ideal and imaginative, though all mechanical minded men fully believe they can grasp it—so palpable it seems, and it will *not* be successful."[4] And this statement in turn leads us to the assurance that in his personal scheme of values Horne is contrasting the materialist, presumably an entrepreneur like Macready—the practical, unimaginative businessman—with himself, the free, unfettered artist, one who seeks to "grasp the main pillars of the ancient, high, mysterious temple of tragedy . . . and to shake the whole fabric to its base, so that mankind may be roused to examine the lofty

---

[3] *Ibid.*, p. 257.

[4] "Robert Browning and J. W. Marston," pp. 278–279.

branches of its power, and to search into the depths and breadths beneath, which support its awful structure."[5]

Horne, then, is not the artist to conceal his intentions from his audience. In the lengthy Preface to his drama *Gregory VII* (1840) he calls for a free discussion on the stage of moral and psychological issues, and states that tragedy creates effects and produces an impact upon the sensibilities not given to any other artistic form. Shelley had upheld much the same position many years earlier; and Robert Browning, in his psychological dramas, already had been groping toward the resolution of dramatic, poetic "action" in much the same fashion. So it cannot be said that Horne is advocating anything radically new, any pathway toward which this new spirit of the age was not already directing itself. The pity is that Horne here is merely codifying a tendency that had been patent for some time past—and now that this particular direction is ending in a blind alley, Horne is simply stating, after the fact, what all along had been an actuality. What he is calling for—a "new order of dramatists"—had been at work for a generation; the irony is that since the age of Romantic drama had already passed, formalization of tendencies as they existed had come too late.

Yet *A New Spirit of the Age* is relevant in another respect— in explaining the demise of Romantic tragedy. Horne is remarkably shrewd, even at this early date, writing as he does when the Victorian novel was still in its earliest stages of development. His grandiose *Gregory VII* contains what have been described as "numerous scenes of stage splendour which would have delighted a Victorian audience."[6] The same can be said for his earlier *Cosmo de' Medici* (1837). In this play, for example, a long scene (III,i) is presented with little excuse than to allow an interminable procession of Florentine dignitaries, from Benvenuto Cellini to Michelangelo, to cross the stage. As we might expect, in this play the customary curtsies are made to "remorse" (II,iii). The play is principally a reversion to type, to the ten-

---

[5] "Essay on Tragic Influence" (p. xxvii), *Gregory VII* (London, 1840).

[6] Reynolds, *Early Victorian Drama*, p. 97.

dency to Elizabethanize. For *Cosmo, Gregory VII*, and Horne's other plays, *The Death of Marlowe* (1837) and *Laura Dibalzo* (1880), are unabashedly neo-Elizabethan, which is to say they conform to Horne's convictions that "the spirit of passionate and imaginative poetry is not dead among us in the 'ignorant present'—it is alive, and of great splendour . . ."[7] We may agree with Horne in this, little as we may be satisfied with this poetry as conforming to Elizabethan models and precedents. We may also agree with Horne when he maintains that a play like Browning's *King Victor and King Charles* "is another proof, among the many already existing, that the unacted drama is incomparably superior to the melodramatic plays and farces adopted by managers."[8] Yet in his efforts to counter these melodramatic plays and farces "adopted by managers," Horne no more than Beddoes, Wells, and Darley selects the proper models for his plays—for as we have already seen, Romantic drama had been led into a complete dead end by neo-Elizabethanism some two decades before Horne's arrival on the scene; what he is fighting for is a cause that is no longer even of minor consequence.

This realization never fully penetrated into the consciousness of other writers, either. Later, with the zeal of the natural crusader and fiery fanaticist, Swinburne would be at work in an effort to resuscitate this moribund Elizabethanism. And others in this same decade of the 1840's were toiling as ardently to reshape into something usable the visible tokens, in print and on the stage, of a glorious Elizabethan heritage.[9] Among them John Westland Marston (1819–1890) must assume the position of principal importance. With him we can say that Romantic drama continues to exist, at least in enfeebled form, even after Browning's time, since neo-Elizabethan dramas by Marston were being played in London until after the mid-century mark.[10] Of major

---

[7] "Robert Browning and J. W. Marston," p. 278.

[8] *Ibid.*, p. 286.

[9] Reynolds, in *Early Victorian Drama,* lists a number of Romantic dramas that never reached the stage; see pp. 115–117.

[10] *Marie de Méranie,* Olympic Theatre, 1856; *Strathmore,* Haymarket, 1849; *Anne Blake,* Olympic, 1852. Reynolds discusses the first two of these plays in detail, pp. 104–112.

interest is Marston's *The Patrician's Daughter* (Drury Lane, 1842), a play that was first produced before the terminal point in our study of Romantic drama. It is a classic example of why Romantic drama had in effect reached its termination—if not as yet an explanation of why poetic tragedy thereafter vanished from the stage. In this same year Browning was beginning work on *A Blot on the 'Scutcheon*, a play with which Romantic drama approached the Olympic heights of Shelley's *Cenci* of 1819—and here, in *The Patrician's Daughter*, much of the same sort of contemporary or pseudo-contemporary background is employed as is found in Browning's play. With these two plays the gap between the past and the present is slowly being closed, for in both average human beings are the *dramatis personae*, rather than legendary Greek heroes or historical personages from France or the Italian Renaissance.

Here all resemblance between Browning's play and Marston's play ends, aside from the fact that both are written in blank verse. Marston is allied much more closely to Bulwer than to Browning; his attitudes toward the drama are much the same as Bulwer's, his lack of feeling for the use of words and his strong sense of the melodramatic. Even in the shaping of its plot *The Patrician's Daughter* resembles Bulwer's *Lady of Lyons* in that in both plays a proud girl is loved by a man whose social station is beneath hers. It cannot be denied, as Marston so cheerlessly states in his Preface of 1876, *The Patrician's Daughter* was produced at a time "when the fierce class animosities excited by the first reform bill had by no means subsided."[11] But this cannot change the facts of the case as they stand in print: like Bulwer, Marston leaves us with the feeling that no burning conviction motivated the writing of this play—other, that is, than the effort to cater to the interest in topical events. Nor can it be claimed that in dealing with everyday reality and everyday life, Marston is any the more real. At least this is true so far as presenting issues behind a veil of half-disguised allusion is concerned. What results must be considered little more than

---

[11] P. ix.

pretentious melodrama, melodrama copiously seasoned with
early-Victorian morality. Nor are the sentiments any more memorable than the verse itself.

> . . . And is it then not sin
> To crush those flowers of life, our freshest hopes,
> With all the incipient beauty in the bud,
> Which knows no second growth? to cast our faith
> In human kind, the only amulet
> By which the soul walks fearless through the world,
> Into those floods of memorie tterness,
> Whose awful depths no diver dares explore?
> . . . .
> Is it not sin? To the unsleeping eye of Him
> Who sees all aims, and knows the wrongs
> No laws, save his, redress, I make appeal
> To judge between us. There's an hour will come,
> Not of revenge, but of righteous retribution. (III,ii)

This is not the stirring cry of the villain struck by remorse as of
old, nor even Browning's variation, a stirring plea for all-ful-
filling love; it is the new voice of the virtuous, Bible-reading
early Victorian, the forgiving voice of a domesticated Ion, meekly
willing to forgive his enemies and to pray for his contemners.
Hardly has the heroine repented of her unjustified rejection of
a worthy man when death overtakes her in the presence of both
father and admirer, a touch appropriate to sentimental melodrama, perhaps, but scarcely worthy of a play intended to be
written in the mainstream of a tradition of poetry.

The goals of Romantic drama have become misunderstood.
And the reasoning of the writers of poetic tragedy has become
confused in an effort to cope with current tastes for the sentimental and the morbidly dramatic. No more than Bulwer does
Marston seem able to decide just what position he wishes to
adopt poetically. In *England and the English* (1833), Bulwer
recommends that the writer select the course of writing about
the Simple and the Magnificent,[12] as much a contradiction in

---

12 *England and the English* (2 vols., London, 1833), II,145 ff.

terms as Hazlitt's remark that the dialogue of Sheridan Knowles "tends to action, all his situations form classic groups."[13] In his efforts to please everyone, the Romantic dramatist now was but ignoring those vaguely suggested concepts that successively had been introduced by the leading figures in Romantic tragedy as the genre had slowly evolved: a fixed intention to capture poetically the language of real life; a concern, psychologically, with the passions of the soul; an absorption with moral redemption and intellectual rehabilitation of the great man, the hero gone wrong; a passionate involvement in the causes of freedom and liberty; an inchoate awareness of the difficulties entailed in reconciling the actual and the ideal, the utopian and the practical; an attachment to a world of liberal values, liberally held and liberally advocated—these issues, time and again we discover, are now being hidden behind a welter of supernumerary details of perspective and presentation and the mechanics of how, poetically, a writer is to resolve the problem entailed by his paper creations' having to say something as simple as "shut the door." This, in turn, brings us back to the beginning of our study and the problems of stagecraft and production, the problem of *mise en scène* that none of our poetic dramatists from Coleridge to Browning ever managed to master, no matter who the manager in question might be, Macready or Sheridan.[14] Indeed, in certain respects poetic drama was doomed from the beginning, caught on the horns of a dilemma presented by the technical limitations of the age itself, problems the writer alone could scarcely be expected to cope with adequately without more able outside professional assistance than stood at his disposal.

But there is more to the demise of Romantic tragedy than mere mechanics. Melodrama, after all, continued to flourish for many years, nor after 1843 did the theatre in any way cease to function. We return, therefore, to Richard Hengist Horne. In our study of the earlier development of Romantic tragedy our most percipient critic and evaluator of current and future trends was Byron; now it is Horne who provides us with clues

---

[13] See p. 136.
[14] Possibly Bulwer is the only exception to prove the rule.

to Romantic drama's decline. "What is the Spirit of an Age as regards the Drama?" he asks. "Certainly the Theatrical Spirit is the most undramatic that can be. Stage-plays are not of necessity Dramas, and more truly dramatic elements may be found in the novelist's works than in the theatrical writer's."[15] In a certain sense this is true for the "Theatrical Spirit" of any age, not alone for the specific "spirit of the age" we have observed in Hazlitt's remarks on the undramatic quality of his times.[16] Horne's remarks, however, do have a certain bearing on the theatrical situation of his day; they are intimately connected, moreover, with the reasons why—aside from the difficulties in understanding exactly what it was a manager like Macready wanted them to write about and the means he wished them to employ—poetic dramatists of the order of Bulwer and Browning should altogether have stopped writing for the contemporary theatre.

The question revolves around the issue of finance: Coleridge's anguished cry, "neither my finances nor my feelings can *afford* it,"[17] by the time of Bulwer and Browning has become that much more to the point. Bulwer, writing to Macready in 1839, declares: "I am in a deadly rage Having just rec'd the accounts for The Lady in the Provinces 17£3s!!!—the Agency at the Dramatic Authors must be shamefully done. I should like to remodel the whole thing. I am the only man of Business of my whole tribe."[18] The truth is that the Dramatic Authors Bill of 1833, one of the reforms recommended by the Select Committee of which Bulwer had been chairman, did not prove to be of as much assistance in protecting the rights of the aspiring playwright as had been anticipated.[19] Successful London plays were

---

[15] "Sheridan Knowles and William Macready," p. 238.

[16] See *supra*, p. 136.

[17] See *supra*, p. 83.

[18] Shattuck, p. 118.

[19] For a discussion of the poor payments received by playwrights in the period, see Ganzel, pp. 394–396. The Dramatic Authors Bill "gave the dramatist complete control of his work for twenty-eight years or his lifetime, whichever was longer . . . ; stipulated that a producer must have an author's permission, in writing, before a piece could be

pirated in England and Ireland as before; the objection was
raised to the bill that "it was impossible properly to police all
the theatres in England, Ireland, the Channel Islands, and the
British possessions to be sure that unauthorized productions did
not take place."[20]

Even so, according to one critic, the Act of 1833 did manage
to provide "most of the protection needed to give incentive and
fair treatment to the dramatic author,"[21] more protection, that
is to say certainly, than ever previously. But this protection was
not enough—and it came too late. Why should a literary artist
force himself to contend with implacable managers and uncertain revenues in the theatre when he could deal with one con-
veniently located London publisher? These were questions all
the more timely (or questions an artist could ask himself with
an all-the-more realistic attitude) now that the age symbolized
by the words remorse, freedom, and liberty was, dramatically
speaking, past. And Bulwer was one who quickly sensed the
change. The title of his greatest success, *Money* (1840), graphi-
cally exemplifies this shift in values and standards. The idea behind the play is that success on a social plane and happiness itself
depend upon "plenty of money" and little else. A new (-old)
attitude has been given the imprimatur of dramatic statement—
and on the stage the way has been opened for theatrical examination and comment on an already widely prevalent early-Victorian commercial point of view. In such circumstances a
concept of poetic literature grounded upon liberal principles
and humanitarian instincts will surely find itself out of step, an
alien in the very field in which so many have labored for so
long to carve out for it a niche that would both be lasting and
significant.

Thus the keynote expressed in Shelley's sonnet "On Political
Greatness," the desire to arouse within the early-Victorian audience an acceptance of liberal convictions based on the glorifica-

---

played; and awarded damages to the author of £10 to £50 for every
night on which an authorized play was presented" (Ganzel, p. 396).

[20] Ganzel, p. 396.

[21] *Ibid.*

tion of the exploits of a people untamed by tyranny while aware
of their historical past—this intention, often unconscious, of the
playwrights of the 1830's and 1840's was destined to be realized
only in part. For the rest, the years that witnessed the rise of
Romantic tragedy to its greatest heights were also the years that
marked its decline and fall. Difficulties in staging and production, Romantic playwrights had been able to face with a certain
equanimity; the exigencies of theatrical conditions, the problems entailed by the uncertain demands of audience and manager, most playwrights somehow had been able to resolve in
their own minds if not in their plays; even the question of financial reward had been ignored by the most dedicated and persistent of the poetic dramatists. But the times had changed. So
long as the poetic playwright was able to satisfy both the esthetic
requirements of his audience and his own personal inclinations
and interests, Romantic drama continued to be written and
performed. But by 1843, the gulf separating the ideal and the
new reality had become too great. The poetic dramatist, born
into a Romantic age, was growing to maturity in an era of realism—commercial, financial, esthetic. In view of these new existing conditions, Romantic drama as an entity and as a concept
no longer represented a stageworthy commodity. Romantic tragedy had become but a monument of a glorious, distant past.

Bibliography

Annual Register, April 30, 1794.

Archer, William. *The Old Drama and the New: An Essay in Revaluation.* Boston: Small, Maynard and Company, 1923.

——. *William Charles Macready.* London: K. Paul, Trench, Trübner and Company, Ltd., 1890.

Aristotle, *Works,* ed. W. D. Ross. 12 vols. Oxford: The Clarendon Press, 1908–1952.

Ashe, Dora J. "Byron's Alleged Part in the Production of Coleridge's 'Remorse'," *N & Q,* CXCVIII (1953), 33–36.

Babbitt, Irving. *Rousseau and Romanticism.* 3rd edition. New York: Meridian Books, 1957.

Babcock, Robert W. *The Genesis of Shakespeare Idolatry, 1766–1799.* Chapel Hill: University of North Carolina Press, 1931.

Baillie, Joanna. *Dramatic and Poetical Works.* London: Longman, 1851.

——. *A Series of Plays.* London: T. Caldwell, Jr., and W. Davies, 1802.

Bair, George. "The Plays of the Romantic Poets: Their Place in Dramatic History." Unpublished dissertation. University of Pennsylvania, 1951.

Baker, Henry B. *History of the London Stage and Its Famous Players (1576–1903).* London: Routledge, 1904.

Barnett, Howard A. "Robert Browning and the Drama. Browning's Plays Viewed in the Context of the Victorian Theatre: 1830–1850." Unpublished dissertation. Indiana University, 1959.

Bate, W. J. *From Classic to Romantic: Premises of Taste in Eighteenth-Century England.* Cambridge: Harvard University Press, 1946.

Bates, Ernest S. *A Study of Shelley's Drama "The Cenci."* New York: Columbia University Press, 1908.

Baugh, Albert C., ed. *A Literary History of England.* New York: Appleton-Century-Crofts, Inc., 1948.

Beddoes, Thomas Lovell. *Works,* ed. H. W. Donner. London: Oxford University Press, 1935.

Bernbaum, Ernest. *Guide Through the Romantic Movement.* 2nd edition, revised. New York: The Ronald Press Company, 1949.

Blackwood's Magazine. Vol. VII (June, 1820).

Blessington, Lady. *Conversations of Lord Byron.* Philadelphia: E. L. Cary and A. Hart, 1836.

Boyer, Clarence V. *The Villain as Hero in Elizabethan Tragedy.* London and New York: E. P. Dutton and Company, 1914.

Brandl, Alois. *Coleridge and the English Romantic School.* London: Murray, 1887.

Browning, Robert. *Letters, Collected by T. J. Wise,* ed. T. L. Hood. New Haven: Yale University Press, 1933.

———. *Poetical Works.* Cambridge edition. New York and Boston: Houghton Mifflin and Company, 1895.

Bulwer, Edward Lytton. *England and the English.* 2 vols. London: Richard Bentley, 1833.

———. *Dramatic Works.* 2 vols. London: George Routledge, 1876.

———. *The Duchess de la Vallière.* 2nd edition. London and New York: Saunders and Otley, 1837.

Bunn, Alfred. *The Stage: Before and Behind the Curtain.* 3 vols. London: R. Bentley, 1840.

Burgum, E. B. "The Literary Career of Edward Bulwer, Lord Lytton." Unpublished dissertation. University of Illinois, 1924.

Bush, Douglas. *Mythology and the Romantic Tradition in English Poetry.* Cambridge: Harvard U. Press, 1937.

Byron, George Gordon Lord. *Works.* Cambridge edition. Boston: Houghton Mifflin and Company, 1905.

———. *Works: Poetry,* ed. E. H. Coleridge; *Letters and Journals,* ed. R. E. Prothero. 13 vols. London: Murray, 1898–1904.

Cambridge Bibliography of English Literature, ed. F. W. Bateson. 5 vols. Cambridge: The University Press, 1940–1957.

Cambridge History of English Literature, ed. A. W. Ward and A. R. Waller. 15 vols. London and New York: G. P. Putnam's Sons, 1907–1933.

Cameron, K. N., and Horst Frenz. "The Stage History of Shelley's *The Cenci,*" *PMLA,* LX (1945), 1080–1105.

Campbell, O. J., and Paul Mueschke. *"The Borderers* as a Document in the History of Wordsworth's Aesthetic Development," *MP,* XXIII (1925–26) , 465–482.

Campbell, Olwen W. *Shelley and the Unromantics.* London: Methuen, 1924.

Campbell, Thomas. *Life and Letters,* ed. William Beattie. 2 vols. New York: Harper, 1850.

Carhart, M. S. *The Life and Work of Joanna Baillie.* New Haven: Yale University Press, 1923.

Chambers, E. K. *Samuel Taylor Coleridge.* Oxford: The Clarendon Press, 1938.

Charlton, H. B. "Browning as Dramatist," *Bulletin of the John Rylands Library,* XXIII (1939) , 33–37.

Chew, Samuel C. *Bryon in England: His Fame and After-Fame.* London: J. Murray, 1924.

——. *The Dramas of Lord Byron.* Göttingen: Vendenhoeck and Ruprecht, 1915.

Christensen, Francis. "Three Romantic Poets and the Drama." Unpublished dissertation. Harvard University, 1934.

Coleridge, Samuel T. *Biographia Literaria,* ed. John Shawcross. 2 vols. Oxford: The Clarendon Press, 1907.

——. *Collected Letters,* ed. E. L. Griggs. 4 vols. Oxford: The Clarendon Press, 1956–1959.

——. *Complete Works,* ed. W. G. T. Shedd. 7 vols. New York: Harper, 1853.

——. *Poetical Works,* ed. E. H. Coleridge. London: Oxford U. Press, 1912.

Coles, William A. "Magazine and Other Contributions by Mary Russell Mitford and Thomas Noon Talfourd," *SB,* XII (1959) , 218–226.

Colman, George. *Random Records.* London: H. Colburn and R. Bentley, 1830.

Colvin, Sidney. *John Keats: His Life and Poetry, His Friends, Critics, and After-Fame.* 3rd edition. New York: Charles Scribner's Sons, 1925.

Cottle, Joseph. *Early Recollections; Chiefly Relating to the Late Samuel Taylor Coleridge.* 2 vols. London: Longman, Rees and Company and Hamilton, Adams and Company, 1837.

Cunliffe, J. W. *Short History of English Drama from 1825.* London and New York: Harper and Brothers, 1927.

Darbyshire, A. *The Art of the Victorian Stage*. London: Sherratt, 1907.

Darley, George. *Complete Poetical Works,* ed. Ramsay Colles. London: George Routledge, n.d.

De Selincourt, Ernest. *Oxford Lectures on Poetry*. Oxford: The Clarendon Press, 1934.

———. *Wordsworthian and Other Studies,* ed. Helen Darbishire. Oxford: The Clarendon Press, 1947.

De Vane, W. C. *A Browning Handbook*. 2nd edition. New York: Appleton-Century-Crofts, 1955.

Donner, H. W. *Thomas Lovell Beddoes: The Making of a Poet*. London: Oxford U. Press, 1935.

Doran, John. *Annals of the English Stage*. 3 vols. New York: Bigelow, Brown and Company, n.d.

Du Bois, Arthur E. "Beginnings of Tragic Comedy in Drama of 19th Century." Inaugural dissertation. Johns Hopkins University, 1934.

———. "Robert Browning, Dramatist," *SP*, XXXIII (1936), 626–655.

Eastlake, Charles L. *History of the Gothic Revival*. London: L. Longman's, 1872.

Edwards, Maldwyn. *Methodism and England*. London: The Epworth Press, 1934.

Elton, Oliver. *Survey of English Literature, 1780–1830*. 2 vols. London: E. Arnold, 1920.

Evans, Bertrand. *Gothic Drama from Walpole to Shelley*. Berkeley and Los Angeles: University of California Press, 1947.

———. "Manfred's Remorse and Dramatic Tradition," *PMLA*, LXII (1947), 752–773.

Fairchild, Hoxie N. *The Romantic Quest*. New York: Columbia University Press, 1931.

Filon, Pierre M. *The English Stage, Being an Account of the Victorian Drama,* trans. Frederic Whyte. London: John Milne, 1897.

Firkins, I. T. E. *Index to Plays, 1800–1926*. New York: The H. W. Wilson Company, 1927.

Fitzgerald, Percy. *A New History of the English Stage*. London: Tinsley Brothers, 1882.

Forster, John. *The Life of Charles Dickens*. 3 vols. Philadelphia: J. P. Lippincott, 1874.

Fox, Arnold B. "Political and Biographical Background of Coleridge's *Osorio*," *JEGP*, LXI (1962), 258–267.

Fraser's Magazine, vol. XIII (1836), April.

Fricker, Robert. *Das historische Drama in England von der Romantik bis zur Gegenwart*. Bern: A. Francke, A.G., 1940.

Ganzel, Dewey. "Patent Wrongs and Patent Theatres: Drama and the Law in the Early Nineteenth Century," *PMLA*, LXXXVI (1961), 384–396.

Garrod, H. W. *Wordsworth: Lectures and Essays*. 2nd edition. Oxford: The Clarendon Press, 1954.

Genest, John. *Some Account of the English Stage*. 10 vols. Bath: H. E. Carrington, 1832.

Gifford, William. *The Baviad and the Maeviad*. 8th edition. London: Murray, 1811.

Goode, Clement T. *Byron as Critic*. Weimar: R. Wagner Sohn, 1923.

Gosse, Sir Edmund. "The Revival of Poetic Drama," *Atlantic Monthly*, XC (1902), 156–166.

———. *Robert Browning: Personalia*. New York and Boston: Houghton Mifflin and Company, 1890.

Graham, Walter. "Contemporary Critics of Coleridge." *PMLA*, XXXVIII (1923), 278–289.

Greever, Garland, ed. *A Wiltshire Parson and His Friends*. New York, Boston: Houghton Mifflin and Company, 1926.

Griffin, H. W., and H. C. Minchin. *Life of Robert Browning*. 3rd edition, revised. London: Methuen and Company, Ltd., 1938.

Griggs, Earl L. "Coleridge and Byron," *PMLA*, LXV (1930), 1085–1097.

Haller, William. *The Early Life of Robert Southey: 1774–1803*. New York: Columbia U. Press. 1917.

Hamilton, M. P. "Wordsworth's Relation to Coleridge's *Osorio*," *SP*, XXXIV (1937), 429–437.

Haney, John L. *The German Influence on S. T. Coleridge*. Philadelphia: n.p., 1902.

Hanson, Lawrence. *The Life of Coleridge: The Early Years*. New York: Oxford U. Press, 1939.

Harper, George M. *William Wordsworth: His Life, Works, and Influence*. 2 vols. New York: Charles Scribner's Sons, 1916.

Harrison, John W. "The Imagery of Byron's Romantic Narratives and Dramas." Unpublished dissertation. University of Colorado, 1958.

Havens, R. D. *The Mind of a Poet: A Study of Wordsworth's Thought with Particular Reference to "The Prelude."* Baltimore: Johns Hopkins Press, 1941.

Hawkes, Terence, ed. *Coleridge's Writings on Shakespeare.* New York: Capricorn Books, 1959.

Hazlitt, William. *Complete Works,* ed. P. P. Howe. 21 vols. London and Toronto: J. M. Dent and Sons, Ltd., 1933.

Herford, C. H. *The Age of Wordsworth.* London: Bell, 1897.

——. *Sketch of the History of the English Drama.* Cambridge: n.p., 1881.

Hicks, Arthur C., and R. M. Clarke. *A Stage Version of Shelley's Cenci.* Caldwell, Idaho: The Caxton Printers, Ltd., 1945.

Hinck, H. W. "Three Studies in C. R. Maturin." Unpublished dissertation. State University of Iowa, 1954.

Honan, Park. *Browning's Characters.* New Haven: Yale U. Press, 1961.

Horne, Richard Hengist. *Cosmo de' Medici.* London: Rivers, 1875.

——. *Gregory VII.* London: Saunders and Otley, 1840.

——. *A New Spirit of the Age.* New York: Harper Brothers, 1844.

——. *Orion.* 9th edition. London: Ellis and Green, 1872.

Houtchens, L. H., and C. *The English Romantic Poets and Essayists: A Review of Research.* Modern Language Association, 1956.

Hunt, Leigh. *Dramatic Essays,* ed. William Archer and Robert W. Lowe. London: W. Scott, Ltd., 1894.

Idman, N. *Charles Robert Maturin: His Life and Works.* Helsinfors: Centraltryckeri, 1923.

Irish Quarterly Review, 1852.

Jeffrey, Francis. *Contributions to the Edinburgh Review.* 3 vols. 2nd edition. London: Longman, Brown, Green and Longmans, 1846.

Johnson, Charles E., Jr. "The Dramatic Career of Robert Browning: A Survey and Analysis." Unpublished dissertation. University of Michigan, 1959.

Johnson, Reginald B. *Famous Reviews.* London: Sir I. Pittman and Sons, Ltd., 1914.

——, ed. *Shelley-Leigh Hunt.* 2nd edition. London: Ingpen and Grant, 1929.

Keats, John. *Complete Poetical Works,* ed. H. E. Scudder. Cambridge edition. Boston: Houghton Mifflin and Company, 1899.

Kessel, Marcel, and Bert O. States, Jr. "*The Cenci* as a Stage Play," *PMLA,* LXXXV (1960) , 147–149.

Knight, Joseph. *History of the English Stage During the Reign of Victoria.* London: n.p., 1901.

Knight, W. A. *Coleridge and Wordsworth in the West Country. Their Friendship, Work, and Surroundings.* London: Elkin Mathews, 1913.

Knowles, James Sheridan. *Dramatic Works.* London: Routledge, Warnes and Routledge, 1859.

Knowles, Richard Brinsley. *The Life of James Sheridan Knowles.* London: James McHenry, 1872.

Lamb, Charles. *Works,* ed. E. V. Lucas. 7 vols. London: Methuen and Company, 1903–1912.

Lee, Harriet. *Canterbury Tales.* London: n.p., 1799.

Legouis, E. *Early Life of Wordsworth,* trans. J. W. Matthews. London: J. M. Dent and Sons, Ltd., 1932.

L'Estrange, A. G. K. *Life of Mary R. Mitford.* 2 vols. New York: n.p., 1870.

London Magazine, April, 1820; July, 1820; April, 1823.

Longaker, John M. *The Della Cruscans and William Gifford.* Philadelphia: n.p., 1924.

Lounsbury, Thomas R. *The Early Literary Career of Robert Browning.* New York: Charles Scribner's Sons, 1911.

Lowes, John L. *The Road to Xanadu: A Study in the Ways of the Imagination.* New York: Vintage Books, 1959.

Lucas, E. V. *Life of Charles Lamb.* 2 vols. London: Methuen and Company, 1905.

Lytton, The Earl of. *The Life of Edward Bulwer.* 2 vols. London: Macmillan and Company, Ltd., 1913.

Machule, P. "Coleridge's Wallensteinübersetzung," *Englische Studien,* XXXI (1902) , 182–239.

Macready, William Charles. *Diaries,* ed. William Toynbee. 2 vols. London: Chapman and Hall, Ltd., 1912.

——. *Reminiscences,* ed. Sir Frederick Pollock. New York: Macmillan and Company, 1875.

Madariaga, Salvador. *Shelley and Calderon.* New York: E. P. Dutton and Company, 1920.

Mandeville, G. E. "A Century of Melodrama on the London Stage, 1790–1890." Unpublished dissertation. Columbia University, 1954.

Marston, John Westland. *Anne Blake*. Boston: William V. Blake, n.d.

———. *The Patrician's Daughter*. London and New York: Samuel French, n.d.

Mason, Francis C. *A Study in Shelley Criticism*. Mercersburg, Pennsylvania: privately printed, 1937.

Matthews, Brander. *A Study of the Drama*. Boston: Houghton Mifflin and Company, 1910.

Matthiessen, F. O. *American Renaissance*. London and New York: Oxford U. Press, 1941.

Maturin, Charles R. *Bertram*. London: J. Murray, 1816.

McCormick, J. P. "Robert Browning and the Experimental Drama," *PMLA*, LXVIII (1953), 982–991.

McNeill, W. E. "A History of the English Drama from 1788 to 1832." Unpublished dissertation. Harvard University, 1909.

Medwin, Thomas. *Conversations of Lord Byron*. London: H. Colburn, 1824.

Meeks, Leslie H. *Sheridan Knowles and the Theatre of His Time*. Bloomington, Indiana: The Principia Press, 1933.

Milman, Henry Hart. *Poetical Works*. 3 vols. London: J. Murray, 1839.

Mitford, Mary Russell. *Works, Prose and Verse*. Philadelphia: Crissy and Markley, 1854.

Moore, Thomas. *Life of Lord Byron*. London: J. Murray, 1860.

Moorman, Mary. *William Wordsworth: The Early Years, 1770–1803*. Oxford: The Clarendon Press, 1957.

Morgan, Bayard Q. "What Happened to Coleridge's *Wallenstein*," *MLJ*, XLIII (1959), 195–201.

Morley, Edith J., ed. *Correspondence of Crabb Robinson with the Wordsworth Circle*. 2 vols. Oxford: The Clarendon Press, 1927.

Morley, Henry, ed. *Parodies and Other Burlesques of the Anti-Jacobin*. London: George Routledge, 1890.

Nag, U. C. "The English Theatre of the Romantic Revival," *Nineteenth Century and After*, CIV (1928), 384–398.

Nicholson, E. W. *The Struggle for a Free Stage in London*. New York and Boston: Houghton Mifflin and Company, 1906.

Nicoll, Allardyce. *A History of Early Nineteenth Century Eng-*

lish Drama. 2 vols. London: The University Press, 1930.

Orr, Mrs. Sutherland. *Life and Letters of Robert Browning.* 2 vols. New York and Boston: Houghton Mifflin and Company, 1892.

Our Corner, June 1, 1886.

Pater, Walter. *Appreciations.* London and New York: Macmillan and Company, 1889.

Peck, Katherine M. *Wordsworth in England.* Bryn Mawr, Pennsylvania: n.p., 1943.

Pedicord, Harry W. *The Theatrical Public in the Time of Garrick.* New York: King's Crown Press, 1954.

Pierce, Frederick E. *Currents and Eddies in the English Romantic Generation.* New Haven: Yale U. Press, 1918.

Potter, Stephen, ed. *Minnow Among Tritons: Mrs. S. T. Coleridge's Letters to Thomas Poole.* London: Nonesuch Press, 1934.

Praz, Mario. *The Romantic Agony,* trans. Angus Davidson. 2nd edition. London: Oxford U. Press, 1951.

Previté-Orton, Charles W. *Political Satire in English Poetry.* Cambridge: Cambridge U. Press, 1910.

Prior, Moody E. *The Language of Tragedy.* New York: Columbia U. Press, 1947.

Procter, Bryan Waller. *An Autobiographical Fragment and Biographical Notes.* Boston: Roberts, 1877.

——. *Life of Edmund Kean.* New York: E. Moxon, 1835.

——. *Mirandola.* London: John Warren, 1821.

Pückler-Muskau, Hermann L. W. *A Tour in England of a German Prince.* 4 vols. London: Wilson, 1832.

Quennell, Peter. *Byron in Italy.* London: Collins, 1941.

——. *Byron, The Years of Fame.* New York: The Viking Press, 1935.

Quinlan, Maurice. *Victorian Prelude: English Manners, 1700–1830.* New York: Columbia U. Press, 1941.

Rannie, David W. *Wordsworth and His Circle.* London and New York: G. P. Putnam's Sons, 1907.

Raysor, Thomas M., ed. *The English Romantic Poets, A Review of Research.* Revised edition. Modern Language Association, 1956.

Rea, Thomas. *Schiller's Poems and Dramas in England.* London: Unwin, 1906.

Read, Herbert. *Coleridge as Critic.* London: Faber and Faber, 1949.

Reed, Joseph W., Jr. "Browning and Macready: The Final Quarrel," *PMLA,* LXXXV (1960), 597–603.

Reynolds, Ernest. *Early Victorian Drama, 1830–1870.* Cambridge: W. Heffner and Sons, Ltd., 1936.

Rice, Charles. *The London Theatre in the Eighteen-Thirties,* ed. A. C. Sprague and B. Shuttleworth. Printed for the Society for Theatre Research, 1950.

Richards, I. A. *Coleridge on Imagination.* New York: Harcourt, Brace and Company, 1935.

Robinson, Henry C. *Diary, Reminiscences, and Correspondence,* ed. Thomas Sadler. 2 vols. 3rd edition. London and New York: Macmillan, 1872.

Roscher, H. F. G. *Die Wallensteinübersetzung von S. T. Coleridge.* Leipzig: R. Noske, 1905.

Rowell, George. *The Victorian Theatre: A Survey.* London and New York: Oxford U. Press, 1956.

Sandford, M. E. (Mrs. Henry). *Thomas Poole and His Friends.* 2 vols. London and New York: Macmillan, 1888.

Schelling, Felix. *English Drama.* London and New York: E. P. Dutton and Company, 1914.

Shattuck, Charles H., ed. *Bulwer and Macready: A Chronicle of the Early Victorian Theatre.* Urbana: University of Illinois Press, 1958.

——. "The Dramatic Collaborations of William Charles Macready." Inaugural dissertation. University of Illinois, 1938.

Shaw, George Bernard, *Dramatic Opinions and Essays.* 2 vols. New York: Brentano, 1906.

Sheil, Richard Lalor. *The Apostate.* New York: Samuel French, n.d.

——. *Evadne; or The Statue.* New York: William Taylor and Company, n.d.

Shelley, Lady Jane, ed. *Shelley Memorials.* 3rd edition. London: Henry S. King and Company, 1875.

Shelley, Percy Bysshe. *Complete Poetical Works.* Cambridge edition. New York and Boston: Houghton Mifflin and Company, 1901.

——. *Letters,* ed. Roger Ingpen. 2 vols. London: Sir I. Pittman and Sons, Ltd., 1909.

Shipp, Horace. "Shelley and Chevalier," *English Review*, XXXV (1922), 522–525.

Smiles, Samuel. *A Publisher and His Friends*. 2 vols. London: J. Murray, 1891.

Smith, Horace and James. *Rejected Addresses*. 22nd London edition. Boston: Ticknor and Fields, 1860.

Southey, Robert. *Selections from the Letters*, ed. J. W. Warter. 4 vols. London: Longman, Brown, Green, Longmans, and Roberts, 1856.

States, Bert O., Jr. "Addendum: The Stage History of Shelley's *The Cenci*," *PMLA*, LXXII (1957), 633–644.

Stevenson, E. *Early Reviews of English Poets: 1786–1832*. London: W. Scott, Ltd., 1890.

Stokoe, F. W. *German Influence in the English Romantic Period, 1788–1818*. Cambridge: The University Press, 1926.

Summers, Montague. *The Gothic Quest*. London: The Fortune Press, 1926.

Swinburne, Algernon C. *Complete Works*, ed. Edmund Gosse and Thomas J. Wise. 20 vols. London: W. Heinemann, 1925–1927.

——. *Miscellanies*. London: Chatto and Windus, 1886.

Talfourd, Thomas Noon. *Critical and Miscellaneous Writings*. 3rd American edition. Boston: Phillip, Sampson and Company; New York: James C. Derby, 1854.

——. *Dramatic Works*. 11th edition. London: Edward Moxon, 1852.

——. *Tragedies*. New York and Boston: A. S. Francis and Company, 1846.

Taylor, Henry. *Philip van Artevelde*. 4th edition. London: Edward Moxon, 1846.

Thorndike, A. H. *Tragedy*. Boston: Houghton Mifflin and Company, 1908.

Thorslev, P. L., Jr. "The Byronic Hero: Types and Prototypes." Unpublished dissertation. University of Minnesota, 1959.

Trevelyan, George M. *English Social History*. 3rd edition. London and New York: Longmans, Green, 1955.

Watson, Ernest B. *Sheridan to Robertson: A Study of the Nineteenth-Century Stage*. Cambridge: Harvard U. Press, 1926.

Watson, Vera. *Mary Russell Mitford*. London: Evans Brothers, 1950.

Wellek, René. *A History of Modern Criticism, 1750–1950*. Vols. I and II. New Haven: Yale U. Press, 1955.

———, and Austin Warren. *Theory of Literature*. New York: Harcourt, Brace and Company, 1956.

Wells, Charles. *Joseph and His Brethren, A Dramatic Poem*. London: Oxford U. Press, 1908.

White, Henry A. *Sir Walter Scott's Novels on the Stage*. New Haven: Yale U. Press, 1927.

White, Newman I. "The English Romantic Writers as Dramatists," *SR*, XXX (1922), 206–215.

———. *Shelley*. 2 vols. New York: A. A. Knopf, 1940.

———. "Shelley's Dramatic Poems." Unpublished dissertation. Harvard University, 1918.

Whitman, Robert F. "Beatrice's 'Pernicious Mistake' 'in *The Cenci*," *PMLA*, LXXIV (1959), 249–253.

Wilson, John. *Works*, ed. J. F. Ferier. 12 vols. Edinburgh: Blackwood, 1855–1858.

Wordsworth, Christopher, ed. *Memoirs of William Wordsworth*. 2 vols. London: Edward Moxon, 1851.

Wordsworth, Dorothy. *Journals*, ed. Ernest de Selincourt, 2 vols. New York: The Macmillan Company, 1941.

———, and William Wordsworth. *Letters*, ed. Ernest de Selincourt. 6 vols. Oxford: The Clarendon Press, 1935–1939.

Wordsworth, William. *Poetical Works*, ed. Thomas Hutchinson. New York: Oxford U. Press, 1933.

———. *Poetical Works*, ed. Ernest de Selincourt and Helen Darbishire. 5 vols. Oxford: The Clarendon Press, 1940–1949.

Year's Work in English Studies, ed. Frederick S. Boas. London: The English Association, 1917 f.